Humanism in the Classroom

Humanism in the Classroom

an eclectic approach to teaching and learning

Wesley C. Huckins

Wright State University

Harold W. Bernard

*Oregon State System
of Higher Education*

ALLYN AND BACON, INC.   Boston, London, Sydney

Library of Congress Catalog Card Number: 73–89265

Printed in the United States of America

Second printing ... March, 1977

Contents

Preface *vii*

PART I **The Person in the School** 1

Chapter 1 A Humanistic Approach to Teaching 3
Chapter 2 Facilitating Learning Processes 22
Chapter 3 The Teacher and a Learning Milieu 48
Chapter 4 Communication and Interpersonal Transaction 75
Chapter 5 Teachers: Agents and Victims of Change 105

PART II **Innovative Practices and Techniques** 131

Chapter 6 Teachers and Technology 133
Chapter 7 Programmed Learning, Open Education, and Creativity 165
Chapter 8 Nongraded Schools and Continuous Progress 196
Chapter 9 Independent Study 222

PART III **Organizing for Innovation and Change** 239

Chapter 10 The Team Approach to Learning 241
Chapter 11 Organizing for Innovation 286

Glossary 319
Bibliography 324
Name Index 347
Subject Index 352

v

0379795

Preface

This book evolved from a series of visits which we made to innovative schools all over the nation. Our purposes were to investigate and evaluate current educational innovations and to formulate a rationale for the innovative process.

Our presentation is addressed to those school personnel who see the need for improvement regardless of the category in which their school falls. Marked improvement is possible when goals are (1) stated clearly and (2) accepted and acted upon by all staff members. Such clarification will require time and study.

We begin with the premise that an innovation is effective only to the extent that it facilitates pupil learning. From this and from an extensive review of the literature, we have formulated a number of propositions as a framework for these observations. The material which resulted is presented and analyzed in this book. We have the not very modest objective of furnishing school personnel with practical suggestions for making teacher-pupil, teacher-teacher, and teacher-administrator transactions effective and satisfying. But teacher attitudes in successfully innovative schools indicate that this effort is likely to bear abundant professional dividends as well as personal satisfaction.

We emphasize people and process rather than subject matter and its presentation. This position is taken because differing personal needs and developmental status mean that no one method of education will work for all pupils. Varied styles of learning require study and adaptation of teaching methods. Some schools are highly effective in meeting the needs of academically talented pupils; others are noteworthy for stimulating the culturally different; and some demonstrate concern for the social-emotional aspects of development. But there are others which are relatively inept by any evaluative criteria. In some schools, pupil morale is high, paralleling a high degree of teacher dedication. In others there is a feeling of drudgery and discouragement on the part of both teachers and pupils. These differences are, we believe, largely due to the quality of the interpersonal transactions within the school.

Because no plan is better than those who use it, Section III is concerned with the process and the people. The major emphasis is "how teachers come across" to their pupils and their colleagues. Members of the staff, meeting in small groups, with some previously trained as facilitators, are asked to help each other perceive the effects of their behavior more objectively and accurately. The aim is not to change personality by psychotherapy—it is to bring about new perceptions of the role of self and of others, to learn how one is seen by associates so that one may better manage interpersonal behavior. Group members are asked to formulate objectives for self-directed growth and also to use colleagues, pupils, and video equipment as feedback agents.

We do not perceive this process as the traditional imposition, management, and evaluation by outside sources. Instead, it can be teacher instigated and controlled. It can operate for teacher as well as for pupil growth. We believe that staff members presently on the job have the capacity to affect substantially the caliber of the local teaching-learning milieu and their own satisfaction as participants.

PART I

The Person in the School

CHAPTER 1

A Humanistic Approach
to Teaching

Rapid change in our culture is indicated by many alarming events: The population explosion, the knowledge explosion, disasters in the schools, and riots in the ghettos have claimed the attention of school personnel. Many critics claim that, with retention rates at an all-time high, the schools have failed. The man on the street is swayed by this failure propaganda—swayed to the extent that he has defeated school support issues in epidemic numbers.

There is urgency in meeting the needs of increasing numbers of school children and in knowing how to deal with rapidly accelerating rates of knowledge, so that constant study, and modification, of teaching-learning transactions are merited. Student strikes, sit-ins, youth "demands," and questions of educational relevance suggest that many schools have not made enough of the needed changes in time. It has been said that one who has been absent from this world for fifty years would, on returning, have difficulty recognizing a bank or a hotel but that he would quickly recognize a third grade classroom. Population growth, knowledge increase, and changing social relations and demands are such that revolution in instruction is desirable. While many would disagree with the implications of such words as explosion, catastrophe, and failure, few would oppose the need for continuous improvement of the school—or of any other human institution.

HUMANISTIC ORIENTATION AND ACADEMIC DISCIPLINES

A humanistic concept

There are several psychological views regarding how adjustments to the rapidly changing world should be made. In some the emphasis is on teaching and conditioning; with others, on learning and being. The authors favor a humanistic orientation defined in the following manner: Humanistic psychology postulates and promotes a lively, selectively perceptive, unique person who reacts and *proacts*. (See Bonner, 1965, pp. 21ff.) Humanistic psychology does not repudiate the concept of drive that pervades psychoanalysis but would add love, goal-seeking, and personal choice. The humanistic view does not ignore scientific approaches but its adherents do profess that science cannot separate physical causes from the active and sentient human being. Bonner uses the term "proactive psychology" to describe the projection and propulsion of psychological events into the future. This forward and future movement is made possible by the human's ability to choose, to dream, and to act now because of intangible stimuli. Man propels himself into the future by virtue of his aspirations.

Maslow (1968) also places the human in the leading role. Reinforcement and conditioned reflexes work, he says, but they cannot be separated from the human personality. Associative learning is a valuable concept if one wants to learn about habits, but man's projection of himself into the future and his attempts at self-improvement, self-fulfillment, and self-actualization are the real concerns of psychology.

Weiner (1972) might be considered a humanistic psychologist for his "attribution theory." Briefly, this means that one's future actions are determined and are at least partly predictable from attributions made by the perceiver. For example, a pupil possesses achievement motivation in terms of what he thinks of himself—having or not having ability, working hard or just drifting along, facing what he perceives is an easy or difficult task. As a humanist also, Wiener perceives motivation not simply in terms of rewards or threats or punishment but in terms of what those rewards, threats, or punishments mean to individual humans.

Bruce (1966) explains the nonexclusive character of humanistic psychology by examining the history of psychologies. For sixty or seventy years each new psychology started as a rebellion against deterministic and analytic trends as represented by associationism and psychoanalysis. Humanistic psychology as represented by Maslow, Combs, and Rogers seeks to coalesce data into a comprehensive theory, including not only historical psychologies but also embracing contributions from sociology, anthropology, and psychiatry. Adding man's social and cultural nature to his biological and instinctual equipment constitutes an appropriate concern for humanistic psychology, says Bruce.

Humanism has a philosophical as well as a psychological aspect. As a philosophy it recognizes the uniqueness and individuality of persons. This implies that creativity, spontaneity, and distinctiveness of life styles and learning styles must be a conscious part of teacher-pupil transactions. Routine and mass approaches would be suspect. It implies that the child is no simple tabula rasa upon which stimuli write their irretrievable messages. Rather, the child elicits (even as a "hard" or "easy" baby) the kind of stimuli that are presented to him by adults, who in turn may be kind and accepting or harsh and punitive.

Humanism as a philosophy attributes to man the capability of creating a peaceful, salubrious climate in which the preciousness of human beings is recognized (Aiken, 1973), or of destroying himself and others with him. In contrast, humanism stresses happiness, freedom, and growth as man's highest goals. It welcomes joy and beauty (Lamont, 1973). Hence population problems, ecology, and interpersonal relations are a crucial part of the new curricula. Thus teacher-pupil transactions should be characterized by mutual respect and acceptance and recognition of pupils' needs for safety, identity, achievement, and differential (or individual) treatment. Ego-demeaning, authoritarian practices have no place in a humanistic curriculum.

With such an orientation, humanism is an approach to coalescing psychological knowledge and beliefs about the nature of humans as individuals. Now, the means by which various academic disciplines shape our emphasis on the centrality of persons can be considered. How is the school, as an institution, designed to fulfill the needs of pupils so they may become fully functioning persons?

Psychology

How one views and uses psychology influences his teaching methods. This is recognized in virtually all states by requiring course work in educational psychology for teacher certification. The content of such courses can be shaped by many theories and points of view, but, for the sake of brevity and fitting the scope of this presentation, three orientations are considered. Behavioral, psychoanalytic, and humanistic psychology have achieved some prominence in formulating classroom theory, in contrast to the intuitive, habitual, and traditional practices which actually obtain.

Contiguity and reinforcement are concepts considered under the behavioral orientation and are illustrated by Thorndike's (1924, 1932) laws of learning:

Law of effect: A response that produces pleasant effects tends to be repeated and consolidated.

Law of exercise: The more frequently a stimulus-response bond is exercised the stronger the bond becomes.

Law of readiness: When a stimulus-response bond is ready to act the effect is pleasurable.

Much of such psychology prevails in today's schools. Drill, recitation, review, and reward find justification in the Thorndikian rationale. Feedback and reward recently have been given impetus by Skinner's (1971) emphasis on positive feedback, as is noted in his endorsement of programmed learning. The need for success and approval are important in behavioristic psychology as well as in humanistic orientation. Goal seeking is recognized by behaviorists as being important; but, unfortunately the goals are more likely to be those of the teacher than those of pupils.

Freud was not primarily interested in the psychology of learning in the classroom but some basic assumptions made by him are pertinent here. He emphasized that mental events are automatically regulated by the pleasure principle (Freud,

1920). He also noted that there is a tendency toward repetition-compulsion; i.e., some things are repeated even though they do not yield pleasure. Thus overlearning makes an activity resistant to extinction. The idea that anxiety creates a drive has been used as a rationale for the threat of low grades or failure to pass. The notion of unconscious drives as a source of motivation is, it seems, consistently ignored despite our verbal recognition that home influences may interfere with mental set for learning school tasks. Repression of unpleasant thoughts or memories may be another factor that is too often neglected as a possible barrier to learning. Teachers should also remember that hostile impulses may be displaced on innocent objects or persons, as when they find pupils acting very aggressively with classmates or themselves.

Humanistic psychology provides an interpretation of teaching-learning transactions that was previously implicitly recognized but not openly and consistently stated, i.e., the teacher and the learner, as persons, take precedence over the lesson plan, the hardware, or the software (see Glossary) of education. Teachers must be good examples as learners and as persons. They teach what they *are* quite as much as what they *do* and *say*. They must accept pupils as being important, likeable, and unique persons. They need to be more concerned about processes and interpersonal transactions than about subject matter mastery.

Pupils in a humanistic school environment also have much responsibility. They must participate, listen, respond. Pupils must and will do their own learning. They are responsible for their reactions to the external events that surround them. Pupils are responsible for their own perceptions. Whether they wish to be or not, or whether they recognize it or not, pupils have the "awful burden of choice."

The interdisciplinary approach

At one time it was believed that, to understand the learning process, psychology was the most appropriate academic tool. Now it is apparent that learning is interdisciplinary and that sociology, biology, anthropology, and chemistry also can make solid contributions to understanding how people learn. At the same time government, the community, and religion have

7

KNOWLEDGE
EXPLOSION

THIS COULD BE
EXCITING!

WILL THE BOMBING
EVER STOP?

Things which are perceived as challenging to one person may be experienced as threatening to another.

considerable influence on curriculum content and on attitudes toward educational institutions. All these are determinants of the personality of the individual and of his attitudes toward self and others.

Sociology. The family has considerable influence on the pupil as a learner, as studies of motivation, social class, and family composition clearly reveal. One sociological study of the relationship of family to children's education (Brookover and Erickson, 1969, pp. 71ff.) demonstrated parental influence on learning patterns and levels of aspiration. Most boys who had high achievement motivation had mothers who were kind but exacting and who had high expectations for their sons, but such mothers often had an opposite effect on their daughters. In other cases, children said they could not disappoint their fathers. The impact of parental expectation was precarious either way—too much expectation, or too little, on the part of parents lowered the children's levels of motivation. Related sociological studies have dealt with "father absence," particularly in terms of the personality and school performance of boys and girls (Biller and Bahm, 1971; Hetherington, 1973). These and other studies by sociologists—studies of parents, siblings, peers, classroom groups, and home and community values and attitudes—contribute more to understanding about the teaching-learning process. Achievement orientation, peer affiliation, nonconformity, and autonomy are related to such things as identification with parents, peers, and teachers (Weiner, 1972). And all of these affect the attitudes of the pupils sitting in the classroom and the attitudes of the teachers standing at the blackboard.

Anthropology. Anthropology is the study of the processes by which individuals learn and transmit the particular behaviors which are characteristic in their culture. Cultural anthropology, through analysis of social class structure, has made highly pertinent contributions to our knowledge of some of the major successes, defeats, and problems of education.

One of these contributions describes the effect of social class on the ability to learn in school. Social class refers to the comparative distribution and incidence of prestige, disdain, opportunity, or discrimination among the people of a total population. Such stratification in a society is based upon a number of factors, or criteria, which indicate relative worth. The amount of money one has or earns is often an important factor, significant enough so that social class also is referred to as socioeconomic status. Education, source(s) of income, kind and location of residence, occupation, and family background are other important factors that combine to determine one's status. However, one must have, or develop, the behaviors, language, attitudes, styles, and ideals of the particular class, determined by the attributes cited, in order to be accepted and to remain in that class.

Twenty years ago, when cultural anthropologists began to publish their findings on American social structure, the idea of class was repudiated by the typical citizen. Supposedly, this is a classless society in democratically oriented America. Such differences which exist in income and status are attributed to brains, ambition, and developed skills. One can rise to the top if he just works hard enough, and some just are born with more of what it takes.

9

Anthropologists have rendered that ideal untenable. Today it is recognized that educational opportunity, legal justice, job availability, and access to medical services are unequally distributed. Teachers who once believed that pupils stayed in school, got good grades, and conformed to expectations because they had brains and good dispositions, now will accept that:

Being a dropout or finishing school is closely associated with social class (Binzen, 1973; Jencks, 1968);

School grades and assessment of intelligence are frequently based on class lines (Havighurst and Neugarten, 1967; McClelland, 1972);

The behaviors, ideals, and attitudes toward education which teachers find acceptable reflect middle-class values (Stalcup, 1968, p. 38);

Teachers, who are mostly middle class or upper lower class, feel most comfortable and accepting and most readily identify with middle-class children (Stalcup, 1968, p. 38);

Intelligence and achievement tests are devised by middle-class experts in terms of middle-class culture with the result that lower-class children compare unfavorably with those of the middle class (Kagan, 1972);

The temptation to regard those who are different as inferior, not only in status but also in ability, is widespread (Jensen, 1969; Shockley, 1972); and

Children from the lower class who have comparative deficiencies in verbal and conceptual functioning may come to be regarded as slow learners and negativistic toward structured learning (Bernard, 1973, p. 157).

Anthropologists have demonstrated that a number of pupil differences, formerly thought to be innate and irremediable, are—upon scientific analysis—culturally imposed and perhaps susceptible to alteration. They have emphasized that pupil variations are not necessarily matters of deprivation and deficiency but rather that they are essentially cultural differences (Gage, 1972). Teachers who appreciate that there is a vast difference between cultural deprivation or cultural handicap and cultural difference increase their own stature as accepting human beings and also increase their professional ability. Anthropology thus underscores, for the humanistic psychologist, the centrality of the person.

Business and Industry

One new scheme after another has been tried to improve education and then failed to make a lasting improvement. The Lancastrian model, the contract method, progressive education, the comprehensive high school, ability grouping, special education, aptitude testing are among those proposals that have provided a false hope. Today, many people think business and business methods will solve the problems of education in the United States.

With formal education occupying the full time of about twenty-five percent of the population, schools present an attractive market for businessmen. Books, films, projectors, school furniture, maps, art supplies, and the whole realm of building construction and management are big business. Now businessmen have shown a desire to get into an active role in the teaching-learning process. Using the methods with which they are familiar—assembly line, tested efficiency, measurable results, and guaranteed product—they emphasize responsibility and accountability. In effect, they say "Let us agree upon the specific results you want, and we will either deliver the goods or refund your money."

The initial trial of "accountability" with business and industry in charge has been completed and some of the results are in (Elam, 1970). In Texarkana, Texas, where teacher salary levels, per capita income, and pupil achievement are near the lowest in the nation, pupil performance with business-in-education has exceeded expectations. The schools of Texarkana are being studied as models of school efficiency. Although the data are not yet complete, the tentative conclusions are exciting.

In September 1969, the Texarkana Schools contracted with Dorsett Educational Systems to operate Rapid Learning Centers (RLCs) for ninth graders on a guaranteed results basis. The Centers, enrolling over 400 students before the academic year was completed, had the goals of preventing dropouts and raising achievement levels in reading and mathematics. Participants had been identified as potential dropouts. They attended the Centers about two hours per day and participated in regular classes and student activities the rest of the day. Twenty local teachers took special training in order to become "expert consultants," who were paid regular salaries and bonuses to compensate for longer working hours.

Even to a child, the thrill of accomplishment often exceeds the "green stamp" incentive!

The instructional program consisted of programmed reading and mathematics material. The branching version of programming (see Glossary) which was used capitalized on feedback from tests to determine needed program modifications. Feedback and reward were provided in the form of Green Stamps. When a child gained one grade level, he was given a transistor radio. The pupil who made the greatest advance in grade level, as measured by the Iowa achievement tests, won a portable television set.[1]

---

[1] A delicate question is posed by such an extrinsic reward system. It often gets results (it certainly did in Texarkana), but it seems useless except in formal school situations. Who provides the Green Stamps, grades, credits, certificates, diplomas, and degrees for reading quality magazines and serious books and for independent quests for knowledge? When does, and can, a shift be made from the extrinsic rewards to the intrinsic rewards of satisfying curiosity and knowing that one is growing as a person? It should be noted, in this context, that programming is not dependent upon such an external reward system as is described above. The hazards of extrinsic incentives are recognized but until the pupil can get his incentive from achievement, this kind of reward has an appropriate place.

Pupils at least two years behind grade level but with an IQ above 70 or 75 (depending on the school) were chosen. Results in terms of pre- and posttest results were gratifying, particularly since no one student spent more than approximately three months in the program.

On February 2, fifty-one students were posttested with the Iowa Tests of Educational Development (which the schools used in pretesting) to determine extent of progress. Results indicated that in a total of eighty-nine hours of instruction, the average student had achieved an increase of .99 grade levels in math and 1.50 in reading. In vocabulary subtests even better results were realized.

A second posttest, involving fifty-nine students, was conducted on March 2. Results indicated that in a total of 120 hours, equally distributed between reading and math instruction, students averaged 2.2 grade level increases in reading and 1.4 in math.

These, remember, are averages. It was somewhat surprising to note that as many as 32 percent of the pupils had made *no* progress—had even slipped back from .1 to between 3.0 and 4.0 grade levels in one or another subject. For example, of fifty-one pupils taking the March 2 test of reading comprehension, thirteen had slipped from .1 to 1.0 grade level and four had slipped between 1.0 and 2.0 grade levels.[2]

There were other tangible results which accompanied the program and which indicate the impact of the school on its pupils.

Vandalism in the cooperating schools was cut in half.
Only one of the 301 participants voluntarily dropped out of school.
Voters switched from a segregation stance to an integration stance in order to get federal aid to save the program.

In addition, there is a possible chance, not yet confirmed, that per pupil costs will be reduced by $100 per year, and there is the possibility and hope of extending the RLCs to grades 4–6 and 7–12.

Those close to the experiment—the contractors and the teachers involved in the program as aides and consultants—do

[2] Stanley Elam, "The Age of Accountability Dawns in Texarkana," *Phi Delta Kappan* 51 (June 1970): 513.

not believe that business-in-instruction is the bright star that will enlighten all the problems of education. For doing a particular job—subject matter mastery in certain areas—and for pupils whose learning style programming suits, it has advantages. It may be, as its proponents say, that Rapid Learning Centers and private industry are well-suited to reducing the incidence of dropouts but would be inappropriate for other student and student-teacher problems. It should be noted, however, that the failure of many education experiments in the past has been caused by the lack of such an objective appraisal.

Ostensibly this is a sounder approach than the historical practice of hiring an unemployed preacher as "schoolmaster," superior to employing teachers to "keep school" or allowing teachers to remain on the payroll regardless of how much or what kind of impact they have on pupils. However, when it comes to teaching a love for learning, bolstering the self-respect of a bewildered pupil, or fostering the divergent thinking of a creative pupil, the art and skill of a real teacher is without equal. It cannot be compared with the guaranteed outcome of business-in-education. Performance contracting has not done much to advance scientific knowledge about education (Miller, 1973).

Several important lessons have been learned from the partnership of business and education. Communities must be ready for the new plan or must go through preparatory processes to get ready for it. Success in Texarkana was accompanied by training teachers to act as consultants. The relationship of teachers and pupils remains central. Business-in-education uses methods that have been criticized by educators and psychologists: teaching for the test and extrinsic rewards. However, the methods work for some or, to the extent that they do not work, the students depart from the program.

Business-in-education has yet to resolve the difference between assembly line efficiency and the uniqueness of the human individual; many conventional schools have not achieved this goal either. Classroom teachers and businessmen must continue to look for some way to bridge the gap between immediate results and long-term retention of knowledge. The search for an avenue to the cultivation of the habit of continuous and independent learning must continue.

THE ROLE OF THE TEACHER

Teacher-pupil influence

In scores of studies of the teaching-learning milieu in this century, the relationship of teachers and pupils has always proved to be the critical element. In 1914, a survey in Locust Point, a section of Baltimore, Maryland, revealed 166 pupils out of a school population of 1,502 who were so socially, emotionally, or mentally handicapped that they were expected to become community dependents, delinquents, criminals, or alcoholics. It was predicted that they had little chance of becoming independent and/or contributing citizens (Fairbank, 1933). Seventeen years later a second survey of these same 166 persons was conducted. Surprisingly, very few had lived up to the prediction of general social inadequacy, even during a time of marked economic depression. Developing an awareness of need, involving parents, and special classes had been part of the project. But it was to the teachers, selected for their sympathetic and insightful understanding of disadvantaged children, that most of the credit was given for transforming the lives of these youngsters.

> Here, again, we find the effect of contacts in those early years with teachers who were not convictionless, but aggressively determined not to lose an opportunity to inculcate good old-fashioned morality, embodying principles of decency and respect for individual personality and cleanmindedness. The most striking result of this survey is to be found in the lasting impression made on these people in childhood by one of the teachers who came in closest contact with them. Science has no tests to evaluate the influence on personality, but the tests of life on growth and development tell the story.[3]

Flanders (1965) made a study, involving thirty-two teachers and over 1,200 pupils, of the impact of teacher behavior on pupil attitudes and learning. He contrasted direct and indirect influence. Direct influence consisted of statements made by the teacher which restricted freedom, focused on a selected prob-

---

[3] Ruth E. Fairbank, "The Subnormal Child—Seventeen Years After," *Mental Hygiene* 17 (1933): 208.

Teaching is an interpersonal transaction!

lem, and interjected teacher authority. Indirect influence consisted of statements that expanded freedom and encouraged participation and initiative, questions which clarified the students' feelings and ideas, and praise and encouragement of the students. Flanders posed these three hypotheses for the study.

Hypothesis One: Indirect teacher influence increases learning when a student's perception of the goal is confused and ambiguous.

Hypothesis Two: Direct teacher influence increases learning when a student's perception of the goal is clear and acceptable.

Hypothesis Three: Direct teacher influence decreases learning when a student's perception of the goal is ambiguous.

All three hypotheses were supported by Flanders' research. Pupils achieved more when their teachers used indirect methods than when teachers used direct methods. Teachers who used direct methods were consistently less flexible than indirect method teachers when pupils did not understand the goals. Flanders concluded that ". . . direct influence decreases learning, except when goals have been initially clarified and made acceptable by use of indirect methods." [4]

[4] Ned Flanders, *Teacher Influence, Pupil Attitudes, and Achievement* (Washington, D.C.: United States Office of Education, 1965), p. 109.

The implication seems to be inescapable: *Teachers teach not only what they say but also what they are and do.* Pupils scale their aspirations and activities to the kinds of influence which teachers exert (Robinson, 1973). Kounin and Gump (1961) reported that punitive teachers, in contrast to nonpunitive teachers, had more pupils who manifested aggression, displayed misconduct in school, and cared less about learning and school-related values. Leeper (1967) concluded that pupils learn school subjects more easily when teachers are courteous, friendly, and respectful. Pupils have trouble when teachers are impersonal, hurried, and autocratic.

Rogers (1969) has asserted that teaching is a vastly overrated function, because the emphasis should be on the process of learning—if there is no learning there has been no teaching. Lesson telling, lecturing, keeping school, and covering the text are not teaching unless the pupil learns. The major contribution of Rogers, which actually summarizes the findings of many investigators, is a summary of the characteristics of the teaching-learning transaction that maximize learning. He emphasizes that:

Teachers must enter the teaching-learning relationship without fear, front, or facade. They must be real persons by being their real selves.

Learning is facilitated when the pupil is prized, is valued and respected, by the teacher who can care without being possessive.

Empathic understanding, an awareness of how the pupil is feeling about the situation, facilitates learning. Understanding is quite different from judging and evaluating.

Trust facilitates learning processes because it permits the three foregoing characteristics to emerge. It consists of believing that the learner need not be crammed with information that is of the teacher's choosing but that the pupil has capacities for developing his own potential.

Rogers makes it clear that this type of teaching is not a one-sided transaction. It has exciting implications for the personal growth of the teacher and for the enhancement of the joy of living and being for the teacher as a person. The teacher changes by developing the characteristics that are described above and that are essential to learning. By granting freedom for students to live, learn, and be, the teacher gains freedom for himself. In several decades, traditional teachers will have largely disappeared (Rogers, 1968).

An evolving concept of teaching

It would be an overstatement to claim that this constitutes a trend toward a new concept of teaching. There are, however, educational leaders, or visionaries, and a few classroom teachers who see, as does Rogers, a vastly altered role for teachers. But the change can be tersely stated: *The responsibility for learning is shifted from the teacher to the pupil.*

Goodlad (1967) says that there is no assurance that the revolution that is tearing at the edge of the education establishment will reach to the inner core. But he hopes that, by the 1980s, schools will abandon the "telling" procedure which is so widely extant and shift to "discovery" and "inquiry" approaches. The emphasis will shift from teacher activity (teaching) to pupil activity (learning) and responsibility, from instruction and materials to the children themselves. Instead of subject matter mastery, the goal will be a warm, positive, and accepting human quality in the classroom. Information acquisition will be a natural by-product of such a relaxed environment.

Tyler (1967), in accord with Goodlad, does not recommend the elimination of subject matter but he emphasizes that the new task of the schools and teachers is that of teaching pupils how to learn and developing in them the motivation and skills required to keep alive their learning processes after formal schooling is complete.

Miller (1967) reports a shift from regarding the student as a passive learner to making him an active participant in the learning process. The teacher, instead of depending on drill, recitation, and repetition (thus lagging further behind the accumulation of knowledge), will design plans and use technological aids appropriate to needs of each individual. The teacher then may find that once-over is enough, and gain greater satisfaction by giving the pupil an experience in independence and self-reliance.

Goldhammer (1967) perceives the well-prepared teacher as a director of a team who leads trained assistants in the coordination of teaching-learning activities. He will spend no more than half of his time in the classroom, using the rest for planning, developing materials, and coordinating learning activities.

Lee (1966) believes that teaching roles are changing from the diversified to the specialized (counselor, supervisor, social worker, and curriculum coordinator) and, secondly,

". . . the teacher is moving away from the position of being exclusively or predominantly a source of data and a dispenser of information. . . . The growing stress upon 'learning how to learn' means that the elemental ingredient in education is not discrete fact but underlying principle, not details of information but insight into intellectual processes. This means that the *teacher must function more as a catalyst, as one whose prime obligation is the stimulation of the urge to inquire and the oversight of individual, independent study.* Facts and information are vital, of course, but in this perspective they become instruments for teaching and learning rather than ultimate ends in themselves.

"Third, and in line with the foregoing, the conception of the teacher's role grows less didactic and more tutorial; he becomes less the source than a resource for information, which is to say that he tends to stand increasingly as a mobilizer of materials for learning. . . ."[5]

Because no one program can fit more than a few pupils in a class, Hart (1969) suggests that planned, sequential teaching must give way to trust in random learning. The role of teachers is to give learners three As—acceptance, applause, and attention. This does not mean that no guidance is provided. The random approach uses goals but no timetable. Random learning permits pupils to take responsibility for their own learning.

Much evidence suggests that the innovative teacher of the future will serve as a resource person in the guidance of pupils' learning activities, instead of being an instructor. In the future, the art of teaching will reside less in being unusually well informed in a subject matter area—though this would be no handicap—than it does in knowing where information might

---

[5] Gordon C. Lee, "The Changing Role of the Teacher," *The Changing American School*, National Society for the Study of Education, 65th Yearbook (Chicago: University of Chicago Press, 1966), pt. 2, p. 24. Italics added.

be found and how a pupil might best use his own style of learning. Pupils' interests will be recognized, even if their interests are not traditionally academic. Such individuality of content not only makes pupils increasingly responsible, but it also nourishes the teacher's ingenuity and creativity.

SUMMARY

Many changes have taken place in education but student unrest, knowledge explosion, education of the culturally different child, and the need for continuous, lifelong learning have thrust new challenges onto the schools. Psychology, sociology, anthropology, and business and industry have provided substantial clues regarding better approaches to the complex problems of improved schooling.

Without ignoring the matter of materials and methods, it is a tenable thesis that teachers are at the heart of improved learning processes. It is not only a matter of what teachers are as human beings but also a matter of their perception of their role in the classroom. This role seems to be shifting from that of a tutor to that of learning catalyst—of placing more responsibility on pupils.

It is herein postulated that humanistic psychology, with its recognition of contributions from other psychological orientations and its emphasis on the centrality of the individual, puts the teacher closer to a resolution of some of the many dilemmas of creative, innovative educational processes, by stressing the person who receives this education. Furthermore, humanism reconciles such academic disciplines as anthropology, sociology, and psychiatry in acknowledging the individual as an active agent in learning and behavior.

SUGGESTED ADDITIONAL READINGS

Berscheid, Ellen, and Walster, Elaine. "Beauty and the Best." *Psychology Today* 5 (March 1972): 42–46. This statistical study shows how a child's perception of his physical attractiveness and the teacher's perceptions of the child's attractiveness color expectation and evaluations and, consequently, the child's achievement motivation.

Coleman, James S. "The Children Have Outgrown the Schools." *Psychology Today* 5 (February 1972): 72–82. Schools were designed historically to supply textbook information in an information-poor environment. Now in crowded cities, with radio, television, and vehicular mobility, our environment is information-rich and children are being stifled in schools. Coleman advocates community action schools or releasing children to work at earlier ages.

Ellison, Alfred. "The Myth Behind Graded Content." *Elementary School Journal* 72 (January 1972): 212–21. Pupil variation in achievement, potential, socioeconomic status, and interests make graded content impractical and dangerous. At a time when children should be questioning, curriculum improvement depends on children's search for answers.

Erikson, Donald A. "The Trailblazer in an Age of R & D." *School Review* 81 (1973): 155–74. The burdens and hazards of educational reform are described. Research and development have a place in educational reform but cannot bypass the teacher. Conversely, it takes more than trying harder, loving pupils, and altering subject matter to achieve significant results.

CHAPTER 2

Facilitating Learning
Processes

The previous chapter dealt with some of the culture-wide conditions which influence pupil and teacher behavior. This chapter builds upon the framework of psychology that was outlined in Chapter 1. Herein the position is taken that sociology, anthropology, and the view of the individual adopted by psychiatry make it somewhat easier to perceive the uniqueness of persons. It becomes somewhat easier to avoid a search for panaceas in method and content. Knowledge of such conditions marks the difference between the professional teacher and the teacher as technician. A technician wants proven, prescribed methods and content. He needs answers and formulas and usually works best in structured settings. The professional knows the many conditions that influence pupil personality and learning, recognizes them in action, and adapts his approaches accordingly. While the technician knows what to do, the professional supplements this by also knowing why. Thus the role of the professional teacher is that of a manager of learning activities. His is the job of orchestrating use of the curriculum and technological aids, facilitating the work of school personnel, and promoting learning activities of pupils.

22

The propositions that follow are designed for discussion and evaluation, in the hope that teachers and teachers-to-be will gain new perspectives on innovative, creative learning processes.

PROPOSITIONS ON THE FACILITATION OF LEARNING

The study of psychology, anthropology, sociology (especially the insights derived from the study of socioeconomic class) and the experience of business-in-education encourage a new and careful look at what occurs in classrooms. Much of what is done conventionally is not wrong, or even bad, so much as it is insufficient or inappropriate for some pupils. Formal education has not reached so many pupils as is necessary, and it has not fostered as much continuous learning as rapid change demands. Concern about methods, techniques, materials, and organization must give way to concern about the learning atmosphere and the interpersonal relationships which prevail in the classroom. These will predominate regardless of the subject being taught: Unless they are established, nothing else can be expected to work very well.

Heterostasis and homeostasis

Proposition I. *Children will learn more effectively when their heterostatic urges—their normal, healthy, and innate curiosity, their urge to explore and find out, to experience, to grow, to learn, to become, and to cope with their environment—are recognized and encouraged by teachers.*

Homeostasis is the tendency of the organism to remain as it is, or come to a state of rest, balance, or repose. Heterostasis is its polar opposite—the urge to be active, to explore, and to grow. Both are normal biological and psychological tendencies but heterostasis largely has been ignored until recent years. Menninger (1963, p. 34) used the word to indicate the drive to reach out and to develop. Rogers (1965) called the tendency "directional growth." Maslow (1970) remarked of a healthy person, "What a man can be, he must be" and developed the concept of self-actualization. Proactive indicates a move to-

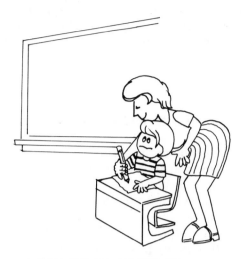

I CAN DO IT MYSELF!

The heterostatic urge can be dampened by oversolicitous child care.

ward the future as contrasted to man as a reactive being, reacting to stimuli, circumstances, and history. A central theme in proactive psychology is man's desire and capacity to choose, dream, aspire, and otherwise reveal a forward thrust. Although one may be a product of his past, he himself is a factor in what he will become (Bonner, 1965).

The heterostatic impulse is shown in the young child who grabs the spoon and wants to eat without assistance, who repeatedly picks himself up and tries again to walk, and who wants to go to kindergarten without holding mother's hand. Later, a normal adolescent rebels against continued dependence upon parents.

The heterostatic urge can be dampened by oversolicitous child care, by "momism" and possessive love with the adolescent, and by teachers who insist on following the course of study and making all decisions. A boy who is apathetic in school may be an enthusiastic reader of baseball records, biographies of sports heroes, and rule books. A teacher who can accept this as a good learning experience and who can reinforce the pupil's learning his "own thing" at his own rate and in his own style is keeping the heterostatic urge alive and fostering real learning. Chase (1966) claims that the major function of the early school years is to keep alive the child's natural, spontaneous quest for meaning and to equip him with the essential tools for pursuing learning on his own.

It is the pupil inhibited by the threat of failure, cowed by the presence of power, and thwarted from the pursuit of his own curiosity who seeks the security of homeostasis, the safety of conformity, the routine, and the familiar. Motivation for learning is more dynamic and enduring when it stems from the heterostatic urge than when external rewards or symbols (grades, marks, degrees, Green Stamps, and gold stars) are used. The heterostatic urge does not have to be learned or taught, but it can be shriveled by experiences which discourage its manifestations. When the heterostatic urge is stifled it is necessary to do more than remove restrictions, it is necessary to reteach and relearn.

It may be unrealistic to hope that all educational practice will capitalize on the heterostatic urge. However, Hart (1969), Goodlad (1969), and certainly many others stress the benefits of curiosity, individualized learning, and the self-actualization of the lives of unique pupils. Goodman (1968) and Coleman (1972) predict the demise of contemporary schools unless such an alteration is effected. Gross and Gross (1970) report that much in this direction is being done in British Infant Schools. Ellison (1972) says that graded content must go.

In this proposition and the following one, the matter of teacher growth and development is fundamental. Teachers encourage more effectively by demonstrating than by directing. They are more likely to teach what they are than what they say. Heterostasis is encouraged when all aspects of what the teacher does carry the message that a really helpful relationship is established. Heterostatic behavior can be learned, or perhaps relearned, by teachers as well as by students. If something is to be taught, it must be known and practiced by those who would develop the behavior; hence teacher growth, in this respect, is a prerequisite to pupil learning. And through growth teachers can improve their style of life and enhance its enjoyment.

The whole child

Proposition II. *Children will learn more effectively when their total personalities (physical, emotional, mental, and social) are considered within their environmental context and when teachers do not attempt to isolate the cognitive from the affective or to consider pupils apart from their environments.*

For more than half a century psychologists have described human behavior as "holistic," meaning that each individual functions as an organized system within a unique perceptual field (see Glossary). Nevertheless, school learning tends to be viewed as an essentially intellectual function. The futility of this is shown by the difficulties experienced with Blacks, Mexican-Americans, and Indians in school settings. Coleman (1972) believes that helping youth become adults demands changes in the family, business, community, and industry. Changes therein will make it possible for school to shift from its present role of baby-sitting. He says that when students do not have responsibility they become irresponsible, when they are not allowed to produce they become unproductive, and when they are kept from independence they become dependent. They must, in short, learn to work, learn to get along with others, learn to be wives, mothers, husbands and fathers, learn concern for others, and learn to take responsibility. The curriculum of the school is thus not a purely cognitive function.

Maslow (1970) conceptualizes human needs as being arranged in hierarchical order. The lowest, most basic, needs are those which relate to physical requirements such as food, water, and maintenance of a restricted range of temperature. Next are the safety needs which, when satisfied, conserve the individual both physically and psychologically. The next higher level of needs consists of those relating to the need to love and be loved, to belong and be accepted, and to be respected and have status. Finally, at the highest level of needs are those least urgent but most specifically human—the needs for satisfying curiosity and gaining knowledge—the need for self-actualization.

Learning will occur most rapidly and efficiently after lower level needs have been satisfied or are on the way to becoming satisfied. Hungry and emotionally upset children have difficulty concentrating and focusing on school tasks (Wright, 1937; Dayton, 1969). Needs are not fully satisfied at any level. They are in a continuous process of ebb and flow. The very essence of pupil self-direction and independent learning is that pupils will in some way use their psychosocial environments (school, family, community) in attempting to fulfill their recurring needs.

Recognition of holistic functioning calls for teachers to examine their own attitudes and actions. It calls for a consideration of pupils' out-of-school experiences as well as the materials, tasks, and equipment within the school. Those innovative practices which focus on the improvement of teacher perceptions (such as hope, faith, and trust) along with novel approaches to content are likely to be most productive. Basic questions in innovation are: (1) How can teachers come to realize that the intellectual aspects of pupil environments cannot be dealt with separately from the emotional, physical, and social factors which exist concomitantly in a dynamic system? (2) How can the contributions of the behavioral sciences best be utilized by educators to improve this holistic system of relationships?

Varied learning styles

Proposition III. *Pupils will learn more effectively when the uniqueness of their learning skills, potentials, and styles, as well as the learning modes which they share with all or many of their peers, are recognized by teachers.*

There are many similarities in the learning patterns of different pupils. We know, for instance, that the affective aspect of human behavior is no less important than the cognitive. For all pupils, the desire to learn is a partner of opportunity to learn. Yet no two persons memorize, recall, or recombine information in exactly the same way (Hammer, 1972). It appears possible that one of the significant advances in the teaching-learning transaction will be routine identification of varied learning styles and appropriate classroom adaptations to them (Nations, 1967; Riessman, 1964). For example, experienced teachers are sometimes surprised, and even disappointed, when a child who did not read his assignment does well on the test. Another pupil who did not listen and who was frequently absent also does surprisingly well. The explanation is at hand, although there is some reluctance to accept it. Pupils have different learning styles—some do (in accordance with conventional expectations) learn by reading, but some learn by talking, some by listening, some by acting

27

and doing, and still others by observing. Some learn by readily accepting but others must dispute and argue, some need direction and structure while others need freedom, and some need independence but others learn better in groups.

What is needed is an inventory, resembling a personality inventory, of learning styles. This might include pupil self-assessment, teachers' anecdotes about learning behavior, and a check list of self and others' observations. Such a schedule might make the learner observant of how he learns, and the teacher aware of the reality of pupil differences in the classroom.

It is not suggested here that learning styles are genetically determined. It is not implied that styles cannot be changed, or that one cannot develop a new style. It is suggested that a pupil's self-concept can be bolstered and his heterostatic impulses can be enlivened if teachers progress from strengths to weaknesses. Specifically, if a child can learn by listening, then acceptance and positive feedback for his distinctiveness will also constitute a solid approach for his learning how to learn by reading. If he can draw and paint and learn, then those should not be neglected and made to consume less time than is given to instruction in reading.

One of the major concerns of educators today—that of keeping culturally different children in school—can be handled by recognizing differences in learning styles. These children, even more than others, need to touch, feel, act out, and directly experience those things which are to be understood. "They are at a disadvantage only in developing skills and attitudes that schools and other mainstream social institutions require." [1] Other children, because of prior varied experience, can depend much more on linguistic and symbolic representation.

The self-concept

Proposition IV. *The learning of school tasks will proceed most expeditiously when teachers acknowledge, in attitude and action, the relationship between pupils' self-concepts and their readiness and aspiration to learn.*

[1] Marian Sherman Stearns, "Early Education: Still In Its Infancy," *American Education,* 6 (No. 7): 5, August–September, 1970.

I MAY DESERVE A "D" BUT IT SURE WRECKS MY SELF-CONCEPT.

The typical teacher enjoys having pupils who best achieve school goals, who are confident, industrious, accept guidance, do not vie for attention, and who accept teachers as their friends. Such pupils approach their tasks expecting to accomplish them. Doubt and fear do not shrivel their capacities. These pupils know that they are able, accepted, and are of such worth that they may maintain their individuality. It should also be noted that pupils who dare to think divergently are often disliked by teachers. Most teachers prefer the convergent, passive, conforming type of learner (Getzels and Jackson, 1962).

Believing that one is socially unacceptable, intellectually inferior, or racially excluded tends to inhibit optimum learning. Emaciated, negative self-concepts are the outgrowth of rejection, excessive criticism, ignorance and punishment for attempts to have one's presence acknowledged. Such self-concepts are the result of being forced to participate in experiences for which one's background is inadequate and then being branded as a failure for not competing successfully with more experienced rivals. Low self-concepts may be the result of being placed in remedial classes and being branded as, *then becoming,* a remedial case.[2]

---

[2] The teaching approaches of remedial teachers are not questioned. Their emphases on individualization, success, emotional poise, and acceptance of

Jensen (1969) does not believe that the intelligence quotients of disadvantaged children have been changed much by compensatory education. The more positive claims, he says, are reportedly favorable effects on self-confidence, motivation, and attitudes toward school. The teacher with the humanistic orientation says that this is, indeed, a highly desirable result. Few persons, perhaps none, would argue that the tools of learning—reading, writing, and computation—are unimportant. There are many who would argue that having the tools of learning is not very important unless there is a concomitant inclination to use them. Every bit of subject matter and every teaching technique might well be evaluated in terms of "What does it do for the pupil's self-concept?" Emphatically, what an individual will aspire to is dependent upon what he sees as being possible.

Self-fulfilling prophecy

Proposition V. *Learning will be facilitated when teachers recognize the centrality of the ego-concept.* They will interrupt the self-perpetuating aspects of a low self-concept. They will nurture the reinforcing aspects of the ego-concept.

Kelly (1955, p. 367), for instance, cites the example of young men in training to become military officers who do become leaders although they showed no previous indications of leadership abilities. He believes it is "amazing" that an obsolescent mass promotion policy such as that used in the United States Navy works as well as it does.

Experienced teachers who trust their pupils to behave when they leave the room will not be amazed at confirming research findings. Teachers were deliberately misinformed about the intelligence of their pupils and, when they treated those pupils as if they were bright, follow-up tests showed I.Q. gains as high as twenty-four points (Rosenthal and Jacobson, 1968). A New Jersey study found that pupils who were classed as failures and treated as failures succeeded in verifying teachers' expectations ("Research Discloses. . . . ," 1967).

---

children are commendable and should be incorporated in the classroom. It is the identification and separation of different children that is questioned.

Taylor (1964, p. 41) reports that, after past achievement, the best predictor of creative performance is self-rating, based on what others think one can do.

The self-fulfilling prophecy is a double double-barreled phenomenon. It can promote expansive, striving, heterostatic behavior or it can generate retiring, defensive, and homeostatic actions. It can result from the expectations one has for himself or from the expectations of others. It is self-perpetuating because, when doubting their own ability and viewing themselves as inadequate, people hesitate to risk new experiences and limit awareness of that which is self-enhancing and developmental. Defense mechanisms, for example, help the organism to remain comfortable by reducing awareness of painful realities. In contrast, the confident person attacks the new with vigor, enjoys new experiences, and acts with full energy because he can afford the risk.

Human functions that are not used either fail to develop or tend to atrophy with continued nonuse. Just as practice contributes to the efficiency of an athlete, so the disposition toward openness and learning is enhanced through use. The point is both illustrated, and contained within, educators' attitudes toward compensatory education. Jensen (1969) believes such programs are largely futile, Bloom (1964) believes they are ineffective after the adolescent years, and White (1972) says the question is still open, that compensatory education has not yet really been tried.

Often, unfortunately, the most learning some pupils acquire is a clear notion that they are stupid, dirty, and undesirable. Yet the steady support of just one person can be enough to teach a child that he is intelligent, dependable, and acceptable. When self-regarding attitudes can be influenced so that the individual comes to see himself as more adequate, he tends to become less defensive and more open to experience. Learning is facilitated, and feelings of personal worth are enhanced.

Origins of the self-concept

Proposition VI. *The self-concepts most conducive to optimum learning are nourished in a milieu in which teachers recognize that self-concepts stem from interaction with the social and physical environment.*

31

The "and" in this proposition merits consideration. The self-concept originates, in part, from the way key persons in the individual's environment regard him. Doting, biased, and emotionally astigmatic parents who regard their offspring as being the smartest, best behaved, and best looking child on the current scene are providing part of the milieu needed for a robust self-concept. In addition the child must have his lower level needs for food, warmth, and protection from the elements satisfied; he must feel safe from insult and injury and he should experience more success than failure in his endeavors.

Both positive and denigrating concepts of self are learned from experiences with people, situations, and things. The "organization" man and the "other-directed" person both tend to act as they perceive others want them to act. The desire of adolescents for approval and the phenomenon of peer pressure tend to keep many young people in line. Yet, theoretically, we prize distinctiveness. It is largely the different and creative person who is responsible for innovation, change and progress. Philosophically, we admire the one who is his own person; actually, such persons tend to make others feel uncomfortable, so those who are on the borders of self-actualization often have their nascent tendencies discouraged. It is in this area that school personnel have most perceptibly failed to promote effective learning. The failure may be due in some part to teachers' suspicion and distrust of deviation.

Self-concepts may be weak because teachers have not used or have misused peer influences (see Proposition XI). Typical is the teacher who puts pressure on a pupil to inform on his peers: "Who's smoking pot in the rest room?" "Who is the pusher?" A less familiar example is the use of the competitive grading system, where the success of one implies the frustration of another. When one must compete to gain status, it is difficult for any of the competitors to have meaningful interpersonal relationships. Peer influences are also neglected when there is failure to take advantage of the lessons that sociometry might teach, though other techniques for assessing interpersonal attractions and those viewed as comfortable persons could be used. Permitting the exercise of democratic classroom procedures is a powerful means of validating the worth of individuals. The feeling that "I am needed" is a powerful incentive to learning (Pfeil, 1969).

HOW DUMB DOES ONE HAVE TO BE TO GET INTO A LEARNING OPPORTUNITY CENTER?

The self-concept as a factor in learning, and the cause of its self-perpetuating nature, may be seen in the reaction of a school staff to the challenge of innovation. Some personnel will welcome the opportunity to grow. Some will resist subtly and logically, but will resist. In part, the resistance is an inability to trust others or reluctance to give trust a trial. And the path of the helper is risky because trust is both a result and a cause. Help must be given without belittling. Schools, nevertheless, are proving that enhancement of teachers' and pupils' self-concepts can be achieved (Cottle, 1969; Harrison, 1970).

Words are more than symbols

Proposition VII. *Learning will be facilitated when the implications of the verbal-symbolic method of dealing with problems and actualizing the self are purposefully used by educators.*

The old charm "Sticks and stones may break my bones but names will never hurt me" is grossly erroneous. Whether or not damage is physical is of little import; words (allegedly only

33

symbols) can, and do, injure psychologically. The "stupid Swedes," the "dumb Pollacks" of immigration days, the "dirty Jews" of World War II, can attest to the tangible reality of words.

Early childhood education for the culturally different places heavy emphasis on language development. This is because words and language are not only clues to the culture but because words are an indication of identity with a culture (accents, dialects, standard English indicate one's exclusion or inclusion in this culture). Communication with others, which is largely verbal and largely abstract, is a major determinant of the development of the mind and in the maintenance of the self-concept.

Technology, automation, population explosion, knowledge explosion and the quest for personal identity are causing a shift from a physical to a psychological world. It becomes necessary to diminish reliance on direct experience and accelerate dependence on ideas, symbols, and abstractions. Because words are abstract, it is necessary that adults use words and provide experiences that are appropriate to the developmental level of children.

Failure to provide such experiences is not so much a matter of teachers' being unappreciative of the verbal-symbolic aspect as it is of their monopolizing its application. Estimates and measurements indicate that about eighty percent of the talking in classrooms is done by teachers. To the extent that learning is doing—that we learn what we do—the proportion of teacher vs. pupil talk should be reversed. Even culturally different (sometimes called linguistically handicapped) pupils, when encouraged, have surprising linguistic skills (Mickelson and Galloway, 1972).

Although research has indicated that many things are important, the chance for children to verbalize has been, and remains, an important component of compensatory education programs in early childhood (Stearns, 1970). The chance to talk with peers and with accepting, nonjudgmental counselors has been found to reduce significantly the anxiety of adolescents transferring from high school to college. Studies show that the greatest development and modification of behavior takes place in small, face-to-face groups.

Scholars in the field of linguistics are both telling educators what to look for and supporting teachers' findings with respect to the centrality of verbal-linguistic activity in the development of self. Becker (1962, p. 103) asserts that the self "is primarily a linguistic device." The most prominent findings from the communication studies of Watzlawick and others (1967, p. 84) affirm that the self-concept, and mental development, spring from the confirming aspects of human communication.

Much of traditional education emphasizes the teacher's verbalization and minimizes that of the pupil. The pupil's opportunity to test his perceptions, knowledge, and feelings is limited largely to answering teachers' questions and reporting the contents of books. Discussion is a neglected art. Educational innovation has sound psychological and sociological roots when it proposes more opportunity for pupils to talk, discuss, explore, and to live their problems and questions in an interpersonal setting.

A few elementary schools make provisions for pupils' talking. Corte Maderia, California, the Lamphere schools in Madison Heights, Michigan, and the Matzke School in Dallas, Texas, have built corners, rooms, and centers where pupils may convene to discuss those things that are important to them. Nova High School, Florida, has built extra wide hallways and placed benches in them. Instead of requiring pupils to march quietly from one class to another, it is expected that they will and should stop to visit. In Evanston (Ill.) Township High School little cubicles are provided for those important student-to-student talks. No doubt there are many other schools which are recognizing the importance of the verbal-linguistic approach.

Schools have been somewhat successful in teaching the verbal-symbolic method of coping with problems of a tangible, concrete nature. They have been considerably less successful in helping youngsters deal verbally with their more interpersonal, emotional concerns. Yet counselors and psychologists have repeatedly demonstrated that, to a marked degree, it is unnecessary to act out problems when they can be talked out. Behavioral scientists know how to encourage these verbal-symbolic transactions; the question is how long it will take teachers to adopt them. Rogers predicts that this goal will be realized by the year 2000. We wonder, "Is that soon enough?"

His [the student's] learning will not be confined to the ancient intellectual concepts and specializations. It will not be a *preparation* for living. It will be, in itself, an *experience* in living. Feelings of inadequacy, hatred, a desire for power, feelings of love and awe and respect, feelings of fear and dread, unhappiness with parents or with other children—all these will be an open part of his curriculum, as worthy of exploration as history or mathematics.[3]

Involvement and affiliation

Proposition VIII. *Pupils will learn more effectively when the teacher and fellow pupils show, by attitude and action, that they are accepted, belong, and their involvement is desired and significant.*

The optimum school learning situation is one in which there is a contingent relationship (see Glossary) between the teacher and the taught. Unless the pupil feels that he is an influencing member of the group and that he is identified with others in the classroom he may come to view the school, the system, and the establishment as some anonymous "they" who exercise all the power and all the control. The outcome is highly variable, ranging from apathetic resignation to rebellion—no aspect of which is conducive to achievement motivation.

When directions continually come from exterior sources, when experience is limited to that which is prescribed, then people fail to develop the ability and determination to manage their own affairs. In such instances, responsibility falls upon the manager, the director, or the teacher. "The teacher did nothing to motivate me!" The program, the credit, and the blame are all assigned to another. The person who can do nothing on his own can be responsible for nothing. "I did everything I could to make her a moral person," wails the mother of the pregnant, unmarried teenager.

A contingent relationship has not been developed when one has neither power nor control. There is no contingent

[3] Carl R. Rogers, "Interpersonal Relationships: U. S. A. 2000," *Journal of Applied Behavioral Sciences*, 4 (1968): 275.

relationship when each is free to blame another for unwanted results. Pupils blame the teacher, teachers blame the administrators, and administrators blame the board of education (which is an anonymous "they")—there is no contingent relationship.

In an authoritative, evaluative, and blame-placing relationship, it is wrong to fail. One dare not risk divergent or new thoughts or behaviors because he may lose status and acceptance. It is better not to try at all and be able to say, "I could if I wanted to." Youngsters who know that *their* offhand questions and *their* interests beyond the formal course of study will result in lower grades than if they just do the assignments are not experiencing a contingent relationship. Neither are they satisfying their own curiosity or exercising their heterostatic urges. In order to acquire behavior, one must exercise it (Skinner, 1971).

Antidotes do exist and teachers are using them. Teacher-pupil dialogue (see Glossary) can be practiced. Teachers can reduce their lecturing posture and increase their action as learning catalysts. Controversial issues are discussed but are not resolved. Subject matter relevant to the students' lives is sought. The compulsion to cover the syllabus has been allayed (but not eliminated). Much innovation properly is designed to enlarge the incidence of success, which also helps to involve the pupil. Material, curricular organization, distribution of time, and methods of evaluating are, along with the teacher-pupil interaction, matters of serious concern as we consider affiliation and involvement.

Product versus process

Proposition IX. *Pupils will learn more effectively when their teachers regard the process of learning as more important than the product of learning.*

The importance of the products of learning, the basic need for facts, skills, and information are undeniable. The products of learning are, indeed, involved in process; they reward, provide feedback, and influence next steps in the learning process. Moreover, it seems highly probable that if the process is held in high regard, the products will be more readily acquired by pupils. Ultimately, we are judged by what we know or have produced and by the skills we have acquired. However, in a world rapidly changing, the task of the school shifts from what is learned to how learning is learned and how it carries over to continuous, lifetime learning. The mind needs to be thought of as an instrument to be used rather than a storehouse to be filled.

The data-based approach to education is justified when it is assumed that *the* answers and *the* best ways of acting are already known and only need to be passed on to the ignorant. Evaluation based on information acquired may produce a kind of tunnel vision and an inability to perceive the creative and serendipitous. If information is the focus, then computers may well do a better job than the human teacher. Critical thinking does require data, but which data are needed is less readily indicated. Approximately three-fourths of knowledge now existing was unknown at the end of World War II (Tyler, 1966). At this rate, and the rate has actually increased, a data-based education becomes obsolete in less time than it takes to acquire it.

> We find that the emphasis is changed from one of the passive learner to one of an active participant in the learning process. In many cases, the question is more important than the answer. Action upon knowledge is more important than the quantity of right answers.[4]

One of the grave dangers of the content-oriented concept of education is the idea of completion or closure, that a person has "completed his education." A sufficient number of teachers act as if this were true, so that it is alarming to those who believe that, like it or not, teachers are the principal role-models for their pupils.

Whether students' tasks are self-determined or teacher-assigned, the stress should be on the process of learning. Rate of learning, content, points, credits, grades, diplomas, or degrees are of value only as they serve a transitional function

---

[4] Paul A. Miller, "Major Implications for Education of Prospective Changes in Society: One Perspective," in E. L. Morphet and C. O. Ryan, eds., *Implications for Education of Prospective Changes in Society* (Denver: Designing Education for the Future, 1967), p. 17.

from the phenomena of emphasis on content to emphasis on process. Process is a key factor in intrinsic motivation.

Preschooler: "I can do it myself."

High schooler: "Let me be, give me room."

Adult: "I want to be my own kind of person."

The nation which has an educational system geared to developing creative thought and teaching the process of discovery, insures its own self-renewal, survival, and prosperity (Gordon, 1972).

Teachers as models

Proposition X. *Learning will be more effective when teachers act on the premise that pupils' behavior tends to be in terms of the actions and attitudes of significant persons.*

The range of potential human behavior and development, present at the moment of conception, is much less than is commonly believed. The great differences between individuals, social strata, and nations reside predominantly in what happens to hereditary potential (Hurley, 1969). Each experience modifies the individual's behavior. Each human contact presents an opportunity to observe and absorb new and varied ways of acting. Thus the prospects for becoming what one biologically can be reside largely in the quality of key people who are around the individual. This does not ignore the matter of heredity or the matter of individual choice, but it does call attention to the inescapable relationship of self to others.

Allport (1968) found that the impact which teachers generally have on pupils is disappointingly small. He asked 100 college students how many of their prior 4,632 teachers had exerted a strong or reasonably strong influence on their lives. Three out of four teachers already had been virtually forgotten. One teacher in ten was remembered as having a powerful influence. When one considers that the population of this study consisted exclusively of those deemed to be scholastically successful, it is disturbing to think that the matter of the teacher as a model is left to chance.

Because the impact of the teacher is so small, it is even more important that that influence be positive. And this is because the teacher is society's planned representative. Teachers' attitudes, behavior, and influence can be changed. This change can be affected by in-service education, by means of teacher workshops, through psychotherapeutic intervention (Jersild and Lazar, 1962), and by direct emphasis on human relations (Harrison, 1970). The whole concept of the value of an education is denied when we claim that teachers are born and not made. Teacher education programs need to pay more attention to the development of teachers who accept themselves and who can accept others.

The influence of key people as models is so subtle and continuous that it often escapes recognition. The walk of father and son, the word inflections of mother and daughter, the political stance of adolescents and parents are slight indications of a widely pervasive phenomenon. Most teachers, and most people in general, often project attitudes and feelings of which they are not aware, nor are they aware of their own transparency. The necessity for psychological self-preservation makes all individuals much more conscious of the moods, feeling tones, and unexpressed attitudes of others than they realize. The lesson is being learned from the cradle on, long before the learning task is verbalized. Children know and respond to the moods of their parents. This sets the stage for the ambiguous communication called the "double-message."

The pervasiveness of feelings, their ambiguity, and their transparency all promote double message communication. Mothers who have read of the importance of love try to conceal their revulsion for crying, messy babies. Teachers who are impatient, frustrated, and hostile try to conceal these feelings behind the stereotyped role of warm, accepting, and self-controlled teachers. As children and as pupils, young people get both messages, and have some difficulty in knowing which to respond to. It is hard to know how to act to fulfill expectations. Teachers present the kind of problem they should be helping young people to resolve. The model they furnish is confused, ambiguous—worse than none at all.

Too much of today's college preparation for teaching and the theme of most experimentation and innovation within schools relates to what the teachers can do and what they can say to make lessons impressive. Many studies describe the relationship between teachers and pupils but relatively few deal with the experimental improvement of those relations. In addition to the question "What can I do?" both pre-service and in-service teachers should ask "Who am I?" and "How do I come across to others?"

Teachers who are qualified in a content area should be exposed to some type of human relations training that will help them attain the following objectives: first, the ability to use the social skills of accepting, clarifying, and using the ideas of students in planning work and diagnosing difficulties; second, knowledge of those that expand student reactions; and third, understanding of a theory of instruction that he can use to control his own behavior as he guides classroom communication.[5]

In order to function with sincerity and validity and to provide acceptable models, teachers must be and not merely act. If they are to instill intellectual curiosity in pupils, they themselves must be enamored with the process of growth and discovery. If they want youngsters to innovate and create, they must be willing to think divergently. If they will have their pupils tolerant and accepting, teachers have no more potent tool than providing an example.

Peer influence

Proposition XI. *Pupils will learn more effectively when teachers implement the premise that peer influences, interactions, and models are strong detractors or strong reinforcers of classroom instruction.*

James. S. Coleman, Erik Erikson, Lawrence K. Frank, Edgar Z. Friedenberg, Margaret Mead, Frank Musgrove, and Carolyn and Muzafer Sherif are among the more articulate critics who have indicated that the great need of youth today is to be recognized, to have an identity. Because there are so many factors in our culture that deny this identity, the importance of the social or peer group has been intensified.

[5] Ned A. Flanders, *Teacher Influence, Pupil Attitudes, and Achievement,* (Washington, D.C.: U.S. Department of Health, Education, and Welfare, 1966), p. 118.

There are other reasons why peer relationships should be considered in evolving the strategies of innovative education. (1) The theoretical and philosophical bases of our democratic way of life are denied when the posture of the schools is that of superior and subordinate. It is difficult to shift responsibility to those who have learned to defer to, and rely upon, authority. (2) Good human relationships are important factors for success in occupations and professions. Schools should recognize this social aspect as well as the technical and theoretical phases of work. (3) The young person's motivation to achieve, choice of curriculum, and mode of response are influenced, but not dictated, by his peer or reference groups. Although classroom instruction is predominately a group activity, teachers rarely study or experiment with group dynamics.

Caution should be mixed with enthusiasm but it does seem that recognition of the power of peer groups will see an expanded use of discussion in many classes. A few teachers have the skill necessary for the leadership of such discussions. Many will have to unlearn the instructor role and develop an ear that can hear the voices of group participants.

Peer influence is ignored when teachers punish the class for the transgressions of the culprit who will not step forward. Disdain for peer influence is shown by the teacher who uses public ridicule, reprimand, and sarcasm. Such actions are culpable at any time, but particularly devastating when used in the presence of one's peers.

School personnel reveal their ignorance of the strength of peer influences when they teach, preach, and demand differences in mode of dress and grooming from that sanctioned by the peer group. The result of contradicting fads and fashions is to place teachers and pupils into opposing factions. Teachers strive for the manifestation of "common sense," which really means "the way we did it when we were young." Then pupils seek and contrive ways to circumvent the imposed regulations. In extreme cases the conflict of adult and peer perceptions of propriety provides a spark for protests, demonstrations, and confrontations.

When peer influences are recognized, there may be less need for teachers to perform the roles of police, jury, and judge. In fact, it has been found that students often judge each other more harshly, in student courts, than would their teachers who have to intercede for the transgressor.

A system of values

Proposition XII. *Pupils will learn more effectively, and will organize their lives for optimum efficiency, when teachers and other significant persons help them evolve a system of conscious, studied values.*

In order to become a true and satisfied human, an individual needs the momentum and direction of a studied system of values. Man must have, say students of motivation, purposes that pull as well as stimuli that push, if his life is to be full and complete. The advantages of a system of values are: (1) that knowing one's position or direction helps to develop some consistency or authenticity as a person; (2) that knowing one's position is a prerequisite for choosing, providing a vantage point for solving personal problems; and (3) that awareness of position helps to establish a consistent image to which others may refer and to provide the dependability that adds to meaningfulness and trust in interpersonal transactions. Hopefully, the teacher will have a system of values upon which his teaching transactions will be less ambivalent, more consistent, and less likely to be an enigma to his pupils.

Readiness

Proposition XIII. *Learning is facilitated when it occurs during certain developmental phases—sometimes called critical periods or stages of readiness.*

There are many kinds of readiness for learning that tend to make the pupil particularly adept for a period of time. If that time goes by without tutelage in that area, the learner seems to have lost some of his adeptness. Thus, there is what is known as a cumulation of deficiency in ability to learn in school on the part of culturally different children. Probably the most widely recognized readiness is that for reading instruction. Readiness for a second language illustrates the fact that facility for a particular area of learning may be transitory. Penfield (1972) postulates that language centers of the brain—if not exercised by a second language prior to age 12 or 13—are taken over by other functions and some of the facility for language learning disappears. It has been hypothesized that mothers who prevent their adolescent sons or daughters from dating at an appropriate age may prevent their reaching mature heterosex-uality—unless there is therapeutic intervention.

The concept of readiness may have its greatest value in enabling adults to recognize that it is useless to try to teach a child a particular thing when he is indisposed, indifferent, or inefficient; that, for instance, teaching social dancing to pre-adolescent boys would be inappropriate and unproductive.

Reinforcement

Proposition XIV. *Learners tend to repeat those behaviors that are successful for them or result in approval or attention.*

Behaviorists and humanists are much in accord in re-garding success as a positive reinforcement that consolidates behavior. However, the humanist would emphasize that the meaning of success may not be the same in everyone's perception. Babies have repeated temper tantrums because tantrums have been successful. Children play hookey because there is some element of success involved. Occupation by students of the president's office on campus, sit-ins, disruption of classes have been successful or these would not be repeated. Protestors wait to create disorder until television cameramen arrive. The bearded sages who utter words but have nothing to say, when given television time, are experiencing success. Many of them have said, "I detest violence but it works." And so, too, do temper tantrums—with some parents.

Teachers should be charged with the task of analyzing, from the first grade through college, those factors of success that cause students to repeat their actions.

Learning involves ambivalence

Proposition XV. *Learning will be more effective when pupils' feelings of security are bolstered by using established habits and familiar routines while providing new experiences.*

The first proposition emphasized heterostasis, the ten-dency of the healthy organism to move out, to grow, and to become. The polarity of heterostasis with homeostasis was mentioned in the discussion. In this last proposition, it seems practical to return to the elaboration of this polarity.

A corollary proposition is: In constructing something new, whether physical or behavioral, we make it as similar as possible to that which is already familiar. A teacher will encounter areas of resistance to change even in the healthy pupil who is reaching out and exercising curiosity in other areas. When their behavior is already successful, when they determine that change is unimportant, or when they find the subject irrelevant, pupils resist change. In the presence of rapid change even the normal person is attracted to the regular, the routine, the reliable. Kindergarten and primary teachers should appreciate the comfort that a schedule, regularity, and consistency provide to a child who is experiencing a plethora of new things.

However, we are more concerned with the behavior of teachers and their program for learning new and innovative practices than we are with pupils' attitudes toward learning. Thus teachers should look at the phenomenon of resistance to change as it exists within themselves. This self-scrutiny, both individually and in groups, will help them to decide whether the resistance they feel, and see in others, is due primarily to the rationale of the idea or is primarily a rationalization of one's own defensiveness.[6]

Cottle (1969), Harrison (1970), and Parker and Withycombe (1973) have suggested in-service education as one approach to rendering teachers more open to, or at least more accepting of, educational innovation. One such in-service approach would be the opportunity to observe varied practices. This would include leave-of-absence policies designed for "retooling" of teachers. It would include putting college professors into schools to lead in-service classes. It could mean teacher participation and involvement in the formation of administrative policy. It would include expanded use of teacher exchanges.

Many people prefer to leave well enough alone. They point to the many successes of the educational system and to the practices believed to be the best in history and the best in comparison to the rest of the world. Others say that educational change is necessary in a changing world and challenge

---

[6] Contrary to popular usage, defensiveness is not always an undesirable characteristic. One would not have a very robust ego if he could not sometimes defend his ideas and behaviors.

45

the institution of the school to assume leadership in this process. Our support of change resides in the argument that the needs of many pupils are not yet being met in the ways that we already know are possible. It becomes a matter of making the good still better.

SUMMARY

Although schools are today effectively reaching more pupils than ever before, there are many pertinent criticisms of educational processes. Dropouts, alienated pupils, failure to realize potential, and taxpayer resistance—all create doubts of the system. Propositions for facilitating learning are presented as criteria for assessing the merit of teaching-learning innovations and emphasizing the shift in teachers' role from instructing to orchestrating teaching-learning transactions.

The authors propose that learning will be facilitated when teachers:

I   recognize and act upon the theory that pupils want to learn, to grow, and to become;

II   recognize that the emotional, physical, and social, as well as the intellectual, aspects of personality influence learning;

III recognize and accept the uniqueness of each child's learning pace and style and give it a chance to function;

IV   recognize the centrality of the child's self-concept and strive to bolster and enhance a positive self-regard;

V   make the self-perpetuating and self-reinforcing nature of the self-concept a central concern;

VI   act upon the thesis that self-concept arises from contact with others and from success in dealing with the environment;

VII appreciate and make provisions for implementing the implications of the verbal-symbolic nature of living and thinking;

VIII show that the learner is accepted, belongs, and his involvement is desired;

IX   implement the idea that the process of learning is more important than the product of learning;

X   put into action the notion that, inevitably, they are models of behaving and learning;

XI   acknowledge in action that peers influence the methods, goals, interests, and attitudes of fellow learners;

XII   recognize that a well-developed system of values is an integral part of learning efficiency and help pupils develop such a system;

XIII devise their plans to accord with the fact that certain learnings take place at certain times more advantageously than at other times;

XIV   study the implications of the psychological principle that pupils consolidate those learnings that are, for them, successful; and

XV   tolerate the fact that the urge to grow must coexist with the tendency to act on old habits and to resist change.

SUGGESTED ADDITIONAL READINGS

Bogue, E. G. "One Foot in the Stirrup." *Phi Delta Kappan* 53 (April 1972): 506–08. The author recommends honest, trustful communication between teachers and administrators in order to create a productive teaching-learning milieu (See Proposition VII).

Moustakas, Clark. *The Authentic Teacher.* Cambridge, Mass.: Howard A. Doyle Printing Company, 1966. Ways in which teachers have met themselves and brought about change are discussed in a practical, i.e., school, situation (See Proposition XV).

Pearl, Arthur. "There Is Nothing More Loco Than 'Loco Parentis.' " *Phi Delta Kappan* 53 (June 1972): 629–31. The issue in dealing with high school students is neither to assert stronger authority nor to join youthful dissenters. Ways must, and can, be found to make youth more responsible for their own learning goals and achievement (See Proposition VIII).

Tsitrian, John. "The Ferguson Plan for All-Year School." *Phi Delta Kappan* 54 (January 1973): 314–15. Far from abandoning schools, an elementary school in Hawaiian Gardens, California, has made year-round school a success. The key is a continuous progress curriculum based on differences in pupil learning rates.

Zirkel, Perry A. "Self-Concept and the 'Disadvantage' of Ethnic Group Membership and Mixture." *Review of Educational Research* 41 (June 1971): 211–25. The self-concept of school children depends more on the efforts made by society to desegregate and to acknowledge individuality than upon the children's membership in any ethnic group (See Proposition V).

CHAPTER 3

The Teacher
and a Learning Milieu

When one speaks of a learning or a school climate he refers to intangibles, things that cannot be assessed in terms of books, salaries, or equipment, although these may have some influence. He is concerned with the quality of the personal interactions which take place throughout a school. He is thinking of the psychological well-being of participants, their feelings of acceptance, security, and harmony, and their sense of personal importance within a school environment. He is thinking of those aspects of interpersonal transaction patterns which function to maximize or to minimize the self-regarding feelings of individuals. He has in mind the feeling tone of the situation.

SCHOOL CLIMATE

Gorman summarizes climate or atmosphere as ". . . a variable produced by the expectations of members modified by their perceptions of the present situation and their degree of interaction and communication."[1] And Flanders (1965, p. 3)

[1] Alfred H. Gorman, *Teachers and Learners in the Interactive Process of Education*, (Boston: Allyn and Bacon, Inc., 1969), p. 47.

describes classroom climate as generalized attitudes which participants have and share about each other. These attitudes arise from classroom social interaction and refer to those qualities which consistently predominate in teacher-student and student-student contacts. Such an atmosphere tends to be fairly stable once established. This psychological or learning climate is made up of the myriad interpersonal contacts and transactions which take place in classrooms, libraries, hallways, and offices and on playgrounds, athletic fields, and campuses and the feelings and emotional reactions generated by them.

A professor who directed school evaluation teams for the North Central Association of Colleges and Secondary Schools maintained that he could feel how effective a school was by walking up and down the halls a few times. He was unable to state specifically the basis for his feeling but he usually was correct. The schools which felt good also generally proved to be most effective. The authors have had similar experiences with their own school visitations and suspect that most readers can recall a similar sort of intuition of the condition and the emotional load of the interpersonal transactions which they have contacted. The problem is that this feeling for interpersonal climate too often remains intuitive. If school climates are to be improved, as they must be if learning and personal growth are to proceed maximally, then educators must become both concerned and specific about causal factors. They no longer can afford to ignore this and, in effect, to leave the emotional or learning climate of our schools and classrooms to chance or accident (Scobey and Graham, 1970).

The need for examination and change

In order to promote and not inhibit learning, a learning milieu cannot pose threats to the psychological integrity and value of persons. Defensive behavior should be unnecessary and openness to experience should be maximally possible. It should be all right to try new behavior without the risk of being branded as wrong and to innovate without being forced to defend and justify. Individual differences and uniqueness of approach should be encouraged.

Most educators would agree. They believe in the value of individuals and their need to feel positively about themselves. But in too many instances they do not know how to make this happen. It appears to be much easier to describe an effective interpersonal climate than it is to specify the causal conditions and to create the climate itself. The gap between theory and practice well may be as great here as it is any place in education.

Reasons for and difficulties in dealing with climate

One reason for this difficulty in describing causal factors is that effective ways of interacting with other individuals have yet to be considered an important part of what schools teach. Although psychologists and educators (Combs, 1962) have realized the importance of this for some time, this awareness has not been sufficiently reflected in school curriculum changes. In 1962 the Association for Supervision and Curriculum Development of the National Education Association published *Perceiving, Behaving, Becoming*, edited by Arthur W. Combs, as its yearbook. The contributors emphasized the importance of a positive self-image and satisfying and meaningful human interaction for effective living and learning. The book had a tremendous impact upon educators and upon educational theory. But in a relative sense, it made surprisingly little difference in educational practice. Since that time the Association has published, among numerous other publications, *Learning and Mental Health in the Schools* (Waetjen and Leeper, 1966) and *To Nurture Humaneness* (Scobey and Graham, 1970). These books have expanded upon the need for a positive concept of self and an interrelated and concomitant need to relate effectively with others. In each case, teachers and other school personnel have discussed and they have affirmed but implementation has lagged far behind if it has occurred at all. As Green (1968) observed, ". . . our educational system has a remarkable capacity to absorb absolutely any change whatsoever without changing anything."

Presentation and exposure no longer can be assumed to

equal learning. A receptive student also is necessary. If instruction is not to be wasted and a good climate for learning is to be provided, educators must go beyond changing and manipulating schedules and curricular offerings to an active alteration of school psychological environments.

A second reason for the failure of schools to be primarily concerned with the psychological well-being and interpersonal behaviors of learners is that often educational personnel simply do not know how to do anything about this. It is difficult and sometimes threatening to undertake a project when the outcome and even the procedure is uncertain. It is easier to continue to view teaching as the transmission of information and to put out of mind the fact that individuals function holistically. This is true even though it generally is accepted that intellectual and cognitive functioning do not proceed effectively, as the traditional approach assumes they do, when the psychological and affective aspects of the learner's being are not in order. It is fundamental that one's primary concern must be focused on the areas of his greatest discomfort and need. If this were not the case, he could not exist for long either physically or psychologically.

An overdependence upon technology constitutes a third reason for the failure of educators to deal with the human interaction aspects of learning. Along with the tendency to minimize the importance of the individual's psychological welfare and to proceed as though this did not exist can be found the inclination to say "Yes, the human factor does make a difference, but we don't know how to deal with it. So let's work with something we *can* influence." Here one finds the movement to mechanize the teaching-learning process, to adopt programmed instruction, utilize teaching machines, and rely heavily upon computer-based instruction. It is as though the perplexity experienced in dealing with the personal inter-action factor represented by teachers has resulted in attempts to eliminate or limit this by restricting student-teacher con-tacts. But like the other approaches, this begs the issue. People, of whom teachers are representatives, cannot be eliminated. One either learns to promote effective personal interacting or he loses contact with his own source of identity and his means of affirming and validating his self. Bear in mind, however, the appeal which the mechanized approach possesses in this highly technological society. Science and machines have solved many of our problems. It is to be expected that we turn to them with this one.

The alternative, of course, is to become deeply involved with the manner, the effects, and the possibilities of studying and changing human interaction patterns. Specifically, this means such transactions as teacher-student, teacher-teacher and student-student which take place as a part of the school experience. Although it also is highly probable that a youngster's home relationships are strong determinants in his ability to learn, this consideration includes only those relationships that school personnel can do something about. Particularly, it takes in those relationships which teachers maintain and which presumably they have an opportunity to control.

THE CENTRALITY OF TEACHERS

The approach which recognizes the importance and indispensability of teachers and their influence in interpersonal transactions with students also places immense responsibility and pressure upon them. For power and importance do not exist apart from responsibility. Performance expectations tend to keep pace or to exceed both potential and ability. Further, these are of little avail and there is scant comfort in their possession if one does not know how to put them to work. Power, whether actual or attributed, when not applied or when misapplied, creates rather than solves problems. It serves more to furnish its possessor with pressure and threat than with competence and assurance.

The dilemma of teaching

Sources of advice to teachers and expertise in education are many and varied. They range from admirals to psychiatrists to college deans and professors to PTA members and beyond. It seems that almost every person has his own set of ideas concerning how teachers should function. The importance of teacher attitudes, behaviors, and feelings for molding the psyche and future of the young and the aching responsibility involved are pointed out on all sides.

This is analogous to the well-meaning psychologists who have sought to help new mothers by emphasizing the importance that every feeling, word, and action has for the psychological well-being of their offspring. Too often this has induced so much pressure and anxiety that, rather than mothers being able to relax and enjoy their children, they subconsciously reject them as a source of stress and emotional turmoil. Thus inadvertently the experts have added to the very problem they sought to allay. The parallel between motherhood and formal education may be further extended by recognizing that the overall atmosphere of the home produces emotionally stable babies. Whether a baby is fed on schedule, trained early or late in toilet habits, breast- or bottle-fed, spanked or disciplined by words makes little difference when husband-wife relations are felicitous, and when babies are loved, accepted, and fondled by parents (Bernard, 1970, p. 216). The important thing is the characteristic, consistent emotional tone of the home. Considerate, accepting, respectful teacher-pupil relations are more fundamental than the choice of teaching methods.

The pressure to be more adequate and to perform better, which teachers consistently receive from critics, generally comes without specific "how-to" directions. It is not unlike that created by aspiring politicians who are safe to "view with alarm" and pose as experts because they are not in office and do not have to be responsible for what happens. Teachers are told of the possibilities. They are told what they should do and sometimes what they can do but seldom are they told how to do it. As every teacher knows, there is a big gap between such advice as "understand and accept children," and the "nitty-gritty" of putting this dogma into practice. Further, this multiplicity of advice-givers raises the questions of when and to whom teachers should listen. In a sense, they are not unlike the child of a nagging parent who cannot attend to, or cope with, everything he is told to do and is forced to screen some of it out for the sake of psychological self-preservation.

Pilcher described the pattern of outside experts:

The American public school teacher has for years been the 'nigger' of the system. Nowhere is this more obvious than in his relationship with university and other outside experts. Deferentially, he scrapes and bows, listening politely and following obediently the dictates of the obviously superior minds of the outsiders. Just as predictably, when the outsider leaves, the teacher typically reverts to old ways. . . . Indeed, American teachers have proven quite ingenious at sabotaging the carefully laid plans of the most eminent university minds.[2]

Teachers have been in this uncomfortable position for a long time. They have been told that their influence is great. A well-established stereotype and set of expectations has been developed concerning what they should be, what actions they should take, and what feelings they should have. Unfortunately the majority of teachers have introjected this image. When they cannot exert substantial influence and control they feel inadequate. If they do not consistently find themselves loving children, they feel guilty. And if they are not giving and self-sacrificing, with the student's welfare uppermost in their minds, they question their fitness for the job. As might be expected, this combination of idealism and unrealistic expectations has served to disillusion some teachers. It has made cynics of others and it has resulted in considerable self-deceit for many of those remaining.

The real reason for teaching

The authors have conducted numerous classes, workshops, and institutes for teachers working toward graduate degrees. They have asked the question, "Why did you become a teacher?" repeatedly and insistently. The common first answers are: "Because I wanted to help someone" and "To be of service to others." If pressed further, some will say, "For the money," although they usually add that teacher's salaries are not all that good. Then, and only with considerable insistence, some will admit, "Because I get personal satisfaction from relating with young people" and "Because teaching gives me a sense of personal fulfillment." This is the point. The real, basic down-to-earth reason for teaching is because the human interaction opportunities it provides do something for the self-realization and growth of the teacher. *Teachers teach because they hope to get something for themselves from the experience.*

[2] Paul S. Pilcher, "Teacher Centers: Can They Work Here?" *Phi Delta Kappan* 54 (January 1973): 341.

"Schools are for kids" is an old and widely accepted truism. Yet it is only partly true and, like many other part truths, it is dangerous. Schools are for everyone who spends time in them and this includes teachers, administrators, custodians, parents, and children. When they are not, when the mutuality of the teaching-learning relationship is ignored, schools almost inevitably do a poor job of educating. When an interpersonal relationship, and teaching must be this if it is anything, is not mutually affirming, no participant can gain maximally from the interaction (Abrahamson, 1966; Kelley, 1968). When any part of the transaction and the needs of any actor are ignored or minimized, contributions are restricted and the gains any other person can make proportionately are restricted.

To maintain that "schools are for kids" ignores this mutuality in many educational institutions. Assigning a giving role to teachers prevents their seeing relationships with students as a means of self-fulfillment and personal growth. And it is true that a perception of the possibility is necessary for its realization. One cannot actively seek something which he does not acknowledge and when he is led to believe that it is egocentric, selfish, and professionally unethical to do so. He must be free and able to look before he has any chance of finding. Pierson (1965, p. 57) in a survey of counseling institutes stated as one salient principle for effective counseling that ". . . the counselor who cannot receive help himself cannot help others." This is as true of teaching or any other helping relationship as it is of counseling (May, 1967, p. 122).

A teacher who does not expect or seek personal satisfactions and growth from his relationships with students may be doing less than his best job of teaching. Indeed, some such orientation is necessary for teachers if they are to project a positive attitude concerning the personal value of their students. Each youngster presents an opportunity for a new and different interpersonal relationship. The essence of this idea is well expressed in a remark frequently attributed to Carl Rogers. He makes the point that people are just as wonderful as sunsets if they are let alone, adding that we wouldn't try to change a sunset. It is this ability to appreciate and to gain satisfaction from others which, in the authors' opinion, generates feelings of personal worth in students and makes for good teaching.

Along with the skills of dispensing information and maintaining discipline, teachers should be taught and encouraged to formulate and actively seek personal satisfactions and good feelings about themselves from their school and teaching relationships. They should know what there is to be gained from teaching and how to get it.

The classroom observations of the authors have developed the conviction that no personality traits are so essential for good teaching as enthusiasm and whole-hearted involvement. We think these are possible only when personal psychological gain is available in the involving situation. Otherwise, there may be feelings of frustration, of being forced, and put upon. The natural reaction is resistance. There is an inevitable negative effect upon students and learning when this happens. In the words of the poet:[3]

> ". . . if you bake bread with indifference, you bake a bitter bread that feeds but half a man's hunger.
> And if you grudge the crushing of the grapes, your grudge distills a poison in the wine.
> And if you sing though as angels and love not the singing, you muffle man's ears to the voice of the day and the voices of the night."

Limiting aspects of the teacher stereotype

The general public tends to develop certain role expectations about the behavior of people in the helping professions. Television programs, for example, which portray doctors as highly concerned with the welfare of their patients and which show lawyers as dedicated to obtaining justice for the underdog, promote warm, secure feelings for viewers and achieve good ratings. A similar set of expectations exists for teachers. Although changing and admittedly somewhat overplayed here for purposes of emphasis, this stereotypes teachers as largely motivated by a nonmaterialistic love for children. It sees good teachers as warm, accepting, self-sacrificing and possessed of

[3] Kahlil Gibran, The Prophet (New York: Alfred A. Knopf, Inc., 1951), p. 28. Reprinted from The Prophet, by Kahlil Gibran, with permission of the publisher, Alfred A. Knopf, Inc. Copyright 1923 by Kahlil Gibran; renewal copyright 1951 by Administrators C. T. A. of Kahlil Gibran Estate, and Mary G. Gibran.

large amounts of humility. They are viewed as other-, rather than as self-oriented and they are expected to give of themselves rather than receive from others.

This may be fine and heart-warming but it is a limited and limiting perspective. Because it does not permit teachers the luxury of being human and imperfect, it may operate to hinder their development as well as defeating schools and youngsters. A person has only one base of operations and one frame of reference—himself. He cannot, even if he wishes to do so, make it anything but primary and most important. This is the principle of ultimate subjectivity and the inevitability of psychological egocentrism (Thayer, 1968, p. 45). When beliefs and expectations make it wrong to be concerned with self or to be self-centered, as the teacher stereotype appears to do, active seeking for personal growth and increased effectiveness tends to be limited. One cannot honestly and openly reach out for what he needs and what he wants. He is in the position of being frustrated by his own system of beliefs and by the system with which he identifies.

Another distressing aspect of the teacher stereotype is its tendency to promote feelings of inadequacy, guilt, and defensiveness. When a teacher believes that he should be in control and is not, that he should be calm, rational and accepting yet gets emotional and behaves irrationally, then feelings of insufficiency, of lacking something, and of not measuring up are generated. Note here that one is much more apt to feel compelled to defend those areas in which he feels inadequate and also that defense mechanisms, though varied, generally function to distort or screen out reality so that one is more able to like and accept himself. A pretty good rule-of-

PEANUTS®   By Charles M. Schulz

Teachers too often are identified as what is wrong with education. (Reprinted by permission. © 1963 United Feature Syndicate, Inc.)

thumb is that a person usually is defensive in proportion to the doubts he has about himself and his behavior.

Teachers too often are identified as what is wrong with education. From kindergarten instructors to college professors, they too often are indicted when Johnny can't read or when he fails to behave in culturally prescribed ways. The gist of the message is, "Teachers can do so much but do so little. Why, oh why, don't they shape up?" It is especially difficult, when one feels he is threatened, to change, to innovate, to perceive alternatives, and to make advances. For defense, by its very nature, functions merely to consolidate, to maintain, and to justify established positions. In a vicious circle the public blames, criticizes, and uses the schools and teachers as scapegoats. They, in turn, react defensively; they become less able to change and to innovate and more concerned with self-preservation. Consequently, they then deserve the criticism they get.

A further limitation of the teachers' expected role is that it prevents them from seeing things as they really are and any need or direction for change. Just as defensiveness interferes with realistic perception, so an expectation or a perceptual set to see certain things often leads to overlooking others. A blindness to other possibilities is induced. The concern here is that a person must be able to see and to admit having an ineffective behavior before he can change. If he cannot see the flaws in what he is doing and if he is unaware of other ways of acting, he is stuck with what he has.

Restrictive conceptualizations of the teacher's job role prevent or limit the perception of other possibilities. By the time a person is ready to teach, he has been exposed to conventional school and teacher models for approximately sixteen years—for more than half of his life. This exposure to the conventional teacher model occurs during ages of high impressionability. It tends to be incorporated into attitudes and behaviors during the stages of development when actions of significant others are used as standards for learning appropriate conduct. An eye-opening experience in this respect is to watch a group of small youngsters playing school. Teaching behavior is mirrored as it appears to its recipients and the picture often is far from flattering.

Because of this long exposure, the teacher stereotype may be so thoroughly absorbed by most teachers and most people

10-4

1971, The Register
and Tribune Syndicate

BIL KEANE

"We had a substitute today, but she was just like
a REAL teacher. She knew how to
yell and everything!"

*Exposure to the conventional teacher model occurs during
ages of high impressionability.*

that it tends to function below the level of awareness and conscious control. That is to say, teachers behave like teachers because that is the way teachers behave. When they begin to act differently, the expectations of administrators, students, and parents are likely to pressure them to act like teachers are supposed to act. There must be some knowledge of other behavior alternatives if change is to be effected. Realization waits upon an awareness of possibilities and the development of different expectations. It is difficult to order if there is no menu.

A fifth limitation imposed upon teachers by the conventional teacher stereotype is that it tends to limit what teachers do to dispensing information and developing academic or vocational skills. The emotional aspects of relating to one's fellow man, though learned behaviors also, are largely ignored or deliberately avoided as being too personal despite the fact that really meaningful associations and living, like being a parent, a family member, a wife, a husband, or an employee or manager depend upon them (Gorman, 1969, p. 29; Jones, 1968, p. 125).

The result of avoiding the emotional-psychological aspects of learning in teacher education, in-service activities, and supervisory experiences is teachers who are poorly prepared to deal effectively with emotions (Goldhammer, 1969, p. viii). Outbursts or even milder expressions of feeling are discouraged in classrooms and valuable opportunities for teaching students or establishing meaningful contacts with them are lost. This is regrettable, for it is here that many of the immediate satisfactions of teaching can be found. True, one who does not permit himself to become emotionally involved is less vulnerable and in one sense cannot be hurt or disappointed so much. But it well may be that in such a defense of self he removes much potential flavor and zest from his living. The capacity for emotional experience is like that.

It is important at this point to emphasize a concept that many people appear not to understand. *There is a vast difference between denying the existence of feelings and emotions, and controlling them.* Limiting awareness also limits the opportunities for dealing with the environment. When a person ignores or turns his back on the feeling aspects of his existence because he is not comfortable with them, he forfeits not only his chances for experiencing but also his opportunity to learn how to deal with them.

The idea of "ignore it and it will go away" is much less appropriate in the case of emotional involvements than the advice of "learn to deal with it and it will lose its power to upset you." It is impossible, as a matter of fact, to avoid the effects of one's feelings. Choice does not lie in experiencing or not experiencing but only in the manner in which experiences happen or in the effects they will have.

SELF-DIRECTION FOR TEACHERS

New goal for education

A few years ago, James S. Coleman headed a committee (1967)

to investigate the results of racial segregation in the public schools and the effect that different school characteristics have on how much students learn. The school factor which appeared to make more difference than all of the other school factors together was the extent to which the student felt that he had "some control over his own destiny." Being pushed around and dictated to is demeaning and frustrating. It makes angry, hostile, and ultimately apathetic people. Obviously, schools need to be concerned about developing the sense of, and the ability for, self-direction in students in both living and learning. In this age of bureaucracies, big systems, and an overwhelming establishment this is bound to be especially difficult. Unless this happens by accident, it probably will not be done by teachers who themselves are incapable of independent learning, self-improvement and their own self-direction. The first step would seem to be to encourage and develop these traits in teachers by providing opportunities and guidelines.

Suggestions for self-direction

A person who wishes to direct his own living and learning and to behave by design rather than by accident may find the following helpful.

Acknowledge emotions. A self-directed person owns up to the way he feels and the emotions he has. If he is angry he recognizes this. If he feels hurt or happy, he identifies and labels how it is with him. To be sure, one need not act out the feelings or behave in socially inappropriate ways but a knowledge of the condition as one's own is a prerequisite for doing something about it. Suppose, for example, that a colleague's behavior makes me angry and he or someone else notices that I appear upset. Do I deny that I am affected? Do I state that I don't care or that what he does makes no difference to me? Or do I face the fact that I am quite annoyed with him and recognize that I often act hastily and tend to counterprovoke and fuel the fire when I feel this way? One's behavior is

61

influenced most easily by external forces (usually other people) when he is emotionally upset (Shostrom, 1967, pp. 67–75; Beier, 1966, pp. 16, 21). If I wish to influence someone, limit his alternatives, and be able to say what he is likely to do next, I behave to make him angry, I question his adequacy and make him feel guilty, or I praise him and tell him I like him. I know that his choices, alternatives, and self-direction will be decreased in proportion to the adrenalin in his bloodstream or his sense of obligation. Note that it is only as one knows his own feelings and the way in which they affect him that he has much chance of directing his own behavior.

Deal with emotions. The person who wishes maximum influence over his feelings and actions will find it advisable to face and deal with emotions early before they build up and accumulate. Take care of the hurt or anger before it becomes unmanageable. It is easier to handle a molehill than a mountain. Quite often the longer action is deferred, the more threatened, frightened, or angry we feel, the less apt we are to do something, and, because of the increased emotional load, the less chance there is for the action to succeed. The stress generated by negative emotions will not simply disappear if ignored. In fact there is evidence that stresses which are not dealt with as they occur tend to accumulate (Torrance, 1965, p. 57). When the load gets too heavy, the individual may explode at unrelated trivia. Things which he ordinarily would take in stride may trigger disproportionate emotional reactions. Teachers would be a class apart from most people if this did not occur with them also. Probably there are numerous youngsters who can attest that this is fairly common behavior in the classroom.

Denying emotions or allowing the stresses generated by negative feelings to accumulate also affects physical health. Although psychologists have known for years that individuals function as organized wholes, only in the last few decades has the effect of psychological pressure upon such matters as lowered resistance to disease been appreciated. Experiments have shown that in addition to such widespread ailments as heart trouble, ulcers, and migraine headaches, susceptibility to such ordinary disorders as the common cold and tooth decay significantly is also increased by psychological stress (Wolf and Goodell, 1968). A person may be able to convince himself that he controls his emotions by denying them but his body is not so easily fooled.

Seek the real causes of emotions. Another technique for self-direction is to look for the causes in one's own behavior. People have reasons for acting; their behavior does not occur by chance and for no purpose. They do not persist in acting in certain ways unless some satisfaction in terms of need or tension reduction occurs. In the words of the behaviorist or stimulus-response psychologist, a person does not act without some stimulus (reason) to do so and without some reward or reinforcement (satisfaction) for having responded in that manner. Thus behavior can be influenced by manipulating either incentives or consequences or some combination of the two. But it is important to realize that this no more justifies giving others power to regulate any individual than it gives the individual the means of determining and directing his own behavior through the reactions which others have to him. As a matter of fact, a knowledge of the process and an understanding of one's own particular incentives and satisfactions enables that person to recognize and resist some external influences and accede to others. It is only as one is aware of the interaction processes between himself and others (see the Paradigm of Mutual Influence, Chapter 4) that he can exercise a choice in what he wants these to be and hope to change or control them.

Find out how you learned your feelings. Much of the difficulty experienced in becoming aware of the causal factors of one's own behavior lies in the tendency of behaving to become habitual to the point where it takes place without a conscious decision to act in any one of a number of ways (Harrison, 1970). To appreciate this, it is important to realize that most of our ways of interacting with and relating to others were learned early in life. Some ways of acting on our part were approved of (rewarded) by parents while others were not. We came to behave in accordance with their desires without ever being conscious of a learning process or aware of what we were learning (Skinner, 1971, p. 127). While an adult who is conscious that he is being influenced and who knows that he is learning may discriminate in terms of how he wishes to learn to behave, this is not possible for small youngsters even though it is then that basic underlying patterns and modes of behavior are laid down. This important learning usually takes place with none of the participants being aware of what is being taught and learned. Consider this example:

> A ten-year-old boy was given the *Wechsler Intelligence Scale for Children.* He tried hard and gave evidence of being under considerable stress to perform well and to answer correctly. Toward the end of the examination he said that he was somewhat "tired and sick at my stomach." When this was brought to his father's attention, he stated that this was typical of his son's behavior. The boy appeared to respond to stress and to avoid pressure by becoming fatigued and nauseated. A medical examination revealed that the blood sugar level was low. This resulted in the doctor's advice that the boy's teacher have some candy to give him whenever he began to feel tired and upset in order to raise the blood sugar level and alleviate the physical condition.[4]

None of the well-meaning adults involved stopped to think about the kind of behavior that would be rewarded. The question of what the youngster would learn in terms of responding to stressful situations apparently was not considered. His parents, the doctor, and the teacher were unaware of what they were teaching and the boy was unaware that he was learning an ineffective way of behaving. If the stimulus-response-reward pattern had gone undetected, an habitual way of reacting most likely would have been established which would have functioned below the youngster's level of awareness and control. It could not have been prevented and it could not be changed until there was an awareness of the process and the causal factors. On the advice of a psychologist, a box of relatively tasteless dextrose wafers was given to the boy with instructions to take some at a certain time each afternoon. Thus the behavior was not rewarded and the boy did not learn to become nauseated whenever he felt pressured.

This kind of learning and the behaviors which result can

---

[4] The authors neither support nor question this diagnosis and prescription. This was, however, a real incident and as truly described as memory permits.

be contrasted with the more formal type in which both teachers and learners have some idea of what is to be learned and in which both are aware that they are participants. It is learning by plan and design rather than learning by chance or accident. Unfortunately accidental learning, because we are unable to be specific about the behaviors stimulated and reinforced, also may occur to a substantial degree in the average classroom. Teachers probably do not know enough about controlling their own behavior to manage with precision either the stimuli or the reinforcements which they provide. Inattention and negative attitudes toward school, toward self, and toward others may be taught inadvertently to some youngsters while both parties think arithmetic is the subject of the lesson. Thus, a teacher must be concerned with his own behaviors, attitudes, feelings, and self and each school must be concerned with the psychological well-being of its teachers. This is not to say that teachers are more important or more the business of schools than children but unless this priority is recognized, teaching and vital teacher-student relationships will not be improved.

Young people do not learn to live effectively, happily, and with involvement and satisfaction from teachers who themselves are unable to live in this manner (Glasser, 1969, p. 19). And teachers are not helped to do so by good intentions, pep talks, exhortations, or trying harder. They can only do so through a continuous and painstaking observation of their own behavior, its causes and consequences, its incentives and satisfactions.

Discuss emotions. Learn to talk about feelings before they accumulate and begin to exert an undue influence upon behavior. This can be helpful in several ways. It can serve as a substitute for physical action and thus dispel tension; it can help to generate a solution to the causal problem; and, through the sharing of one's personal concerns, it quite often can induce a feeling of closeness and unity with others. Frequently one finds that associates have similar concerns and are willing to share support and understanding.

Few people use this method adequately if they try it at all. We live in a culture which extols the successful, the adequate, the strong, the self-sufficient, and the stoical. To admit to feelings and emotional turmoil is tantamount to admitting

One finds that associates have similar concerns and are willing to share support and understanding. (Reprinted through the courtesy of the Chicago Tribune-New York News Syndicate, Inc.)

weakness, inadequacy, and vulnerability. We have been so successful with the materialistic, objective approach to problems that a concern which cannot be evaluated in terms of dollars, equipment, and schedules either is ignored or increasing amounts of money are more vigorously applied.

It is paradoxical that modern man, who has been so successful in using verbal symbols to solve problems such as those posed by skyscraper construction and travel in space, has been so reluctant to apply this method to those problems arising from his interactions with others. Indeed, divorce statistics—about one in every three to four marriages—indicate that even those who choose to live closely together often lack the ability to communicate effectively enough to maintain the relationship.

Physical outlets for dispelling the energy released by the body's reactions when emotions are generated are more limited today. The average apartment dweller no longer has the physical, socially accepted work outlets which provided the diversionary strenuous action for his grandfather.

Another aspect of our social environment that both generates a need for, and prevents adequate verbalization about, emotional concerns is the tendency for psychological distance to increase as physical distance decreases. This is the anonymity and alienation of such concern to modern behavioral scientists (Ruitenbeek, 1964; Erikson, 1968). Amid a population explosion people appear to have less concern for, and fewer satisfying and meaningful ties with, their fellows than ever before. Schofield (1964) pointed out that one of the functions of the modern psychotherapist is to sell the friendship and concern that people need and which they fail to get from other personal contacts.

Teachers who know how to use the verbal method of dealing with interpersonal and emotional problems and who know how to establish meaningful relationships are much needed today. Such behaviors are learned behaviors and can be taught. But this cannot be done by instructors who themselves are unable to model and to demonstrate.

Use the stimulus-response gap. Another way of minimizing the incapacitating effects of emotional reactions lies in what May terms ". . . *the capacity to be aware of the gap between stimulus and response* and to use this awareness constructively." [5] Again, let us stress that a person should not ignore or repress but rather know of the effects of his own emotional reactions and the extent to which these limit the alternatives he can see and the choices he can make. According to an expanded paradigm of the stimulus-response explanation of behavior (Hull, 1952), what a person will do in a situation

[5] Rollo May, "Freedom, Responsibility, and the Helping Relationship," Presentation given at Arden House, Teachers College, Columbia University, January 6–10, 1963.

depends not only upon how he is stimulated and rewarded but also upon such things as habit strength, need intensity, fatigue, and various other inhibitory or predisposing factors. These intervening variables help to determine what the latter will be (see the Mutual Influence Paradigm, Chapter 4). When one responds to a cue or stimulus quickly, with no gap between the stimulus and the reaction, he lacks time to be aware of either the feelings, attitudes, and predispositions which influence his action or his alternatives for behaving. What he will do is determined and predictable. In a sense his actions are controlled by his feelings and his habits. Choice or personal control is much less possible than when there is a stimulus-response gap.

Freedom, in its most meaningful sense, is not different from this. It is contingent upon an awareness of available choices and the ability to decide among them. For this reason, personal control is a necessity for, and not in opposition to, its realization. According to May, "Freedom is the individual's capacity *to know he is the determined one,* to pause between stimulus and response and thus to throw his weight, however slight it may be, on the side of one particular response among several possible ones." [6] In order to do this, however, one must become aware of his own behaving. He must be able to stand outside himself as a witness to his own actions and to acquire a kind of an emotional disengagement (Beier, 1966, p. 33). A sort of participant observer status must be achieved, as in this example.

> Two men were walking together on the street. One stopped to purchase a newspaper. Despite his cheery good morning and pleasant smile, the newsman merely grunted. He failed to hand the paper to the man and almost threw the change at him. Nevertheless the man thanked him and wished him a good day before walking on. His companion was puzzled. "I would have told him off," he said. "How come you didn't?" The answer illustrates the use of the stimulus-response gap for personal control and establishing psychological climate. "I almost did," he said. "Then I decided that no sour puss was going to determine my actions or spoil the flavor of my day. I did not wish to have *him* control *my* behavior."

[6] Rollo May, *Psychology and the Human Dilemma* (D. Van Nostrand Company, Inc., 1967), p. 175.

The authors speculate that many youngsters are peremptorily sent to the office as a result of a confrontation with the teacher. They may either be cut down by sarcasm or reinforced by their success in getting to the teacher because the latter's response is immediate and emotional rather than considered and managed. The teacher in fact is controlled *by* the situation instead of being in control *of* the situation. What the other class members learn by accident by observing such confrontations can only be guessed but, whatever it may be, these exchanges are not likely to constitute good models for handling interaction difficulties.

Practice self-management. Another basis for dealing with emotionally loaded situations is the knowledge that one influences others in social interactions only as he is able to manage his own actions. One's own behavior and the messages he sends are his most potent tools for influencing the actions or responses of others. He cannot properly say, "If everyone else would shape up, I'd be fine," for his locus of control lies with himself. He renounces his own power and importance when he fails to realize this and attributes the control of his own behavior to some one else.

A person or a teacher who wishes to establish a certain learning or personal interaction climate, initiates contacts on the terms he wishes to promote. He provides initial cues and stimuli for the response of others rather than waiting to respond to those which they may furnish. He sets the emotional tone or psychological climate by moving first. Otherwise, he must overcome or acquiesce to the tone already operating. If a woman meets another with a smile, for example, she makes it less possible for the second woman to frown. But, if the latter's cue is a frown, the smiling of the first woman may be quite unsuitable. One may enact or he may react; he may influence or be influenced. How it will be is determined in a large part by each person's willingness to assume the risk of initiating the emotional tone of the interpersonal transactions in which he participates.

Deal with small behaviors. A further means of managing one's own input for purposeful influence consists in learning to deal with situations in manageable units. An entire repertory of teaching or interaction behaviors cannot be changed all at once. To attempt to do so is merely to spread energy and powers of attention so thinly that little is accomplished. But it is far easier to see a problem in its entirety than to separate out and establish priorities for those aspects which can be dealt with.

The current emphasis on behavioral objectives in education is helping to do this. Emphasis is placed upon breaking down complex behaviors into their smallest components and thinking through the sequence in which they should occur so that each item to be learned is presented in the proper order. If the learning of a specific item depends upon the mastery of other skills, they will be taught first. If other learnings depend upon its mastery, it precedes them. Progress is more easily observed and evaluated.

In keeping with traditional emphases in education, the practice of guiding and gauging learning and change on the basis of behaviorally stated objectives thus far has been limited to student learning and to information retention. Its application generally has been by an agent external to the learner. There is no reason, however, why the use of behavioral objectives as an effective learning technique should require outside manipulation, and there is no reason why it cannot be applied successfully by individuals for self-improvement and for the development of more effective personal behaviors. Certainly teachers must be able to model this process if internally directed, independent learners are to result.

Be alert to overcontrol. One danger in the management of personal interaction behaviors is overcontrol. It is manifest in a lack of spontaneity of expression or a lack of authenticity and realness as a person. A good deal of energy is required just to keep up a front. Some believe that most cases of nervous breakdown may be due to overcontrol and the psychological stress and pressure which this generates (Perls, 1947, p. 224; Shostrom, 1967, p. 72). But this type of behavior is misnamed when the words control and management are used. Overcontrolled people usually are unable to relax and to stop manipulating and structuring even if they want to. Paradoxically, they are not sure they can control so they force themselves to try. They protest too much. The teacher who has no doubt about his ability to manage his classes can allow students considerable freedom because he knows he can prevent disorder. The teacher who is unsure cannot risk experimentation or digression because he basically doubts that he has established his authority.

The person who must overcontrol really is not in control at all. One who must prove his position usually has yet to achieve it. The key lies in the ability to choose to control or not to control. If this choice cannot be made and one must always attempt to control or if he never attempts to do so, he cannot be considered as self-directed.

Spontaneity and naturalness in behavior do not arise from impulsiveness and a lack of restriction. Many of our actions, like walking or eating or dancing, once needed much concentration and attention on our part. A person learning to drive an automobile, a football player mastering a blocking assignment, or a girl learning to knit must be acutely conscious of each movement at first. Only when each action is mastered and coordinated can attention be focused upon something else. This also is true with behaviors which are ineffective and which require changing. A golfer with a bad slice may be advised by a professional to straighten his arm, to reposition his feet, and to alter his manner of gripping the club. If he is to be successful in changing and improving he must (1) become aware that what he does is not working; (2) identify each contributing movement; (3) specify precisely what he will do to change it; (4) consciously control each action and be aware of the manner in which he deviates from the performance he wishes; and (5) repeat and practice the desired behavior with meticulous attention to each component movement until it becomes habitual and until he can do it subconsciously without thinking. Then he will be able to relax, function smoothly and effectively, and really enjoy the game.

The individual who wishes to deal with his own input and who has the responsibility to provide an effective model for others thus may find control of self and of his own behaviors not so much restricting as it is freeing. One inevitably is held responsible for his behavior by those with whom he associates. Whether or not he is able to manage what he does, he must live with the reactions his behavior generates. Loukes has called this ". . . the terrible law of consequence that besets human affairs: the law that as you behave, so shall you be; that the way you do your 'finding out' determines what you will learn;

71

that what we look for in human relationships is what we find." [7]

Especially this is true of teachers. Their job requires a physical and psychological proximity which they cannot avoid. The choice of to be or not to be around people and to influence and to be influenced is not an option available to teachers. Their choice concerns only the manner in which this closeness and interaction will be managed. Effective teachers must be students of their own behavior.

The authors have hoped to furnish a rationale for teacher management of teacher behavior and some workable suggestions for this management in the preceding pages. Admittedly all facets of the process have not been covered for, in keeping with the position taken, we also are learners. We have just begun to encourage our own students and associates to teach us what we can learn from them. We expect to find out more about the effectiveness of our own behavior, about the process of self-directed learning and about the gaining of personal satisfactions with our next teaching contacts. In the meantime, we hope to have persuaded some readers to travel with us. Even if they do not, the sharing of the ideas has left us with a better insight and increased satisfaction.

SUMMARY

A learning or a school climate refers to the feeling tone resulting from the interpersonal transactions which take place within the school. School personnel no longer can afford to leave the emotional tone or psychological climate they generate to chance or accident. They must become both concerned and specific about the causal factors.

Presentation and exposure no longer can be assumed to equal learning. The psychological or listening state of the learner can operate to make this pointless and ineffective.

Most educators not only do not know how to deal with the emotional-affective aspects of learning, they become so uncomfortable when these are manifest that they try to eliminate

[7] Harold Loukes, "Passport to Maturity," *Phi Delta Kappan* 46 (October 1964); 56.

or disregard their effects. The strongest of these attempts is the movement to replace teachers with machines and to deal only with the cognitive, impersonal aspects of learning.

Because much power and influence is attributed to teachers, expectations frequently exceed both their potential and their ability and pressure to perform well is great. This pressure and the introjection of traditional role stereotypes by many teachers have led to the teachers' failure to gain personal satisfactions from contacts with students.

Effective teaching is an interactive process. Teachers can manage it only as they are able to deal with their own cause and effect inputs and with their responses to the inputs of students.

Because teachers must deal with self first in order to function effectively with students, schools must be concerned with teacher satisfaction and psychological fulfillment on the basic sequence of priority. Children, of course, come first in schools in order of importance.

The idealistic teacher stereotype which most people accept and which many teachers have introjected, limits teacher effectiveness by (1) making teachers feel guilty if they are concerned with self and personal growth; (2) identifying them as scapegoats and promoting inhibiting defensiveness; (3) furnishing a perceptual set which limits awareness of other possibilities; and (4) limiting their function to dispensing information while ignoring the emotional aspects of teaching and learning.

Studies indicate that the learner's sense of control over his own destiny exerts a greater impact on learning than all of the other school factors combined. The development of self-directed learning and living in students best can be accomplished when teachers are able to model and demonstrate this behavior.

Because the perception of alternatives and self-direction is limited by emotional upset, teachers need to know how to manage their own feelings to avoid being controlled by them. Some suggestions for doing this are:

(1) admit having the feelings;
(2) deal with them before they cumulate;
(3) bring emotions to awareness;
(4) talk about emotions;
(5) use the stimulus-response gap;

73

(6) recognize that self-control precedes influencing others;
(7) deal with specific emotional subunits; and
(8) recognize the hazards of overcontrol.

SUGGESTED ADDITIONAL READINGS

Abrahamson, Mark. *Interpersonal Accommodation*. Princeton, N. J.: D. Van Nostrand Company, Inc., 1966. The author of this book discusses the need which people have for each other and some of the ways of fulfilling this need. He puts emphases on the psychological mechanisms involved—communication and group interaction. His observations are applicable to teaching-learning, family, and other interpersonal transactions.

Adams, Raymond S., and Biddle, Bruce J. *Realities of Teaching Explorations with Video Tape*. New York: Holt, Rinehart and Winston, Inc., 1970. The point is made here that educators are "spectacularly ignorant" about what really goes on in the classroom. As a remedy for this, video tape is emphasized as a means of recording and studying teacher behaviors and student interaction patterns. There is a good discussion concerning the use of machines versus teachers for effective learning.

Gorman, Alfred H. *Teachers and Learners in the Interactive Process of Education*. Boston: Allyn and Bacon, Inc., 1969. This book describes the use of classrooms as interpersonal relationship laboratories. It emphasizes the part played by communication and sensitivity to others in the process of learning. Some suggestions and techniques for promoting and assessing interaction are advanced.

Meacham, Merle L., and Wiesen, Allen E. *Changing Classroom Behavior: A Manual for Precision Teaching*. Scranton, Pa.: International Textbook Co., 1970. Behaviorism and stimulus-response psychology provide the theoretical and functional bases for this book. The reader is told how to apply reinforcement principles to strengthen desirable and eliminate undesirable behavior in both normal and atypical youngsters.

CHAPTER 4

Communication and
Interpersonal Transaction

This chapter is about a human activity—communication—
which most people take for granted and about which they
know surprisingly little. Although teaching largely is dependent upon the ability to communicate, teachers, teacher-
preparing institutions, and schools pay too little attention to
the dynamics of communicating.

COMMUNICATION DEFINED

Communication, according to one opinion is "the transfer of
meaning" (Fabun, 1968). To another, it is ". . . the process of
effecting an interchange of understanding between two or
more people, . . . that vital process by which individuals and
organizations relate themselves together." [1] Hall makes a good
case for the assertion that "culture is communication" (1959,
pp. 90–98). But definitions often are so limiting or so broad
that they either restrict thinking or offer few practicable

[1] Lee Thayer, *Communication and Communication Systems* (Homewood, Ill.:
Richard D. Irwin, Inc., 1968), p. 13.

guidelines. Neither of the above, for instance, indicates with sufficient weight that communication is indispensible to being human, that it is so necessary to the maintenance of interpersonal relationships as to be almost synonymous with them, or that psychological malfunctioning and mental and emotional breakdowns almost always can be traced to ineffective ways of communicating (Ruesch, 1961; Ruesch and Bateson, 1951).

Importance for teachers

Teachers, more than most people, should be able to communicate with exactitude and with a minimum of meaning distortion if they are to teach by design and if they really are to present what they hope pupils will learn. But such communication may not be assumed. Even though communication is indispensable for what they do, teachers appear to lack information about, and the ability to manage, communication processes. They do not know enough about their own inputs (the messages they send) and they usually fail to concern themselves sufficiently with pupil and student listening and interpretation. Too often teachers assume that presentation equals learning and that transmission equals reception.

Teachers can learn to influence and manage the process of communicating once they realize the necessity for doing so, but they cannot shut it off or ignore it and accomplish what they hope to accomplish. In fact, it is almost impossible even to exist in a social setting without sending some sort of messages and without receiving some sort of impressions. Watzlawick, Beavin, and Jackson (1967, p. 49) rightly assert that, ". . . no matter how one may try one cannot not communicate." True, a person may make no attempt to interact, to share ideas, or to find out or to validate. He may be completely noncommittal but his mere presence communicates something. When others are aware of him, they derive some sort of meaning from what he does or does not do. Even if he says nothing or makes no move whatsoever, interpretations inevitably will be placed on his behavior. He may communicate aloofness and appear stuck up to one person, shy to another, and rejecting to someone else. His choice is not whether or when he will communicate but how he will do it, for one creates the type of social climate in which he lives through the reactions of others to his behavior. Then one's own actions, through the response of others, become a part of the interpersonal environment which influences what he will do next.

The old warning "silence is golden" is questionable advice as far as the maintenance of effective relationships is concerned. In the first place, a considerable amount of discomfort usually is generated by withholding verbal communication. In the second place, the individual who believes that he can choose not to communicate still bears the burden for what is read into his behavior by associates. He must live with their interpretations and consequent reactions. For self-protection, he almost has to talk. A person is seriously handicapped with the interpersonal relationships he maintains when, for any reason, he is unable to verbalize.

Although it has obvious limits, verbalization well may be the best means, short of the exactitude of mathematical symbolization, for being explicit about meaning. The paradox is that, just as it often leads to misunderstanding, talk also must be depended upon as a remedy. But this is true with most of the tools of mankind. Almost any activity of which humans are capable and almost anything which they employ to aid in that activity may be either facilitating or inhibiting, depending upon how it is used. So it is with the manner in which men communicate. One either can solve or create problems with his facility or lack of facility in transmitting meaning.

Understanding and improving communication

In order for a teacher or any other individual to improve his communication processes and his interpersonal transactions at least two things immediately are necessary. First, he must become aware that what he does is not working as well as he would like. And second, he must have some idea of what he needs to do to improve it. One does not embark upon the sea of change without a reason for going and with no course or direction to steer. The following suggestions are offered in order to dispel some of the more common misconceptions concerning communication and to indicate at least in part the breadth and diversity of the possibilities offered by this avenue for increased personal and professional effectiveness.

Humans must communicate. From infancy onward communication is necessary in order best to utilize one's potential for mental and social growth—in order to become more fully human. We help the infant develop his brain cells by stimulating him with sounds, touch, and visual objects (Hunt, 1968). The child develops his concept of self by the messages he receives from his parents and teachers (Gordon, 1969). The adolescent's identity is established through recognition by peers, parents, and teachers in verbal output and feedback (Friedenberg, *Phi Delta Kappan,* 1969). Teachers likewise attain a true professional identity when they can discuss goals, techniques, organization, *and* feelings with their colleagues (Harrison, 1970). Silence raises questions in the other person concerning his worth and importance. It is psychologically threatening.

Communication means developing and maintaining self. This is almost so obvious that one risks redundancy in its repetition. Yet it is this taking-for-granted which often limits both vision and action, and which makes a restatement necessary. Goldstein realized years ago that "language is the means of the individual to come to terms with the outer world and realize himself." [2] Becker indicated that "the proper word or phrase, properly delivered, is the highest attainment of interpersonal power." [3] And King and Neal have stated, "The proper use of language is a prerequisite for the formation of a healthy ego." [4] "Proper" is the key word, for language is merely a tool by which people deal with their environment, and the efficiency of a tool largely is determined by the expertise of the workman. Some individuals use their verbal skills to confuse or to minimize others and to keep people at a distance. Others promote good feelings in, and close relationships with, their associates by the same means. Indeed we believe that verbalization is so powerful a tool that learning to use it effectively, to apply it to all types of human concerns, is completely essential. Being "disadvantaged" in terms of the prevailing American

[2] K. Goldstein, *Language and Language Disturbance* (New York: Grune and Stratton, 1948), p. 23.
[3] Ernest Becker, *The Birth and Death of Meaning* (New York: The Macmillan Co., 1962), p. 104.
[4] Paul T. King and Robert Neal, *Ego Psychology In Counseling* (Boston: Houghton Mifflin Co., 1968), p. 33.

culture may be more a matter of communication deficits than it is a matter of socioeconomic status.

The problem of maintaining self through verbalization is intensifying for a number of reasons. First, too little if anything is being done. Few opportunities exist, short of a psychological breakdown, to learn to verbalize about the emotional aspects of existence and feelings about oneself. Outside the offices of counselors and psychotherapists, there are few individuals who specialize in what might be termed therapeutic communication and who are prepared to teach others to use it. Even Head Start Programs may be too little and too late. Patterns of communication and verbalization may be pretty well established during the ages in which youngsters learn to talk. Thus the best time for learning to verbalize may be from age one or earlier to age two or three. If not accomplished well at that time, this developmental task and this type of behavior may never again be so open to influence and modification.[5]

A second reason for the intensification of the need to verbalize is evidenced by population increase, the tendency for population concentration in certain areas, and unavoidable extended contacts with others. The restriction of physical freedom and physical energy outlets appear to become increasingly necessary as people come to live closer and closer together. It becomes less and less possible to act out feelings and to interact on a trial-and-error basis.

Perhaps it is necessary to replace physical freedom with psychological freedom. As the body is restricted, it may be necessary to find more ways to set the mind free (Schofield, 1964, p. 155). The alternatives of verbal catharsis and communication about possibilities before they happen cannot continue to be ignored if the problems of living very closely to other people are to be dealt with. This will happen best when individuals are taught to communicate with each other about the feelings they have. It is doubtful that it will be effected by committees, by contacts between representatives, or by government decrees and appropriations.

---

[5] A developmental task is ". . . a task which arises at or about a certain period in the life of the individual, successful achievement of which leads to his happiness and to success with later tasks, while failure leads to unhappiness in the individual, disapproval by society, and difficulty with later tasks." Robert J. Havighurst, *Developmental Tasks and Education*, 3rd ed. (New York: David McKay, 1972), p. 2.

A third reason for helping youngsters to verbalize about psychological problems is typified by what Schofield (1964) has termed "The Age of Anxiety." Frustrations are greater and more numerous for more people now because expectations are higher, because change is more rapid, and because answers to social concerns are much more elusive than at any time in history. Americans, once supremely confident of the ability of science and technology to solve almost any problem, have become more and more doubtful. Skepticism has replaced certainty, and the threat and anxiety which people feel have increased in proportion. Under such conditions, the hostility, the riots, and the inhumanity which characterize these times are understandable.

The manner in which the access to power tends to widen the gap between individuals who can gain this access and

When verbalization can take place, aggressive force is spent and does not have to be acted out.

individuals who cannot presents a fourth problem for the verbally disadvantaged. As information increases (doubling every seven to ten years) and machines are improved, the degree to which personal force may be amplified also increases. While physical strength and skill once were the key to control of forces outside oneself, today automation, push-button operation, and computer controlled production operate to transfer this power to individuals with knowledge and the ability to communicate. Amplifiers of physical force include such tools and machines as hammers, bull dozers, and atomic reactors. Intellectual amplification has become increasingly possible with computer memory banks and data processing. Social force and influence is amplified through the use of telephones, television messages, and the like. No amplification agent works for the person who doesn't know how to use it. The more power available, the greater the differential between individuals who can command it and individuals who cannot.

It is important to realize that ways of amplifying personal impact are not limited to physical tools and physical power. An increased understanding of communication and interaction patterns plus a knowledge of the effect of one's own inputs also can provide for this in a psychological sense. The difference between a teacher who has the ability to communicate and one who has not can be large indeed.

Communication means manipulating other individuals

Despite its somewhat disturbing connotations, manipulation of both physical and social environments is an unavoidable aspect of being human. While we recognize and often admire the ability to alter and make use of our physical surroundings, we balk at the realization that we operate in a similar manner both socially and psychologically. Shostrom (1967, p. xi) states unequivocably, "Modern man is a manipulator," and the psychiatrist Beier emphasizes that children learn "the game of manipulation" very early (1966, pp. 20, 21). An infant who does not learn how to get adults to meet his needs will not survive physically. Psychological well-being and existence are no different except that a person may die by degrees by limiting and distorting his interactions with his fellows.

Although we are all psychological manipulators, ethical reservations and an unwillingness to accept such manipulation

81

often prevents sufficient awareness of the process to control or to improve it. It is as though we think that responsibility for behaving in this manner can be evaded by denying that it exists. Hence we continue to transact ineffectively with others and to be victimized by our own inability to comprehend the process. We live with the reactions of associates without allowing ourselves to see that many of the causes for their actions toward us are really reactions to our own behavior. We literally build the interpersonal milieu in which our personality develops without admitting or knowing that we do so. Actually, the often maligned advertiser and propagandist are more honest than most of us in this respect. They admit that their purpose is to manipulate so they are free to study and to improve the process. They are not naive concerning the manner in which they function or about its consequences.

There also are certain expected ways of acting and responding which are ingrained in us by our culture and which heighten our susceptibility to manipulation. Responses often are so automatic and habitual that a person is exploited before he knows what is happening. Hall indicates that these expected ways of responding are learned informally and without awareness. (This is the accidental or informal learning described in the preceding chapter.) He maintains that "entire systems of behavior . . . are passed from generation to generation, and nobody can give the rules for what is happening. Only when these rules are broken do we realize they exist." [6] Beier (1966, p. 21) emphasizes that when the respondent is emotionally involved, he is more easily manipulated, and Becker points out that these culturally expected response patterns put people under compulsion to react in certain ways. "By verbally setting the tone for action, . . . we permit complementary action, . . . not only do we permit it; we compel it, ... By properly delivering our lines we fulfill our end of the social bargain and oblige the other to fulfill his in turn." [7] For example, a person who expresses strong admiration for another creates in the latter some obligation to like him and often some compulsion to return the compliment, for one does not bite the hand that feeds his ego.

[6] Edward T. Hall, *The Silent Language* (Greenwich, Conn.: Fawcett Publications, 1959) pp. 70, 71.
[7] Becker, *Birth and Death of Meaning,* p. 104.

Conversely, behavior also can be constricted (manipulated) by hostile, attacking, threatening actions. Under stress, the number of alternatives which can be perceived and acted upon often are drastically reduced (Levitt, 1967, pp. 117–20). Beyond the point of challenge and stimulation, people seem to lose their ability to think in proportion to the degree of emotionality generated. A frightened, angry, or depressed person is not in control of his own behavior. As such feelings are intensified, responses are limited and actions are made more predictable. Probably the most effective means of compelling another to behave in given ways and of reducing his competence is to cause him to feel attacked or threatened in some way. This is most easily done in those areas where he lacks confidence, feels insecure, and has reason to doubt himself. Thus the teacher who basically questions his own ability is most apt to fear observation, most apt to seclude himself in a classroom, and most likely to be rendered incompetent by the manipulations of his students and associates. And there is scant comfort in knowing that those who feel most inadequate themselves are most likely to attempt to manipulate and control others (Beier, 1966, p. 25). One is most compelled to prove what he is when he is not sure what he is; it is unnecessary to convince anyone of an established competence.

People in general—family members, workers, teachers, and students—are all involved in the process of influencing or manipulating others simply because they are human and because this is a universal human activity. The tendency to deny this limits awareness and possibilities of managing the process. The question to be answered is not whether one manipulates or whether he is manipulated but only how he does this and how he permits it to happen to him. We agree with Shostrom that one has a chance to manage or to actualize himself only as he becomes aware of the manipulative process. "The actualizer is free in the sense that, while he may play the game of life, he is *aware* he is playing it. . . . He realizes that he manipulates sometimes and is manipulated other times. *But he is aware of the manipulation.*" [8]

---

[8] Everett L. Shostrom, *Man, the Manipulator* (Nashville, Tenn.: Abingdon Press, 1967), p. 62.

Message meaning is determined by the receiver. Although two or more persons are needed in order for communication to take place, the interpretation which the listener or receiver places upon the message determines the action which he will take (Thayer, 1968, p. 39). The commonly held assumption that the transmitter fixes the meaning of the messages he sends may be one of the most limiting misconceptions which we have about communication. Yet most people and teachers continue to structure their relationships, and the expectations they have for the behavior of others, upon the assumption that what they say is what is heard, or, even worse, that what they intended to say is what the other person acts upon. Actually, the sender merely furnishes verbal stimuli. The receiver may and often does construct a meaning quite different from the intended message. His experiences, his fears, his habits, and his expectations (perceptual sets) all combine to screen, to limit, and to distort.

Probably no two persons listening to a message can be expected to interpret it in the same manner. Although one person may take a comment as complimentary, another may consider it as demeaning. It may result in smiling, accepting behavior with one and in defensive, angry reactions with another. At least a part of the inconsistency we attribute to the behavior of others can be explained by this. Seemingly perverse pupils and associates may not be obstinate entirely from spite or hostility. They merely may be responding to the message they received rather than the one which we think we communicated.

This means that if one is to know about his own communication and its effects, he must talk about his communications with those with whom he communicates. A name for this process is metacommunication (see Glossary) (Watzlawick, et al., 1967, p. 40). Basically it is not different from the process of soliciting feedback about the effect of one's actions. When it is formalized with a trained observer in order to learn about and to alter ineffective and self-defeating communication and behavior patterns, it is called counseling or psychotherapy (Ruesch, 1961, p. 33). Whatever the label, the mastery of this process is fundamental for good teaching and self-directed improvement.

Message meaning frequently is inexact and ambiguous. Most

"I know you believe you understand what you think I said, but I'm not sure you realize that what you heard is not what I meant."

Message meaning is frequently inexact and ambiguous.

of us, for much of the time, tend to regard the failure to understand our meanings and intentions as the fault of others. We cannot see that the messages we send often are confusing and ambivalent in nature and as easily promote misunderstanding and disharmony as they create understanding and harmony. This is because, consciously or unconsciously, we fail to say what we mean, presenting ourselves as feeling, thinking, or being something we are not. Even when we really do not mean to do so, we either say one thing and mean something else or our statements have a number of meanings. Implicit messages are conveyed at the same time that we think we are being explicit. For example, a person may respond, "I agree with what you are saying but. . . ." or he may indicate, "I like you very much," when his intent is to create a sense of obligation or to insure that he too will be accepted. One may maintain that he doesn't care when he really does care very much or he may say, "Oh well, have it your own way," when this is far from what he means.

Let us emphasize again, however, that these kinds of messages (see "Level five discourse," discussed below) are not necessarily intended by the transmitter. More often than not they probably are employed habitually without his knowledge or control. Interpersonal relationships which are structured by this kind of communication can be expected to lack depth, meaning, and trust. But regardless of intentionality, a person must live with the effects of his communications.

Nonverbal communication

People are less conscious of controlling bodily reactions than they are at managing what they say. The use of the polygraph or lie detector is based on this principle. While one can weigh and edit his speech, such telltale clues as an accelerated pulse, skin moisture, and increase in the rate of respiration combine to give him away. Indeed, there is reason to believe that considerably more is communicated concerning feelings, emotional states, and attitudes by other than verbal means (Birdwhistell, 1970; Longfellow, 1970). Cultural reticence may have something to do with this, for it does appear that those things which we are able to communicate verbally and with awareness have less need to be expressed nonverbally and with less chance of our knowledge and control.

Nonverbal communication patterns are learned early and are so thoroughly assimilated into behavior repertories that they tend to function without anyone's becoming aware of them until a divergent act calls them to attention (Beier, 1967; Birdwhistell, 1970; Thayer, 1968, p. 86; Hall, 1959, p. 71). For example, a woman may embrace and kiss another woman at the airport and provoke no more than passing notice. A man and woman may kiss and embrace also, but imagine the reaction and cultural expectations if two men do so! People transmit and respond to nonverbal messages almost habitually without really thinking. There is little chance of explaining their behavior and making it manageable until observation and research identify specific actions and the meanings which these communicate.

Meanings gained from certain behaviors vary among cultures, geographic locations, socioeconomic groups, and even families (Hall, 1969, p. 50; Birdwhistell, 1970, pp. 50–62). And it may be that at least a part of the inability of middle-class teachers to understand culturally disadvantaged children as well as the difficulties which these youngsters experience in school can be attributed to communication differences. Remedial action will probably not be taken until this is fairly widely accepted as a possibility.

Two implications which teachers may derive from this discussion of nonverbal communication should be valuable to them in their interactions with pupils. The first of these is that people are far more transparent and easily read than they believe themselves to be. Youngsters "psych out" teachers. They can tell with amazing accuracy how much horse play will be tolerated and when teacher limits are about to be reached. The solution may be to stop trying to be something one is not, for this more often generates than prevents interpersonal transaction problems. Misrepresentation, facade building, and problem avoidance use energy that better could be spent in confronting these types of concerns.

The second implication lies with the possibility of ambivalent, double-message communication. This happens when feeling-based, nonverbal behaviors indicate one message and spoken words indicate another. A classroom observation experience of the authors provides an example.

A sixth grade teacher had long standing discipline problems with her class. At her wits end, she asked that she be observed to see what caused the trouble. In discussions preliminary to visiting the class, the teacher described the children involved. She spoke warmly, affectionately, and with understanding of each child.

Later in the classroom, it was hard to believe she was the same teacher. Her voice was flat and her expression was wooden. She performed almost like an automaton, impersonally, giving no indication that she had feelings or that she cared about teaching or her pupils. After an hour or so, the children began to act out and to find out how much she would tolerate. Despite her rather monumental control, the inevitable happened; the teacher lost her temper. Under the stress she stopped feeling one way and acting another. Things went fairly well until she recovered and began to reinstitute more double-message communication.

It was suggested that she risk showing the children that she liked them and let them know her feelings in order that it would be unnecessary for them to push her until they were recognized and treated as persons rather than as things. A more relaxed, happier teacher and less attention-demanding pupil behavior resulted.

The necessity for straightforward communication without ambivalence is illustrated further by a series of interviews by a psychologist with 140 school children. The youngsters explained that they were uncomfortable with a new teacher until they found out about him and about how he operated. "They said that learning the teacher and being learned by him for the purpose of reasonable prediction of behavior led to mutual trust. That was what mattered to them—not technique, not books, not equipment—not anything but being able to trust each other. Then real learning can take place." [9]

THE PARADIGM OF MUTUAL INFLUENCE

In the preceding pages the point has been made that communication, human interaction, and the process of teaching and learning are closely related and similar. These and other human transactions largely are manipulatory in nature, i.e., when people are in contact, each person both influences, and is influenced by, the other. Most individuals, including teachers, are unaware of their involvement in this process and hence not free either to manage their own input or to avoid being victimized by fellow manipulators. And one of the best ways of heightening awareness and understanding of this process is to metacommunicate or to talk about it.

Metacommunication

This type of communication, though unusual and not widely practiced within the culture or by school personnel, can be facilitated in several ways. First, a vocabulary is necessary. Talking, thinking about, and dealing with ineffective communication behaviors is more possible when commonly understood, descriptive terms can be established. Second, an emotionally uninvolved, objective observer who can help to view and

[9] Barbara Ellis Long, "A Climate for Learning," *Today's Education* 61 (September 1972): 51.

describe interaction and communication patterns can be very helpful (Watzlawick, et al., 1968, p. 235). Participants in long standing processes in which emotional involvement is great often are unable to perceive interactions objectively and adequately either in terms of scope or of meaning. When one is caught up in an interaction, the rules, expectations, social pressures, and learned response patterns which govern his behavior tend to be implicit, habitual in nature, and below his level of awareness (Hall, 1959, p. 64; Thayer, 1966, p. 129; Berne, 1964, p. 49).

Classrooms and faculty lounges are among the places in which teachers are involved in such interactions. The poor communication which takes place furnishes some of the reasons for hiring consultants and counselors. An outside observer, particularly if he is trained to do so, often can help participants to become conscious of these implicit situations when they could not do so by themselves. Awareness of their existence and their functioning is a prerequisite for their change.

Description and dynamics

Human behavior and interaction are tremendously complex. A person ordinarily is subject to so many stimuli that the specific causes or reasons for any behavior almost are impossible to isolate. Yet the necessity to avoid teaching by accident and the informal acquisition of self-defeating behaviors make the attempt necessary. To be sure, the following oversimplified description and diagram of the communicative-interactive process is only a beginning. It is offered more to present a point of view and to stimulate thinking than as a model for solving specific interpersonal transaction problems. A number of sources have pointed out that, in communication-interaction situations, each behavior and verbal or nonverbal message, either singly or in combinations, may function simultaneously in three ways (Watzlawick et al., 1968, p. 55; Fabun, 1968, p. 33; Berne, 1964, p. 30). As indicated by Figure 4-1, it may serve as a response to other participant messages or behaviors which preceded, it may function to reinforce that behavior in the sense that being noticed and attended to is rewarding and in the sense that expectations are fulfilled, and it may operate

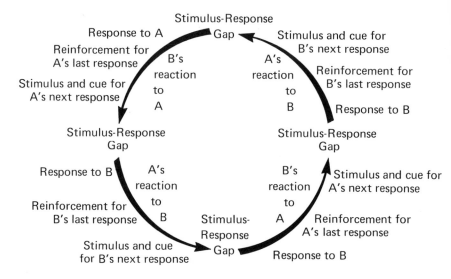

FIGURE 4-1. *The Communicative-Interactive Process.*

as a stimulus to elicit, cue, and direct the next other participant response in the sequence. Such an interaction process tends to be self-reinforcing, i.e., the feeling tone is perpetuated and intensified. If there is an angry, an argumentative, or a competitive one-up response, a similar reaction is aroused and this, in turn, tends to generate an even more vehement return. If the response is conciliatory and friendly, the reaction generally is channelled in the same direction. It is in the gap or length of time which exists between a stimulus and one's reaction to it that a decision may be made to behave in conventional and expected ways or to direct the transaction along dissimilar lines (May, 1967, p. 175).[10] By changing one's own behavior, an altered stimulus cue situation can be presented. Even though the consequent response cannot be specified, it can be conditioned to be different. A transaction can be cumulative in promoting good feelings as well as negative ones.

When two or more persons become involved together in such an interaction process, a number of descriptive points can

[10] See Chapter 3 for a discussion on using the stimulus-response gap for decreasing the effects of emotional involvement and susceptibility to manipulation.

be made. First, the interaction cannot occur as it does without the inputs of all participants. Hence assigning influence, control, and responsibility with any one person is not possible. Although it is tempting to excuse one's own inability by focusing upon the behavior of others as the cause of his acting as he does, the conclusion seems inescapable that interactions are mutually influencing. While some individuals are more easily swayed than others, what happens could not take place without them. Their capitulation and acquiescence are contributing factors in the process. If one is physically present, he can avoid neither participation nor responsibility.

Second, interpersonal transactions are likely to be circu-

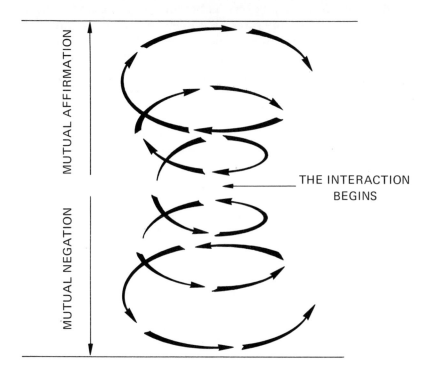

FIGURE 4-2. *The Mutual Influence Paradigm. Notice that the interaction pattern presented tends to increase in magnitude both horizontally (intensity) and vertically (quality). The input of any participant may change movement to either mutual negation or mutual affirmation.*

91

lar, self-reinforcing, cumulative, and repetitive in nature. When an emotion is fed into the system, the feelings of participants often are intensified in that direction, as in Figure 4-2. After an interaction has taken place a number of times, as in families, in classrooms, or between acquaintances of long standing, it tends to become characteristic of the relationship. That is to say, such patterns of stimulating and responding are learned. So any participant not only can influence the interaction by modifying his own behavior, but also he can, through consistent action, teach other participants a different pattern of interacting.

Third, although each participant has power to alter the system, total responsibility cannot be fixed with any one individual. No person reacts as he does all by himself and no interaction pattern operates as it does because of the input of any single person. While it may appear that the behavior of one interactor is directly to blame for the uproar in a classroom or the frigid emotional tone of a school, other individuals inevitably are involved. A person can control nothing without concomitantly submitting to some control himself. Freedom is not gained in the absence of regulation. The operation of an automobile and the freedom of movement it brings, for example, are conditional upon behaving in a prescribed manner.

A psychologist wanted to control the behavior of his cat by training the cat to use a litter box in the basement. He tied a bell to the knob of the basement door, letting it hang low enough so that the cat would find it alluring as a plaything. The psychologist then watched the cat. When it touched the bell and the bell rang, he opened the door and let the cat into the basement. In a few days, he had trained the cat to ring the bell whenever it wanted to go down to the basement. The psychologist congratulated himself upon his ability to control the behavior of his cat until he happened to think, "Who is compelled to open the door when the bell rings?"

If the reader will think back to the systems of psychology which were described earlier, he will recognize elements of both the stimulus-response behavioral approach and the new humanist phenomenological-existential explanations of human behavior. The preceding description of mutual influence made it apparent that psychological theories need not be mutually exclusive. A person may learn to apply stimulus-response and

"I've got him trained—every time I press the button he gives me a piece of cheese." A person can control nothing without concomitantly submitting to some control himself.

behavior modification techniques to himself as well as to others for the purpose of self-management and direction. Independent learners and teachers are not free from, or unaffected by, controls; they merely have learned how to use the human interaction system to gain opportunities for self-expression and personal development.

COMMUNICATING ABOUT COMMUNICATION

If one is to talk meaningfully, a vocabulary or a descriptive terminology is necessary. In classes and publications dealing with human interaction and communication, the authors have found a description of discourse levels to be helpful in providing such a vocabulary. There are, of course, other

93

descriptions and approaches, and no claim is made regarding the superiority of this one. After all, the model one chooses to follow probably is much less important than engaging in the process of examining one's own communicative behavior.

Levels of discourse

When one speaks of levels, he does so with the idea of depth or with the concept of moving in from the outside. Communication, in this sense, suggests degrees or depths of mutual expression or mutual involvement. The communicator may wish to share with and to establish ties and closeness with other persons or he may wish to transact on a superficial and impersonal basis, maintaining certain degrees of psychological distance between himself and his associates. It is when the communicator really wants to promote and maintain warm relationships and yet does not know how to do so that an understanding of the dynamics of discourse may be most helpful.

Figure 4-3 is a graphic representation of the accessibility or closeness to self permitted and facilitated by the various levels of discourse. If the reader can conceptualize the diagram as representing his own self or the selves of others, while the levels of discourse within the concentric rings represent degrees of sharing, openness, amount of defensiveness, and psychological distance, his understanding will be facilitated. Because intended meaning not always is transmitted, the various levels depicted here are called discourse rather than levels of communication.

Level five discourse does not communicate in the sense that what is said is the intended message or that what is verbalized is what is received. Discourse on this level is conducted more for the purpose of psychological self-preservation and the limitation and exploitation of others than to transmit meaning. It is here that ego defense mechanisms function, games are played, and facades are maintained. Level five includes the ambiguous double message described earlier. Level five discourse tends to dominate, often to distort, and to inhibit many of the relationships people maintain. Some of the characteristics and effects of this level which operate to limit meaningful transactions are:

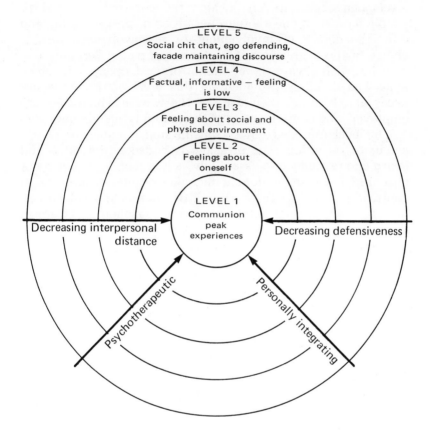

FIGURE 4-3. *Levels of Discourse.*

(1)   trust generally is not generated
(2)   psychological distance is increased
(3)   problems are created rather than solved
(4)   misunderstanding is more apt to result than understanding

Psychologically therapeutic metacommunication, counseling, or psychotherapy is made necessary by this type of discourse.

Despite its propensity for generating insecurity in human relationships, however, level five discourse does serve some purposes. It permits the ice breaking and warming up which

95

need to take place before communication on more meaningful levels can occur. It can cushion the confrontations which people have with one another, permit some prevarication, and offer the choice of involvement or noninvolvement and a choice of the degree to which this takes place. Certainly one does not wish always to be straightforward, open, and vulnerable. The defenses provided by this level of discourse are necessary. It is not their use but the way in which they are employed, and consciousness of them, that is open to question.

In level four discourse, transmission is equal, or nearly equal, to reception. The message is coded as intended and heard and responded to essentially as it is sent. Meaning is not obscured; there are no double messages or ulterior motives. In contrast with level five, there is little emotional involvement. Messages are factual, intellectual, and reasoned in nature in the manner of the laws of physics and the theorems of geometry. Information is conveyed and meaning can be verified.

To be in harmony with the traditional concept of education, instruction in classrooms should be level four discourse. Teachers should speak and pupils should listen. Presentation should equal learning. But discourse of this nature is a rarity. Dropouts and lack of achievement attest to this. Indeed, it may be that the assumption of this level of discourse operates as a causal factor for ineffective school relationships as well as causing disruptions in other interpersonal transactions.

In order to avoid the dangers of such an assumption, three distinguishing requirements of level four discourse are stated. If any of them is not present to a substantial degree the probability is that the discourse is upon some other level. First, message content is unemotional in nature. Second, there is little distortion involved in either transmission or reception. And third, psychological distance between communicants tends neither to increase nor to decrease.

Level three discourse is the first level which may be termed as psychotherapeutic. Discourse on this level operates to counteract the effects of the psychological insecurity and self-doubt brought about by the more exploitative and disruptive aspects of level five discourse. This type of discourse communicates. There is no subterfuge or double message. When a person is interacting on this level, he is talking about his own feelings with reference to his environment. Comments in the nature of "I am concerned about the reactions of my students" and "I feel happy regarding your decision" are representative of this level.

Some ways of determining whether messages can be classified as level three are described below. Knowledge of them can help one to use his own discourse more effectively and to understand the discourse of others. It can help him to metacommunicate. Level three discourse is personal. An individual who is communicating in this manner is speaking of his own feelings and impressions. Emotional involvement characterizes the discourse of persons' interacting in this manner. While no one can speak with authority about how others feel, he, and he alone, really knows of his own emotional experience. Discourse on level three reduces psychological distance and distrust between individuals. It promotes interpersonal sharing and what Buber describes as "I–thou" as opposed to "I–it" relationships (1958, p. 22). Communication is substantially achieved by this type of discourse. The receiver tunes in, understands, and accepts the intended message. He does not question, minimize, or devalue the speaker or challenge his right to feel as he does. If he did so, the discourse would revert to level five and straightforward, single message communication would not be possible. The salient identifying quality of level three discourse is that it concerns the individual's feelings about what goes on outside of him. It is closely related to the next level of therapeutic or personal growth discourse.

Level two discourse differs from that conducted on level three in one important respect. When a person is engaged in this manner, he is dealing with his feelings about himself. He is concerned about what is going on inside rather than outside his own skin and about his reactions to it. Like level three, this is a sharing experience. It promotes trust, decreases psychological distance, and fosters "I–thou" relationships. A person communicating in this manner, for example, could be expected to say such things as "I am afraid," "I doubt my ability to maintain discipline," "I'm happiest when I am able to express warm, positive feelings for others."

The most effective therapeutic communication involves discourse utilizing levels two, three, and four. A person talks of his feeling about himself in relation to his feelings for others with an occasional reference to factual, objective information as an aid to understanding. The process consists in communicating about one's interpersonal transactions or in metacommunicating with an objective observer functioning as an interpretive feedback agent. This can happen, most effectively in a well-facilitated, interpersonal process group (see Chapter 10). Such a group provides the social environment, the listeners, the facilitators, and the observers necessary for the assessment and modification of communication difficulties. Further, it furnishes these in a controlled or laboratory setting in which communication and interaction patterns actually function and are available for observation.

Level one discourse does not communicate for the reason that communication is neither necessary nor possible. A person on this level already has achieved nearly everything that any exchange of feeling or information can get for him. He has reached the "peak experience" state described by Maslow (1968), the condition of being so thoroughly in accord with his fellows which Kaplan termed "communion" (1969, p. 78). More discourse or communication can add little. On level one, there is a feeling of unity, of belonging and harmony, an "All's right with the world," "Oh! What a beautiful morning!" sort of feeling.

Unless one's listener has had a level one experience of the nature he is trying to describe, this is difficult to communicate, for it is something to be felt. Sharing must come through mutual experience. Words are insufficient to describe the feeling one sometimes gets when viewing a beautiful sunset, walking through a grove of majestic redwoods, or gaining a sudden insight. Teachers who have watched a child's face light up with comprehension sense the feeling.

Level one experiences can not come on command. For most of us, they are infrequent and transitory. But some individuals, like Maslow's (1970) self-actualizing people, appear to enjoy many more of them than others and some characteristics and behaviors appear to produce greater numbers of such experiences. Openness and its companion, a lack of defensive behavior, would appear to be one precondition. Others could be a strong personal identity and sense of self and a flexibility and an urge toward the new and the different. Because of high personal involvement and the psychological openness (even nakedness) of levels three and two discourse, it is difficult to stay there. It takes practice and sincerity in the pursuit of growth, to avoid escaping into humor, historical accounts, and theoretical explanations—levels five and four discourse. For the little comfort it may afford, let the reader reflect that growth often requires effort, endurance, and discomfort, even pain, what some authors have described as a trauma of transcendence (Fullmer and Bernard, 1964).

The importance of listening

The traditional concept of teaching as a unidirectional process has operated to cast students in the role of listener and to develop an image of listening as a passive, soaking-up-information process. Students and children have been expected to listen attentively to teachers and parents although, unless these latter also listen attentively, there are no models from whom to learn the process. Indeed, the listening behaviors which children do learn are just as likely to limit the ability to focus upon the speaker and his message. Because the listening skills of most adults are ineffective, ineffective skills tend to be taught, informally and accidentally, to the next generation.

Rather than a passive process, listening actually is a most effective way of communicating. The attentive listener provides a number of important essentials for the process. He furnishes a reason for communicating; cues, direction, and encouragement and reinforcement; and feelings of importance,

Students and children have been expected to listen attentively. (© King Features Syndicate.)

status, and worth for the communicator (Rogers, 1969, p. 224). The listener or audience exerts a pervasive influence over the entire communicative act (Borden, Gregg, and Grove, 1969, p. 215). Listening behavior determines to a considerable degree whether something will be communicated, the duration of the communicative contact, and the subject of the communication. But more than that, and regardless of the subject of the communication, the implicit message which is projected by the listener concerning his feelings about the importance and worth of the speaker is an important factor determining the value which the interpersonal contact may hold. The attending behavior of a teacher, for example, may communicate, without really intending to do so, that a pupil or student is a source of annoyance or that he is unacceptable and lacking in value as a person. In this sense, listening partly carries a double message. It indicates "Yes, I am" at the same time that it shows "No, I am not." Partial attention leaves a speaker in a quandary; he doesn't know whether to try harder and shout louder or to feel hurt and diminished and give up.

Certainly a teacher or a parent cannot be expected to provide total attention each time that it is demanded but there should be times when this is possible. At the very least, a person should be able to recognize the quality of his listening. He should be able to listen totally if he wishes and he should know the impact his partial listening can have. Probably a few minutes of real, total commitment listening does more to assuage a speaker's desire for attention and to bolster his ego than much longer times of the half acceptance, half brush-off attention. Probably the positiveness of a person's concept of self is directly related to the kinds and numbers of people who will listen to him.

Barriers to listening

Real listening, which is totally committed to the self-expression and understanding of another person, is not an easy thing to do for several reasons. To begin with, there are few places in this culture where this type of listening is practiced, short of the therapeutic milieu provided by counselors and psychotherapists. Too much listening is of the cocktail hour variety, not for information or because of concern for the speaker or what he has to say but merely waiting for a chance to speak. Also, listeners typically focus more on verbal content than on the speaker, thus blocking out nonverbal messages. Total listening involves an awareness of visual clues and the use of the listener's feelings as aids to understanding. Furthermore, it is possible to listen and to process aural stimuli at four to five hundred words per minute, while the average rate of speech is only of one-hundred fifty words per minute. Hence the mind may not be fully involved and other stimuli may distract attention. Finally, most individuals have a number of people or tasks competing for their attention at the same time. When one permits himself to be spread too thinly, he makes little difference anywhere. It is thus with listening.

One solution may be to try to experience people rather than simply listening to their words (Fabun, 1968, p. 42). Even though the spoken message may be boring, to assume that the speaker is also may deprive both the listener and the speaker of a satisfying interpersonal experience. For there is more to anyone than just the words he uses. His appearance, clothes, facial expressions, body movements, hand gestures, speaking mannerisms, attitudes, topics of conversation, vocal tone and timbre, and what he shares and what he hides all mean something. When one is using all that he can to understand and experience another person, there is little chance for inattention. Total commitment is necessary. Each human personality offers a transaction opportunity never before experienced. Psychologists, and teachers, can find in such committed listening much of the enjoyment the artist discovers in a landscape or painting. If the opportunities are missed, it is not because they do not exist, but because we are blind to them. Listening behaviors are among the most potent tools we have for influencing interpersonal transactions.

SUMMARY

Communication is essential to human development but most people take it for granted and thereby underestimate its potential.

No person can choose not to communicate. To avoid being misinterpreted, he must express himself as clearly as possible. His only choice is how he will do this.

Human effectiveness and mental health are coordinates of good communication. Emotional and psychological upsets largely can be traced to misleading communication.

The receiver rather than the transmitter really determines message meaning. His actions are based upon what he hears and interprets rather than what the speaker thinks he said.

A large amount of communication is affected by nonverbal factors which tend to occur without the control exercised over speech. A speaker's behavior may belie what he says and he inadvertently may transmit double messages which serve to confuse rather than to facilitate communication.

Because communication is an important means for developing personal identity and a positive sense of self, persons who do not learn to verbalize effectively are seriously disadvantaged.

Communication is the principal means available for influencing the behavior of, and manipulating, other individuals, but reluctance to admit this restricts the opportunity to improve the process.

Although mutual manipulation or influence is universal, the process cannot be exploitative and one-way and still progress effectively. In long-run, meaningful transactions, each party must benefit.

When two or more individuals are communicating or interacting, the response of any one of them furnishes reinforcement for the last action performed by the other as well as stimuli and cues for his next act. Each behavior simultaneously functions as response, stimulus, and reinforcement.

By altering his own behavior, each participant can change the stimulus-cue situation to which his associates react. Transactions (1) cannot occur as they do without the input of each participant, (2) make impossible the fixing of responsibility with any one person, and (3) are circular, self-reinforcing, cumulative, and repetitive in nature.

Improvement of communication involves talking about, obtaining feedback and metacommunicating regarding one's own effectiveness.

Metacommunication can be advanced by a transaction vocabulary. This depends upon an understanding of discourse levels and their effect upon the quality of interpersonal relationships.

If one is to deal with his own communication, he must

consider the effect of his own listening. Constructively used, this can provide associates with a reason for relating, with status, and positive feelings about themselves. The ability to perform committed listening, during which the listener experiences the speaker totally as a person, is a potent tool for good teaching and for maintaining effective relationships. Like all learned behaviors, listening can be modified and improved.

SUGGESTED ADDITIONAL READINGS

Bernard, Harold W., and Huckins, Wesley C. *Dynamics of Personal Adjustment.* Boston: Holbrook Press, Inc., 1970. This book, particularly Chapters 6 and 11, expands upon the topics covered in this chapter. Although youth are its primary audience, its message is pertinent to all ages.

Berne, Eric. *Games People Play.* New York: Grove Press, Inc., 1964. This is a highly readable description of some typical exploitive and manipulative communication-interaction patterns. Readers will see themselves and their associates more clearly through exposure to this classic in the field of human transaction.

Fabun, Don. *Communication: The Transfer of Meaning.* Beverly Hills: Glencoe Press, 1968. This book is a short, well-illustrated exposé of the misconceptions which many of us have about the processes of communicating and interacting. Teachers will find it valuable as a reference.

Hall, Edward T. *The Silent Language.* Greenwich, Conn.: Fawcett Publications, Inc., 1959. This classic in the field of communication provides the happy combination of good scholarship, food for thought, and low price. The author points out many of the things which we take for granted when we communicate and demonstrates how much of the process takes place without our awareness and conscious control.

Shostrom, Everett. *Man, The Manipulator.* Nashville, Tenn.: The Abingdon Press, 1967. The chances are good that this book will point out some possibilities in communicating and interacting which the reader has not considered. The author is very outspoken; and the reader may agree or disagree but he will not be unaffected.

Watzlawick, Paul, Beavin, Janet, and Jackson, Don. *The Pragmatics of Human Communication.* New York: W. W. Norton and Co., 1967. The relationship of communication with human interaction and existence is explored in this book. It describes the values of metacommunication, feedback, and the use of an outside observer for dealing with the problems people have in transacting with each other.

CHAPTER 5

Teachers: Agents and Victims of Change

In the sense that tomorrow is bound to be different, everyone must contend with change. And in the sense that the rate of change constantly is accelerating, each of us must deal with greater differences between yesterday and today than ever before. This dilemma is intensified by the risk of continuing to leave the future to chance. Such problems as pollution, ghettos, riots, and overpopulation heighten the dangers of inaction. The choice is not whether to accept change; it simply concerns the manner in which change will or will not be managed.

Advisability of planned change

During the past decade there has been an increasing realization by scholars in several disciplines that the welfare of mankind may depend upon the ability to apply planned controls to the future. B. F. Skinner (1966) has been one of the foremost psychologists urging that the behavior of individuals be subject to planned control. He has contended that:

(1) Enough is known so that behavior can be managed effectively for both the benefit of the person and society;

(2)   The need is pressing to influence human actions in order to control crime, war, and mental illness; and

(3)   Behavior already is modified and influenced in a haphazard and unplanned manner.

Dobzhansky (1962) among biologists has pointed out the dangers of leaving human evolution to chance and Dubos has advocated a normative planning which is ". . . not based on forecasts of a future that is inevitable; it is concerned rather with imagining a desirable state of affairs and with acting on present conditions so as to bring about desired changes." [1]

In the socioeconomic area, Harrington (1965) has taken a similar position. He has described our era as the "Accidental Century" and maintained that the techniques which functioned well for handling production in an age of scarcity no longer are suitable in an era of abundance. At the same time, consumers rather than producers have become the essential for the operation of the economic system. As Hollomon phrased it, "The education of people . . . will have to do less with their ability to create wealth than with their ability to use wealth which has already been created." [2] Both Harrington and Hollomon urge social planning or engineering in order to develop attitudes and controls more appropriate to this shift in the character of society.

Actually the choice of whether or not to attempt to engineer the future may already have been made by the need to survive. Boyer emphasizes this. He points out that "a society without control over change is a society with its future out of control." [3] Lacking a minimizing of accidental change and a maximizing of intentional change through planning, he predicts catastrophe. He believes that what is needed is not so much a planning *for* the future as a planning *of* the future. Such planning should not assume that people must adjust to trends but should be based upon the idea of adjusting trends to people.

[1] René Dubos, "Man and His Environment: Scenarios for the Future," *New York University Education Quarterly* 11 (Summer 1971): 5.

[2] J. Herbert Hollomon, "Creative Engineering and the Needs of Society," in Daniel V. DeSimone, ed., *Education For Innovation* (Elmsford, N.Y.: 1968), p. 26.

[3] William H. Boyer, "Education for Survival," *Phi Delta Kappan* 52 (January 1971): 258–59.

Difficulties in planning for change

Change which affects the beliefs and attitudes of people is not easily legislated or imposed. On the contrary, pressure to change and be different often carries the implication of inadequacy, unacceptability or culpability. This in turn generates feelings of being attacked and put down which then create immobilizing defensive reactions. An outward compliance can be forced but the inward enthusiasm necessary to make new ideas work rarely is gained through administrative edict. Forced conformity, even if the idea is excellent, will not produce the necessary supporting behavior and complementary ideas from participants. Hence change appears best effected from the inside out and from the bottom up. The authors' visits to innovative schools furnish corroboration. In a number of cases, a teacher or teaching team was designated by the administration and the rest of the staff as being the most innovative and authoritative. Where enthusiasm and support were high, the impetus and leadership for change were furnished by teachers rather than imposed by the school administration or by external agencies.

Some of the considerations involved in anticipating the future were presented by the director of a government sponsored Educational Policy Research Center to a conference of school administrators, counselors, and teachers (Green, 1969). Green spoke of "inventing" the future for the reason that a strictly planned approach may operate merely to extend the present, that what may be needed is not simply an enlargement of what we have but something altogether different. It is important to realize, however, that such an approach may operate no more to make the desirable happen than it may to prevent the undesirable. Perhaps just as important is the realization that the information and expertise to do either cannot be expected to be found in the present. It may be that what one knows today is less important than his ability to discard it and to generate something different (Taylor, 1968). Convictions which tend to set perceptions and to promote inflexibility, as many of them do, may limit rather than facilitate the ability to live effectively.

Power and population increases. The power which men have been able to exert in modifying and exploiting their surround-

107

ings has increased greatly over the years. In addition, the population explosion has caused the character of this environment to become more and more social and psychological in nature. The results of man's efforts to exert control in these areas, however, has been considerably less spectacular than he has experienced in applying physical power and altering the physical aspects of his environment. Masses of people living closely together allow any one person to make more difference, at least in the social-psychological sense, for good or for bad to more individuals than ever before.

Generally the person judged to be effective and accorded status in this culture has been the person who possesses the ability or the power to change or alter the lives of others or the conditions under which they and others live. At the same time that this power has been recognized, however, there has been a tendency to impose controls upon its user. Consider, for example, the rigid licensing of medical doctors and lawyers and the control which the electorate is given through its vote over public officials. One of the conflicts of our time is that so many aspire to power and to status while at the same time protesting regulation and control. The conclusion appears unmistakable that these will be imposed externally.

One of the conflicts of our times is that many aspire to power and status while protesting regulation and control.

Change, as we have indicated, is inevitable. The choice is whether or not it will be planned and deliberately managed or just left to occur haphazardly. Individuals who function as agents of change initiate and influence change processes: They identify promising behavior possibilities and try them; and they conduct pragmatic tests to find out what works. Persons who are victimized by change either resist the new or passively let it happen. Change directs them: They do not function to direct it; they react rather than enact. The unexpected or the unwanted is more apt to limit them than their more innovative and adaptable fellows.

Amplification systems and influence

In that the process of innovation and change usually results in more effective means of doing things, it adds to the power and influence which men can apply. Ferguson (1966) pointed out the historical male preoccupation with power and Bruner (1965) described as "amplification systems" the various means employed by people for increasing the amount of power which any person can exert.[4] In the past these amplifiers, such as shovels, wagons, and bulldozers, were mechanical in nature and served mostly to increase physical strength. But lately, ways of amplifying the force people can employ have moved toward the intellectual. Information is stored in computers, retrieved, combined, and recombined. Other machines are controlled. In a sense auxiliary brains as well as muscles have become available for those who know how to use them.

Psychosocial amplification systems. Although more difficult to recognize or describe, amplification systems also exist in a psychosocial sense. An individual, through good working relationships, knowledge of people, and effective use of communication, can magnify his personal impact to a degree much in excess of what he might accomplish if he did not know how to make the social system work for him. Psychologically one may strengthen his own ego by learning to relate meaningfully

[4] Hall has called these "amplification systems" extensions of the human body. He gives such examples as power tools, glasses, TV, telephones, and books. Edward T. Hall, *The Silent Language* (Greenwich, Conn.: Fawcett Publications, Inc., 1959), p. 60.

109

to his fellows. He can learn to manage what he does with people so that his chances of getting back what he wants from them are increased. It is possible to behave so that interactions with others are mutually self-affirming and self-validating. But we reaffirm and reemphasize, one does not use such amplification systems with long-term effectiveness without also recognizing that the exercise of personal power is never strictly a one-way process. The user also must modify his own behavior and allow other parts of the system some power over his actions. As we have mentioned, one cannot even operate an automobile or train a cat without at the same time modifying and adapting his own behavior.

How psychosocial amplification works. A good example of the use of the social structure as an amplification system comes from the operations of a television master of ceremonies in one of the nation's medium-sized cities. Each Christmas season this man sponsors a fund which is used to buy toys and other things for children confined to hospitals. The businesses and producers advertised on his program furnish prizes to be awarded to donors who are phoned for answers to simple questions, with the whole process televised. Accidentally, or with plan and purpose, this man has been able to combine substantial parts of his environment into a system that works for him. Consider what is happening. The many persons involved—contributors, recipients, business people, and viewers—are all provided with reasons for feeling good about themselves and about others. There is entertainment, publicity, and prizes. Necessary financial inputs, salaries, contributions, and awards all are supplied with gain and without burden for the system operator or catalyst. Products are advertised and associated with a worthy cause. People who need help are helped. And status, ego gratification, and prestige accrue for the person who coordinates and makes the system work. Consider also that all of the components are available. All that is needed is the change agent with the innovative idea for putting them together. He functions as a coordinator, he acts as a catalyst, to provide impetus, and to adjust so that each part meshes and complements other parts and the operation as a whole. Each component is interdependent but not completely dependent. Most of the power and sustaining motivation for making the combination work is generated internally. The operator provides direction and perhaps inspiration. He is not obliged to impose force nor is he responsible for managing any of the interacting aspects of the system.

A kindergarten teacher uses parts of the school environment as an amplification system in a similar manner though on a smaller scale. She asks bored and somewhat intractable sixth grade boys to help her manage, read to, and play games with, morning and afternoon shifts of five-year-olds. Both ages enjoy the experience. The kindergarten group appears to learn as well or better and the older youngsters often improve considerably in reading skills and deportment. The teacher gets greater satisfaction and recognition and status from her work. All parts of the system gain (are amplified) to some extent.

Amplification in organizations. Each school or family or other social organization has its share of those who use it as a personal amplification system and who increase its effectiveness by doing so. Each has a potential for the development of more effective systems. In most, if not all of them, opportunities as change agents and innovators are amply provided for those who are able to analyze and develop new associations and interaction patterns among components.

Successful innovators or change agents appear to be able to recognize, combine, coordinate, and use the various aspects of their environments. They are creative in a social sense. Like the creative individuals described by Barron (1963), they develop new and more effective ways of getting things done and new patterns and structures through which human effort may be applied. The authors, visiting and observing in innovative schools, found that there are certain criteria which can be applied to assess effective change and innovative practices. First, innovators are more successful when they operate within and use the existing system. Power structures and channels of communication are studied and utilized. As a corollary, effective change for organizations as well as for individuals is most apt to take place when the impetus comes from inside. The question, "How can we make it work better?" is much more conducive to change than the statement, "You are doing it wrong." The critic makes it necessary to defend a

111

Each school or other social organization has its quota of those who use it as a personal amplification system.

position and to take a stand against his attack. For this reason he generally must operate outside the system and he often prevents the improvement he wishes to bring about.

Second, once a process of change has begun, it tends to be self-sustaining and cumulative. Once modification is started, further adjustment becomes necessary. Innovative school staffs rarely stop with the initiation of one change. They tend to become involved with the innovative process. An enthusiasm and a sense of cooperation and sharing then tend to be passed on to pupils and students. These feelings, in the opinion of the authors, are more important for effective learning than specific changes in instruction, organization patterns or curricular content. Again, the process appears to be more important than its products.

Third, the process of change, in order to be supported and sustained, must be mutually self-affirming for the majority of those involved. Some satisfaction must accrue and some progress must be apparent. The process must include, not separate, people.

Some effects of amplification. A significant feature of amplification systems is that they inevitably increase the gap between those who have and those who have not. Just as rapid change has widened the rift between generations, so the ever increasing availability of amplifiers has operated to heighten the disparity between individuals who know how to apply them and individuals who do not. Furthermore, the combination of this access to power-expanding agents and accelerating change has served to render choosing to use or not to use somewhat analogous to deciding whether or not to become obsolete and inept. Now one can become out-of-date with astonishing speed. Like other human conditions, this process of becoming obsolescent has cumulative effects. The more one lets himself get out of touch, the fewer ways he has for rejoining the mainstream and the more difficult it gets to be. Indeed, it has been said that if one were to study to the height of his capacity for the rest of his life, he still would be getting continuously less well-informed and backward with reference to the rate of knowledge increase. The teacher or the engineer, the doctor or other professional who believes that he can relax upon receipt of his degree increasingly will be victimized by this delusion. It is becoming easier and easier to get stuck on the have-not side of the efficiency gap without realizing that this is happening.

The mechanics of initiating change

Ideas and theories, no matter how sound and how brilliant, can have little impact until, and unless, they are put to work. And there are big differences between theory and invention on the one hand and innovation and practice on the other. While education appears to abound with and to be beset by the former, not many of these panaceas could endure rigorous testing. The exhilaration of generating and creating is liable to be preempted by outside agents while teachers, all too often, are left with the task of putting someone else's thinking into practice. They are expected to furnish ideas of implementation.

113

They generally are not encouraged to furnish ideas of origin. For whatever reasons, this expectation generally is borne out and justified by teacher behavior. Even though the anticipation may function as a self-fulfilling prophecy, it appears that a majority of teachers fail to suggest educational changes and, except in a few cases, not to function as creative innovators (Meyer, 1969).

Explanations too frequently become rationalizations and excuses. And even though there may be, as Goodlad (1968, p. 5) maintains, "enormous conservative restraints" affecting schools and their administrators, one fact appears fairly well established. As long as schools continue to look primarily to outside agents and administrators for ideas and impetus, as they traditionally have done, needed educational innovations will seldom take place. Despite the obstacles, teachers must be involved. The crucial answers must deal with how to make this happen.

But there is a quandary here which the provision of answers, advice, and directions, no matter how sagacious, does not dispell. Educators who do offer more precise, how-to-do-it statements, are then criticized for being "condescending, patronizing, professorial." The dilemma is that both sides make sense. We know that the really meaningful experiences are those which the individual gets for himself. The process of gaining answers is more important than the answers gained. As the old saying has it, "Give a man a fish and he eats for a day: Teach him to fish and he eats for a lifetime." While giving advice and directions may help to meet the ego and power needs of the giver, this all too often derogates the recipient who is likely to reject the advice at the same time that he urges, "Be more specific." But let us assure the reader that our intent is to suggest rather than to prescribe. We are convinced that the value of any book or attempt to communicate can be no better than what the receiver can get from it. Teacher initiation of change is approached from this frame of reference but admittedly with no ready solution to the above quandary.

Deciding about scope and degree. Innovation, of course, is better accomplished in response to a felt need than just by making a decision to create or vary a situation. But many teachers are aware of numerous needs; for them, deciding to change concerns only where and how to begin. One way might be to determine the amount of innovating needed in order to gain satisfaction and a sense of personal accomplishment. Will the modification of a relationship with a student be enough? Will changing interaction patterns with a single class do it? Must the change encompass a school building? An entire district? How much can one's impact be spread before satisfaction is replaced by frustration?

Levels or types of changes. Another closely related question which a change agent may find helpful to ask and to answer for himself concerns the number of people apt to be affected and whether or not and in what manner they can be expected to react to what he proposes. Miller (1967) and Jones (1969) classified the types of innovation as:

methodological—involving those changes individual teachers can implement with existing space and facilities
instructional—those changes involving more than one staff member and necessitating some modification of time, space, and materials
organizational—the major changes concerning large numbers of staff for long periods and representing a general overhaul of the entire system

Each type of innovation overlaps with the others. Change anywhere in the system does not take place without affecting its other parts or subsystems to some degree.

Figure 5-1 shows that an idea for change may be located both vertically, in terms of the types and numbers of personnel it will affect, and horizontally, in terms of the planning and time required to carry it out. The farther up and to the right an idea for change is placed, the more such factors as the power structure of the school and the community must be considered if theory is to become practice. The farther in this direction, the more teacher ideas must be those of implementation and the more teachers are apt to find themselves working for someone else rather than working on projects of their own. When a prospective innovation moves as specified above, opposition is apt to increase, more proof that the idea will work is likely to be demanded, and those who wish to try it can expect to expend more effort explaining, justifying, and defending. The amount of threat which people feel with change can be expected to increase and the basic merit of any

115

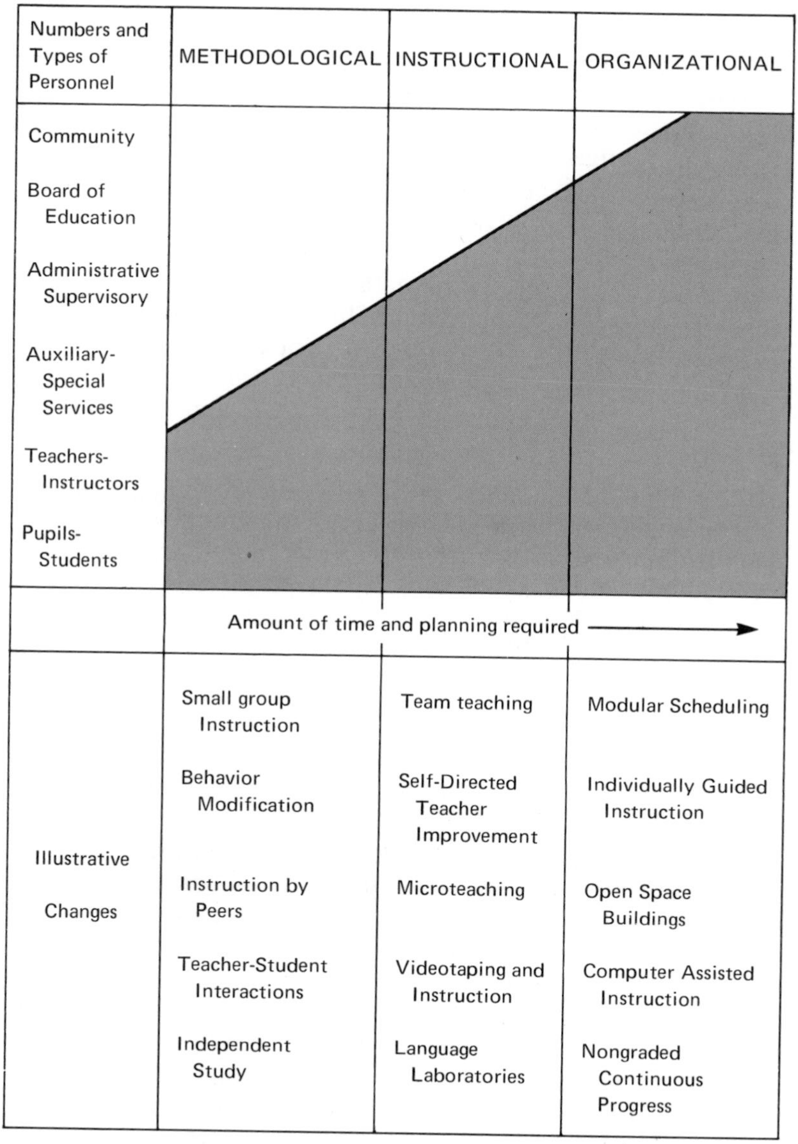

Numbers and Types of Personnel	METHODOLOGICAL	INSTRUCTIONAL	ORGANIZATIONAL
Community			
Board of Education			
Administrative Supervisory			
Auxiliary-Special Services			
Teachers-Instructors			
Pupils-Students			
	Amount of time and planning required ⟶		
Illustrative Changes	Small group Instruction	Team teaching	Modular Scheduling
	Behavior Modification	Self-Directed Teacher Improvement	Individually Guided Instruction
	Instruction by Peers	Microteaching	Open Space Buildings
	Teacher-Student Interactions	Videotaping and Instruction	Computer Assisted Instruction
	Independent Study	Language Laboratories	Nongraded Continuous Progress

FIGURE 5-1. *Types of Innovations. Adapted from Richard I. Miller, ed.,* Perspectives on Educational Change *(New York: Appleton-Century-Crofts, 1967), p. 369.*

proposal is more likely to be supplanted by political considerations. In sum, the larger the number of social power structures

116

involved, the more the issue becomes one of knowing the right people rather than having the right ideas.

Advantages of a small start. But the focus of this book is primarily upon teachers and their interactions with youngsters and upon those changes which teachers can effect through the management of their own attitudes and behavior. Helping people to improve is a more rewarding and lasting achievement than manipulating equipment, materials, or schedules. The authors endorse Brickell's (1961) assumption that the adoption of new techniques and the modification of what is taught are dependent upon fundamental changes in people. Indeed, it well may be that educational personnel in general have been so concerned about the big instructional or organizational changes that they have failed to see and to develop the simpler and often more important methodological changes. A small start which deals with attainable behaviors and manageable units for short periods of time may be the necessary prelude to successful innovation on a broader scope.

There are other advantages. Methodological change is a possibility for every teacher, teaching team, or combination of educational personnel. It does not, for the most part, need to be sold to, and approved by, very many others. It is pertinent to practitioner problems and growth. And it can be carried on with a minimum of exterior direction and intervention. One can get right at it or stop as he wishes and, as far as results are concerned, he need share widely only those which are successful. There is less premium on being right and less risk in introducing variations.

One disadvantage, if it can be so termed, includes fixing at least a part of the responsibility for innovation and in-service growth at teacher rather than administrator levels. A part of the "why-don't-they," expectation and responsibility is lifted from administrators and a defeating rationalization is no longer available to teachers.

Still, administrators do have responsibilities also (see Chapter 11) but these do not, and probably should not, include a prescription of what innovative and in-service activities should be. Just as teachers should not plan educational experiences without considering the individuality and learning style of each student, so in-service experiences for teachers should not be directed entirely toward the group with little or

117

no concern for the individual (Snyder and Peterson, 1970, p. 221). Observation and reaction by peers on the basis of each teacher's own objectives, in each teacher's own classroom, and at each teacher's own request, may well constitute the most effective in-service learning experience. It may also be a very good way of generating and developing innovative ideas for better teaching.

Personal characteristics of change agents

In order to promote a receptivity to change in others (and this must become the essence of educating and learning), it is necessary for teachers to demonstrate this attitude. It is necessary for them to exemplify the process type of learning. If correct answers are more important to them than the process of gaining these answers, that is what they will teach. If their learning is continuous, taking place in the school and in the classroom, then they will teach this to students. As we have emphasized in preceding chapters, teacher change is essential for, and must precede, pupil change. Diplomas and certification no longer are indications that one has learned. They are indicators that one is qualified to continue the process with pupils as emulators and fellow learners. In this sense, the teacher must plan for his own learning if he is to stimulate and structure that of others.

The personal characteristics which enable a person to initiate and to participate in the process of change may also furnish a terminology for describing effective teachers. If good teaching depends upon the ability to communicate and interact with other individuals as we and others (Combs, 1962; Adams and Biddle, 1970; Flanders, 1970) believe that it does, then there is much similarity between the good teacher and the mentally-healthy, socially-effective individual (Waetjen and Leeper, 1966).

Erikson (1968, p. 65) has described the ability to stay tentative and tolerate tension as an essential for psychological well-being in times of rapid change. Hamachek (1969, p. 343) has maintained that the single most repeated adjective used to describe good teachers is "flexibility." Crutchfield (1963, pp. 224–26), under the broad topics of conflict, creativity, and conformity, listed cognitive process deficiencies as one of four personality factors identified with conformity proneness. He indicated that conformists show clear tendencies toward rigidity of thought and a limited ability to perceive openly and realistically. Other characteristics associated with the tendency to conform and to discourage creativity, innovation, and change were (1) a generalized incapacity to cope effectively under stress coupled with a greater vulnerability to free floating anxiety; (2) feelings of personal inferiority and inadequacy along with intense preoccupation with others and the passivity, suggestibility, and dependence which go with these feelings; and (3) a common lack of openness and freedom in emotional expression plus a lack of spontaneity and a low tolerance for ambiguity.

The assumption appears warranted that change and innovation involve the risk of being misunderstood, of being held blameworthy, and of being made a scapegoat. In a success-oriented culture, this is especially hazardous.

People who initiate change appear to differ from those who do not in certain important ways. They are what Torrance and Ziller in their studies involving stress conditions and Air Force personnel have termed "high riskers."

> The personality pattern of the high risker is characterized by self confidence, physical and social adequacy, and self expression. Individuals most willing to take risks feel secure in their own resources and are little concerned that someone may not like them.[5]

Other identifying behaviors are a sense of adequacy, a feeling of power over their environment, greater social aggressiveness, and a history of being highly involved in on-going activities.

Depending on what he expects, one is not surprised to find points of similarity between the high risker as described above and the self-actualized person as characterized in Maslow's research (1954, pp. 203–34), between the creative individual as depicted by MacKinnon (1964, pp. 14–19) and Torrance (1965,

[5] E. Paul Torrance and R. C. Ziller, *Risk and Life Experience: Development of a Scale for Measuring Risk Taking Tendencies* (Lackland, Tex.: Air Force Personnel and Training Research Center, 1957), pp. 198, 299.

pp. 326–31) and the good teacher as outlined by Combs (1965, pp. 70, 71). These sources list or imply the common personality characteristics of:

(1) flexibility or the ability to fit in and to adapt
(2) openness to experience without distortion or shutting out because of threat and defensiveness
(3) a feeling of being adequate, of being competent to function acceptably and effectively
(4) a sense of involvement and of being an important part of what is happening
(5) an awareness of influencing and of making a difference, of being internally rather than externally controlled, of being more than a pawn, and of enacting rather than reacting.

The authors wish to emphasize several points in this respect. The first of these is that people learn to be what they are, i.e., human behaviors are acquired. If a person is fearful, rigid, and inflexible, it is because he has learned to act in this manner. Second, any thing that has been learned is subject to change; different behavior can be learned as a replacement. Individuals can adapt to or alter almost any situation in which they find themselves. Third, this change or learning can be self-initiated and self-directed, at least to the point of recognizing a need and taking advantage of learning opportunities. Fourth, if the capacity for learning and change is not exercised, it will tend to atrophy like other human capacities. In a sense, one must use it or lose it. Fifth, learning, even for teachers, never becomes impossible. No one, as long as he is alive and conscious, ever becomes completely unable to modify his behavior and to learn. He may use age or work load as reasons for not trying and as pretexts for maintaining a comfortable niche but these should be recognized for what they are— rationalizations and excuses. As we have said, to live is to change. Some modification is inevitable even if it is merely to become more fixed and more inflexible; to become more locked in or to wear the rut a little deeper.

The Hawthorne Effect

A school, a teaching team, or an individual teacher should not change just for the sake of changing or just to keep up with those down the hall or with other schools, even though a good argument can be advanced for this. Perhaps the reader is familiar with the Hawthorne Effect (Roethlisberger and Dickson, 1939). In a series of experiments under a variety of working conditions, investigators at the General Electric Company's Hawthorne Works found that, regardless of whether or not the level of illumination was raised, lowered, or held constant, production continued to increase. They concluded that something similar to the placebo in medicine tended to operate in experiments involving people and that the mere fact of being singled out, involved, and given attention in the process of change and innovation often is all that is needed to increase performance.

Implications for schools. The Hawthorne Effect has important implications for teachers and for education. It raises the definite possibility that involvement and feelings of importance are at least as significant in those innovations and changes which encompass people as the specific goal sought. A change may not need to work as expected or to be the cure for many of the recognized ills and shortcomings of a school in order for positive results to accrue. It may even be good practice to instigate a process of changing although outcomes are not clearly specified. Often it is less difficult to perceive that all is not well and that things are not working as they should than it is to prescribe what to do to correct such situations. Further, it is possible, as Green (1968) suggested, that the setting of goals from the limiting perspective of the present may function more to restrict than to advance what can happen in the future. After all, perhaps movement in a consistent direction is all that can be hoped for and all that may be necessary. A continuing Hawthorne Effect may do a lot of good in many educational institutions.

Change and threat

But people look for permanence and the sure thing. Some of them find the unsettled situation uncomfortable and threatening. And there appears to be some basis for believing that, although pressure up to a certain point is perceived as a challenge and operates to generate performance increases, problem solving, experimentation, and innovative behavior, pressure beyond the point where such coping and adaptive actions are no longer successful results in a return to early and overlearned behaviors (Torrance, 1965, pp. 24–25, 57). This is in accord with the Yerkes-Dodson Law which states that, while a small amount of pressure and anxiety is insufficient to improve performance, a moderate amount will improve it (Levitt, 1967, p. 120). Any further increments are likely to be disruptive. In other words, pressure which rouses real doubts concerning ability and shakes self-confidence tends to decrease the ability to try new ways of doing things. It limits flexibility and the capacity to induce and assimilate change.

"You nag me, the boss bawls at me, traffic cops yell at me... Once a week I have to come over here and make faces at the goldfish."

Pressure . . . may result from a single threatening situation or it may come because of a number of minor concerns which are not dealt with and which accumulate.

Innovation and stress. Pressure of this nature and scope may result from a single threatening situation or it may come because of a number of minor concerns which are not dealt with and which accumulate. Thus a person may carry such a load that a small happening, incidental in itself, may trigger a disproportionate emotional reaction. One's tolerance for stress, and probably the flexibility of his behavior and his propensity for change, may hinge to a considerable degree upon the expectations he feels he must meet, his attitude toward himself, and the pressure he is experiencing. Imaginative and creative thinking, and presumably this is essential for innovative action, has been found to vary among children as they move from one developmental stage to another (Torrance, 1965, pp. 101–03). The transition points, for example, which occur between the small child and middle childhood and adolescence are characterized by decreases in creative thinking abilities. Furthermore, these low points in creative development correspond to peak ages for referrals to mental health clinics and similar agencies. The relationship between psychological well-being and the ability to think appears both causal and unmistakable. Generally it is true that crises which require adaptation and which generate undue psychological pressure at any time of life tend to result in performance decrements.

Pressure and teaching effectiveness. Just as little is done about the psychological well-being of people in this culture until a breakdown occurs, so the schools seldom are concerned with helping teachers to deal with pressure and threat until they become noticeably incapacitated (Brenton, 1971). Even then, the common response of the school system is to terminate the teacher's contract. This is true although teacher effectiveness, and consequent student learning and emotional health, substantially and directly may be affected. Despite the expressed desire for creative teaching and the innovative approach, the necessary psychological health in teachers tends to be taken for granted by most school systems. Programs, facilities, and concern, if they exist at all, are obscured by the culture's timidity in dealing with the emotional aspects of life and interpersonal relationship problems and by the preoccupation with the cognitive as opposed to the affective aspects of learning. This continues even though the most economical way

123

of influencing youngsters is through teachers who have more contact with larger numbers of children under conditions which can be controlled than anyone else in the culture. Paradoxically, teachers are credited with great influence and threatened with accountability for using it well at the same time that they are provided with few definitive guidelines beyond the injunction to do better. Public denunciation and pressure thus raise the level of threat for schools and teachers to the point where the desired changes are unlikely to happen.

But we do not wish to furnish excuses or rationalizations, pass the buck, or identify someone to blame. The process of attack and counterattack is more likely to limit than to encourage. We wish merely to describe conditions which need to be faced and dealt with. It is almost axiomatic that when one is able to see those things which influence his attitudes, feelings, and behavior, he no longer is so threatened and dominated by them.

Institutions and stress. Social institutions and groups are not different from individuals in that stress beyond a certain point operates to inhibit effective performance and innovative action. Schools which are under criticism and attack find it difficult to depart from established patterns or to encourage or even permit their personnel to do so. In the same manner that the self-fulfilling prophecy or the expectations of significant others were found by Rosenthal and Jackson (1968) to exert a significant influence over performance in classrooms and laboratories, so institutions such as schools are affected by the attitudes which communities manifest toward them.[6] If they are criticized and described as inadequate, that expectation tends to be fulfilled. In proportion to the doubts which are generated concerning their coping abilities, schools, like people with their self-concepts, are limited in their capacity to tolerate the pressure and risk which go with trying something new. The process is circular, self-sustaining, and cumulative.

[6] This research has been questioned but even though the influence may not be so substantial as claimed, the authors still have raised a worthwhile issue. Brophy and Good (1972, p. 277) surveyed current research on the topic and concluded that there is little doubt as to the reality of teacher expectation effects but that these probably are not so strong or important as some enthusiasts suggest.

The more schools are found to be ineffective and the more the need for change is pointed out, the more defensive they are likely to feel, the more rigid and inflexible they tend to become, and the more difficult it may be for them to experiment (Janowitz, 1969). Paradoxically, with institutions as well as with people, those who need most to alter their behavior and to adopt new ways of doing things may find it most difficult to do so.

Reactions to change differ. Individuals and institutions manifest vast differences in their abilities to initiate and adapt to change. These may be ranged on a continuum from welcoming alterations indiscriminately just for the sake of change to regarding anything new as threatening. While other positions, descriptions, and refinements are possible, we conceptualize this continuum as follows:

Becomes indiscriminately involved in change for the sake of variety, for kicks, and to avoid boredom.	Innovates, conceptualizes, and initiates change. Influences others and furnishes leadership for new ways of behaving. The administrator-management role.	Tolerates and goes along with change, which usually is imposed. A float-along-and-let-it-happen approach.	Actively attacks "new fangled ideas," advocates return to "the good old days."
Superficial enthusiasm and bandwagon adoption of most new ideas as solutions.	Carries out and makes new ideas work. Follows lead of innovators. The technician-consultant-worker role.	Uncomfortable with new ideas and methods, resists change automatically, and rationalizes not wanting to try anything different.	

Managing personal change

No person is all one way or another. Probably most of us feel, at the same time and with varying intensity, that we want to change and we want to cling to the habitual and familiar. Also there probably are unrealized possibilities and capacities in us all. It has been estimated that most individuals develop and use only a part of their potential (Kubie, 1956). Any professed inability to change or to learn new behaviors may be less a matter of incapacity than it is a matter of disinclination because of threat, defensiveness, laziness, or simply preference. Yet even the individuals involved find it difficult if not impossible to assess their own reservations with objectivity. The ego defense mechanism of rationalization, particularly for its user, is hard to distinguish from well-considered and fair-minded opposition. Self-limitation and exclusion of possibilities from consciousness thus operate to cast teachers and schools as victims of, rather than as benefitters from, change. For example, teachers who persist in stressing rote memorization, information, and the right and wrong answers are performing a function which can be accomplished more effectively through programmed learning materials and machine or computer presentation. Teachers who are able to change are no longer so restricted by the responsibility for this type of instruction and are free to develop thinking and problem-solving expertise with their students.

It has been aptly said that almost any behavior of which men are capable either can be facilitating or inhibiting depending on how it is used (Tyler, 1966). The value of any tool depends upon the skill of the workman. No machine can function efficiently with an inefficient, uninformed, or recalcitrant operator and no process or technique is independent of those who put it into practice. This particularly is true of the process and products of change in education. They wait upon people for their effectiveness and it is futile to consider them apart from the personnel who develop and operate them.

It is not the computer or the schedule or the use of space which renders individuals comparatively inept or obsolete. These do not of themselves affect anyone. Only as the new ideas or innovations are put into practice by others do those who are unable to use them become their victims. So it happens that one experiences change and innovation as a victim or as a beneficiary in terms of his own behavior toward them. He can become obsolete or his personal and professional systems can be amplified depending upon his own actions.

SUMMARY

Pressing psychosocial problems force the realization that the choice which people have is no longer whether or not to live with change but rather the manner in which change will be managed.

There is widespread agreement among authorities in the social sciences that mankind no longer can evade the responsibility for creating his own future by design rather than continuing to let it arrive by accident.

Among the difficulties to be faced in planning the future are that (1) much of what we know may not be applicable; (2) more and more people are affected by the population explosion; and (3) the exercise of power is becoming increasingly an intellectual and psychological rather than a physical function.

Amplification systems for increasing personal influence can be developed in a social as well as in a physical sense.

Internal management is necessary for the most effective amplification of social system influence. Once successfully initiated, such amplification tends to be cumulative, i.e., the power to influence extends as it is exercised.

Personal psychosocial amplification systems increase efficiency and status gaps between those who know how to use them and those who do not. One can become obsolete with a greater rapidity than ever before.

Teachers can begin to function as change agents most effectively by starting with manageable units at the methodological innovative level.

The personal characteristics of effective change agents include (1) the ability to communicate and interact with others; (2) a facility for staying tentative and flexible with a high tolerance for tension; (3) the self-confidence necessary for risk taking; (4) inner-direction; and (5) a strong sense of importance and involvement in what is happening.

Effective change agent behaviors can be learned, and such learning can be self-initiated. Some learning and behavior modification is possible regardless of age or any of the other rationalizations employed to justify staying in more comfortable routine.

The Hawthorne Effect indicates that change is a valuable process in and of itself. The attention and status which accrue from being involved in experimentation and change often is sufficient to improve significantly achievement and production.

In individuals and institutions, feelings of insecurity and stress often are generated when change proceeds too rapidly and drastically. Then the consequent psychological threat and stress may limit or defeat the innovative process.

As new ideas and innovations are put into practice by others, those who resist change tend to become victims of the process rather than its beneficiaries. Because individuals and institutions seldom are able to view themselves objectively, it is difficult for them to tell whether or not they are defeating themselves by rationalizing away the need to improve and to innovate. It well may be, therefore, that the more one attempts to avoid the risks attendant with change, the greater the risk he actually incurs.

SUGGESTED ADDITIONAL READINGS

Cummings, Susan N. *Communication for Education.* Scranton, Pa.: International Textbook Company, 1971. A series of penetrating questions of concern to change agents and innovators in education are posed by this book. Particularly, the importance of language and communication in relation to learning, mental health, and effective living is stressed. It should prove valuable toward the process of understanding self and others.

Dubos, René. "Man and His Environment: Scenarios for the Future." *New York University Education Quarterly,* 11 (Summer 1971):2–7. The author advocates planned change and maintains that the present emphasis upon the quantity of production needs to be changed to stress the quality of life. His discussion of the movement from technology to ecology furnishes a valuable perspective on one of the salient issues of our time.

Flanders, Ned A. *Analyzing Teacher Behavior.* Reading, Mass.: Addison-Wesley Publishing Co., 1970. This book departs from the usual more theoretical approach about changing and improving teacher behavior and offers implicit directions and methods for accomplishing this. Even though interaction analysis techniques are advocated, teachers who prefer to develop their own ideas and state their own objectives for improvement can gain some valuable how-to suggestions from this book.

Hamachek, Don. "Characteristics of Good Teachers and Implications for Teacher Education." *Phi Delta Kappan* 50 (February 1969): 341–44. The vigorous contention that "there are clearly distinguishable characteristics associated with 'good' and 'bad' teachers" is advanced. If this is the case, then some goals and objectives can be found in this article by the teacher who is interested in professional and self-improvement. The old cliché that we really do not know what makes a good teacher no longer can be used to justify aimlessness and inactivity in teacher education.

MacDonald, W. Scott. *Battle in the Classroom.* Scranton, Pa.: International Textbook Co., 1971. This book emphasizes that changes in education must take place in the classroom if any real impact is to be made; teachers exercise a powerful influence in the classroom; and teachers are not likely to consider a change in their own behavior unless they believe their efforts will be effective. The author endorses the concept that changes in pupil behavior are best brought about by preceding changes in teacher behavior.

Torrance, E. Paul. *Constructive Behavior.* Belmont, Calif.: Wadsworth Publishing Co., 1965. This book has furnished a guide for understanding personal behavior and the actions of others for one of the authors and it is recommended on that basis. Valuable insights as well as ideas for self-improvement, dealing with stress and developing more creative living, can be gained through its study.

PART II

Innovative Practices and Techniques

CHAPTER 6

Teachers and Technology

Americans are members of a culture in which both technology and individualism are admired and set as goals for development. They are convinced of the value of the person yet rely upon science and machines, insist upon personal independence and move toward greater economic interdependence. At the same time that self-direction and personal autonomy are held as ideals, masses of people and ghetto conditions are alienating people and limiting opportunities to develop personal identity.

MAN VERSUS MACHINE

In theory at least, the underdog has been of greater concern to Americans than the able and the rich. But the conviction that money is very important has been deep and widespread. A faith that, given funds, machines, and technical know-how, most if not all problems can be solved has existed concurrently with the feeling that scientific breakthroughs often create greater and more insoluble problems than those they help alleviate.

Out of these seemingly conflicting attitudes has developed a tendency to view the person and society in opposition, to see the system as inimical to the needs of the individual, and to

133

think of men as victims of the machines and the technology they have created. Unfortunately, competition is not restricted to athletics and economics. It operates throughout the culture, limiting the ability to trust and limiting cooperative relationships with both men and machines.

Many years ago Rugg (1947, pp. 484, 729) pointed out the effect of a "competitive thing society" and the basic conflict between it and the individual. More recently, a vice-president of the United States commented, in a statement indicating the depth and scope of these attitudes, that the average man must compete with the machine created by the exceptional man (Humphrey, 1966). The paradox is that, viewed in this light, technology winds up doing a disservice to those whom it supposedly functions to serve, for the curve of normal distribution indicates that slightly more than eighty percent of all people can be classified as either average or below. So, while the average American uses and relies upon science, technology, and machines on the one hand, he tends to be suspicious˙ and distrusting on the other (Michael, 1967). Saturday morning television cartoons offer a number of. good examples of this. Check to see how many times some mad professor is pictured as developing a diabolical plot or machine in order to subjugate and exploit the majority. Usually, however, the person who understands and applies the technology or the machine power is not threatened. Instead, this happens to those who lack the knowledge necessary to exert control over machines. Too often the sense of challenge and the openness required to gain the necessary expertise are obscured by the distrust and the threat. In such cases the worker or the teacher indeed may be victimized and displaced. He may be forced to "compete with" and his power and influence may be minimized rather than maximized by technological amplifying agents.

Representative psychological theories

This ambivalence in the feelings of Americans, relying heavily upon science and the machine on the one hand and viewing these as manipulative, competitive, and dehumanizing on the other, is reflected in differences among current theories of psychology, learning, and human behavior. It is manifest in schools and by teachers who use a mechanistic, information dispensing approach to learning at the same time that they profess to be teaching youngsters to be self-directing, creative individuals.

The stimulus-response, behavioral modification approach. This explanation of learning and behavior attributes what men do and learn to the rewards and satisfactions gained. When a behavior satisfies a need, it tends to be repeated until it is learned. A corollary proposition is that any person or agent who can control rewards and consequences also can control behavior. People as well as animals can be conditioned or taught (socially engineered) to act or not to act in certain specified ways. They can be habituated to perform according to the expectations of an exterior manipulator. A diagram of the basic concept underlying this theory can be accomplished with a number of different terms, as shown below.

stimulus-------------response--------------reinforcement

cause------------------action-------------------effect

reason----------------behavior--------------consequences

input------------------output----------------feedback

As might be expected, this theory of learning and behaving possesses special attractions for the results-conscious, production-oriented American. First, outcomes are measurable and can be empirically verified. The number of words a child can recognize and spell or the speed at which a rat can run a maze can be observed and confirmed. Second, it works. As indicated above, behavior can be modified by this process. There is something to be said for the claim that if a person acts better, he is better. Third, the process is relatively simple, easy to apply, and easy to understand. Such imponderables as the emotional state and attitude of the learner are not of great concern. The idea is merely that if a behavior results in tension reduction and gratification it will tend to be repeated.

Those who believe strongly that an effective person makes his own choices and directs his own behavior probably think that a manipulation of stimuli and rewards and a conditioning of behavior by agents outside the individual are questionable

135

practices. They feel that dependent learners, convergent thinkers, and conforming individuals result from an emphasis upon this type of process and they tend to associate it with the mechanical, right answer oriented, stimulus reinforcement teaching done through programmed learning, teaching machines, and computer-assisted instruction.

Educational technology, however, is no more characterized by a reliance upon mechanical ways of doing things than it is by certain attitudes and concepts. Teachers, according to Cohen (1970, p. 57), tend to be—often pridefully—"antitechnology." In their minds, technology signals mechanization, dehumanization, and automatism. Their claims to knowledge about instruction stem from what they perceive as a humanistic position as opposed to a technological stance. Too often reactions and associations are so strong that an either/or, negative set, and a knowledge of disadvantages makes teachers unable to utilize and experience the advantages.

The idea that behavior depends upon its consequences was not originated by the stimulus-response psychologists of the twenties. It was merely reaffirmed and formalized then. Probably people unconsciously always have smiled and responded in an affirming manner to associates who have behaved according to their expectations and rejected those who have not. Teachers traditionally have dispensed gold stars and other marks of approval for desired behavior and attached painful consequences to unwanted actions. Parents have molded the personalities and behavior patterns of their children through the reinforcing power of their own responses without being aware of the learning affected by their actions.

It is something of an enigma that people oppose a process which they consistently have practiced and will continue to practice. The possibility is good that modern educator and psychologist proponents of this approach merely are formalizing a process that is as old as human nature. Their contribution may not be so much in insisting on new and different ways of learning to behave as it is in emphasizing the importance of being specific about the process and of applying formal, purposeful controls rather than continuing to modify behavior informally and accidentally.

The new humanistic, existential approach. For purposes of comparison let us review some of the basic concepts of

© *King Features Syndicate*

humanistic psychology as cited in Chapter 1. Along with an emphasis upon inner as opposed to outer direction, this approach stresses that:

Human beings have an intrinsic urge toward growth and self realization.

Responsibility for one's own behavior cannot be avoided.

Awareness is basic to choice-making.

People behave in a holistic manner—cognitively, affectively, and socially.

Each individual determines his own meanings.

137

The argument and its effects

The existence of opposing points of view is both desirable and undesirable. While this difference forces protagonists to look closely at their actions and beliefs and serves to eliminate errors, it also serves to fix beliefs and limit flexibility and an openness to new ideas. When an attack–counterattack interaction occurs, with the consequent need to defend and justify a point of view, participants mainly stress the merits of their own position and the faults rather than the strengths of the opposing stand. Thus the humanists are disposed to view behaviorists as too mechanistic and impersonal and as ignoring much of what makes people human. They emphasize that the results of experiments with animals in laboratories, no matter how rigorous and scientific, cannot be generalized to cover human beings in real life situations. As May has pointed out, "The chief trouble with behaviorism . . . is that it leaves out so much behavior." [1]

On the other hand, those who favor the stimulus-response model for explaining behavior find humanist emphases upon such intangibles as the self, awareness, and feelings difficult to accept. They ask for proof and tend to feel that unless quantifiable results and cause-and-effect relationships can be shown, no claims for validity and application can or should be made. Because they feel that they have the answer, or at least the process, for studying human learning and behavior, stimulus-response people tend to dismiss humanist concerns as either idle speculation and a waste of time or as decidedly secondary to the generation of observable and appropriate behavior. Their attitude seems to be, "Why bother with incidentals when you can be concerned with the basics?"

The emphasis which science and technology have placed upon specified and tangible results unfortunately has served to identify them with the experimental-behavioral theory of human function (Finn, 1966). Educators who disagree with this theory have been inclined to look with suspicion upon mechanical aides and techniques. Just as unfortunate, however, has been the tendency for the advocates of competency-based, result-oriented educational programs to brand those who find

---

[1] Rollo May, *Psychology and the Human Dilemma* (Princeton, N.J.: D. Van Nostrand Co., 1967), p. 190.

the self-concept, identity, and becoming to be of high importance as guilty of loose and unrealistic thinking and as lacking
the ability for objective, valid, and meaningful research.

A possible rapprochement

For the reasons mentioned above, both ambivalence and
conflict concerning the nature of human learning and behavior
can be found in most schools whether or not they are aware of
its existence. Many school personnel subscribe to humanistic
ideals and goals in a philosophical and theoretical sense at the
same time that they employ the instructional methodologies,
teaching techniques, and attitudes of a behavior-reinforcement
nature. Educational theory proclaims a primary concern for
the individual as a self-directed, choosing entity at the same
time that educational practice is preoccupied with information
and right-answer conformity, with the cognitive, intellectual
aspects of functioning to the disdain of the affective, emotional
aspects.

The experts and policy makers may have been so intent
upon establishing one or the other points of view that neither
has been used very well. The regular teacher/practitioner may
have been so confused and threatened by the difference
between what was verbalized and what was expected that the
traditional and habitual have been what has wound up in
application.

Just as marked differences tend to promote disagree-
ments, opposition, and attack-counterattack relationships, so
they also possess possibilities for complementary, mutual enhancement interaction. The authors see and have experienced
some real possibilities in such an approach. In our opinion and
practice, we find *no good reason why experimental-behavior-
istic techniques cannot be applied to the achievement of
existential-humanistic objectives.* We concur with the approach which Meacham and Wiesen (1969) have described as
a "humanistic behaviorism." We think that personal amplification systems, both social and technological, become most
possible to the extent that this can be accomplished. To a
considerable degree it is true that one position is high on how
to do it and the other is high on what needs to be done. Only
with their combination is it possible to facilitate maximally

both the conceptualization and the learning of effective behavior.

Conditions for combination. If the advantages of both experimental-behavioral and existential-humanistic techniques and attitudes are to be brought to bear on the process of learning and living, certain requisites and guidelines must be observed. First, self-direction and self-management must become the primary, overriding, and continuing concerns. Behavior modification and reinforcement techniques and procedures should be taught to individuals as methods of changing and managing their own behavior. Control and responsibility should be interior rather than exterior. Every effort should be made to make the individual aware of, and knowledgeable about, the nature and operation of those aspects of his environment which function to modify his living, learning, and behaving.

Second, human interaction effectiveness, including relationships both with people and machines and including the emotional and affective as well as the cognitive aspects of functioning, must become a major subject for study and instruction throughout the school experience. When feelings are overlooked, important reasons for behavior are disregarded. A person must know of his own influence and of those things which influence him if he is to become self-directing. This is possible only if one knows where he wishes to go.

Third, the process of stating personal objectives involves, and whenever possible should be accomplished by, the individual himself. An important part of self-direction is the ability to describe what one wishes to do in such a way that he can tell when and how well he does so and in such a way that his own observations can be validated through the perceptions of others. Rather than being the earmarks of exterior control and manipulation, behavioral objectives, if formulated by the learner, can be the essence of self-directed learning.

Fourth, learning how well one is functioning is most possible when desired behaviors can be described in observable terms. This is because directed observation is more effective. When observer feedback agents know specifically what to look for, they can say with greater certainty whether or not and to what extent the desired behavior occurs. But it is important for self-direction that the individual learns how to get and to use this feedback for himself. When it is imposed by exterior agents, rather than internally solicited, the recipient tends to feel attack and to become defensive. Then the awareness necessary for intelligent self-direction is inhibited and the traditional person-demeaning process of education is not changed. Both the description of desired ways of behaving and the determination of accomplishment through feedback must remain under the control of the individual if the goal of self-direction is to become more than a theory.

TECHNOLOGICAL AGENTS

When considering technological agents for amplifying personal and professional teaching effectiveness, it may be helpful to bear the following suggestions in mind.

First, technological aids should be thought of no more as machines and gadgets than as ways of thinking, attitudes, and techniques. Systems analysis and interaction analysis procedures, for example, well may have an impact on teaching and education which compares in magnitude to anything which may result from the use of teaching machines and computers.

Technological agents should be considered as tools, whose value and power to generate either desirable or undesirable effects depend upon who uses them. Whenever the preoccupation with machines, gadgets, and scientific manipulation leads to their use merely to satisfy scientific curiosity and meet research requirements and whenever people are exploited in the process, then machines, science, and technology are being misused. Whenever the means to an end becomes the end, then the layman's concern with the ethics of the scientist/technologist becomes justified.

A third suggestion for considering technological agents is that new and different approaches, and especially technological devices in a machine-oriented culture, tend to be invested with cure-all qualities (Martin, 1967; Ruark, 1967). Education and educators are no exception. From time to time certain techniques, ways of organization and equipment are heralded as the answer to all or most of the problems faced by the schools. When this happens, it often is difficult to distinguish between wishful thinking and actuality, between what the theorists say can be and what takes place, and between what

Oettinger (1968), examining the "Myths of Educational Technology," has termed "ultimate promise and immediate possibility."

Computers in education

The application of computers to education furnishes a good example of a technological agent to which the preceding points apply. A number of ideas and techniques which may have considerable impact on education have been generated by computers. Despite the impression conveyed by some enthusiasts, computers are not superhuman. Though highly sophisticated, they still are tools; men must operate them. What they produce is contingent upon what is fed into them. In few of the current new ideas in education is it more difficult to separate claimed possibilities and promises from practice than with computers and their school function. Supporters tend to be so enthusiastic that the impression is gained from their contributions to the literature that computers are financially feasible, readily available, and more and more widely used in schools. This is not the case. The utilization of computers and other technological agents in the process of education is in its early infancy ("Instructional Technology," 1970; Slaughter, 1967; Vriend, 1970). Although this use is increasing, some authorities are skeptical about any really significant progress or change during the next decade (Oettinger, 1968). As Koerner has pointed out, "Educational technology to date cannot be said even to run. . . . Hardly a system today is equal to its propaganda. The most advanced hardware systems have had serious debugging problems, low reliability, high maintenance." [2]

At this time it probably is more realistic to describe the use of computers in education mostly as managed by universities and colleges for research purposes. They are far more often employed for this purpose and for storing, retrieving, and processing data than they are for presenting learning situations to students. Most instructional programs involving computers are still experimental. Only a comparatively few school children have the opportunity to learn directly or indirectly

[2] James Koerner, "Educational Technology," *Saturday Review of Education* (May 1973), p. 43.

The computer didn't read me. I needed to go to the bathroom.

from computers. This, of course, is another way of saying that the immense potential of computers in education is only beginning to be realized. Some of the ways in which this is being accomplished are computer assisted instruction (CAI), educational data processing (EDP), computer mediated instruction (CMI), and computer or modular scheduling.

Computer assisted instruction

The term computer assisted instruction usually is considered to apply only to the direct interaction and dialogue which takes place between the individual student and the computer. It has been defined as ". . . a means of teaching students individually, the contents of a course or series of courses through progressive units electronically manipulated."[3]

With some possible exceptions (Loughary, 1970, p. 190), advocates of computer assisted instruction do not claim that machines will replace teachers or that they are capable of

[3] Louis Hausmann, "The ABC's of CAI," *American Education* (November 1967), p. 15.

providing necessary human and interpersonal contacts. The word "assisted" indicates this. They do point out, however, that computers can store, process, and communicate facts and information with greater facility than people. Instruction can be individualized by accommodating presentation to rates and styles of learning. This is done privately by a computer in a milieu where individuals are not compared or forced to compete but are free to experiment and to make mistakes without risking censure or loss of status. CAI can insure acquisition of the necessary basic skills by presenting material again and again until it is learned. Because each youngster works individually, the quick learner does not force the class to move on through before every child has mastered needed concepts and skills. No child is handicapped because he does not possess the tools which he needs to gain more information.

Computers can handle the routine, drill, and practice aspects of teaching without fatigue, boredom, exasperation, or any risk of negative feedback. CAI does compel curriculum planners, teachers, school psychologists, administrators, and other school personnel to think through the learning process and to integrate and orchestrate instructional material and methodology in logical steps and order. Instantly accessible records of the achievement of each youngster can be maintained. Areas in which further preparation is necessary can be recognized, and help in terms of units specifically designed to remedy given deficits can be suggested by the computer. With such a feedback agent incorporated into the learning situation, neither pupil nor teacher effort needs to be duplicated. Finally, CAI can free teachers for more personal and individualized interaction with students. Relationships unhampered by the need to pressure youngsters to do assignments and conform to standards can be possible. Teachers can have time to serve in a counseling capacity and to take a personal interest in their charges, not merely as pupils but as individuals as well.

Types of computer assisted instruction. There are several ways, ranging from the now possible to the eventually probable, in which computers can assist teachers and students in the learning process. The first of these can be described as the *drill and practice mode.* Material to be learned is presented in a fixed, linear sequence with definite limits upon the branching needed to meet individual differences in response. Only one pathway through the curriculum is available. Little choice can be exercised in terms of what is to be studied and little opportunity is provided to deviate from a straight question-answer-move on if correct-reroute and repeat if incorrect sequence. This is the type of instruction, presented by programmed learning textbooks and teaching machines, which has been available for a number of years. While computers can present these programs, it is not necessary or financially defensible to use them in this manner.

A second type of instruction with which computers can assist may be termed *tutorial.* Learning programs of this nature can provide students with separate and diverse paths or branches through a curriculum, depending upon individual performance and response patterns. Although instruction can be adapted to individual learning needs, rates, and styles to a considerable degree, branches and the amount of direction a student can exert over his own learning experiences are restricted by programming limitations.

The tutorial mode of interaction is in its developmental phase at this time. In education, at least, the capacity of the hardware (see Glossary) exceeds the ability to use it because of a serious lack of instructional programs or software (see Glossary) necessary for computer function. Estimates of the time and cost necessary to generate these have varied from forty man-hours (Caffrey, 1967, p. 31) and several thousand dollars (Bundy, 1968) for each one-hour unit of instruction to around 200 man-hours (Ruark, 1967) and somewhere in the neighborhood of ten to fifteen thousand dollars per student-hour. Though seemingly prohibitive for most schools at the time these figures were quoted, once developed, instructional programs may be channeled through computers to millions of users, new methods and expertise can be generated continuously, and computers will be capable of serving many users simultaneously so that costs can be shared. It is becoming increasingly apparent, however, that many schools either lack resources or refuse to commit the funds necessary to incorporate expensive computers into their programs, especially since such equipment becomes obsolete so quickly that capital investments for new hardware, once begun, are a continuous drain on finances.

Student computer *dialogue* programs constitute the third mode of CAI. With them there will be no need for typewriter keyboards or coding and decoding. Naturally spoken language will be the means of interacting with computers and their services will be available to more and more people. Loughary (1970), for example, describes a system which is able to substitute totally for counselors with regard to such specific functions as catharsis and listening. He predicts, within a decade, there will be personal assistance and planning systems which can help an individual direct and develop his own potential. The dialogue mode, of course, is more in the realm of possibility than actuality. It should be some time before many school children will learn by interacting directly with computers in this manner.

The Stanford-Brentwood Computer Assisted Instruction Laboratory, East Palo Alto, California, has pioneered in this area and is one of the most widely known of these programs based on the tutorial mode. Sixteen computer stations (interfaces) are employed in presenting reading and mathematics instruction to elementary school children. Visual and auditory stimuli are presented and pupils are asked to designate correct words and answers. They are reinforced by a smiling face on the screen when they are successful. When they are not, the face frowns and they are requested to try again. Items which are not recognized are presented over and over at intervals until they are mastered.

At Willowbrook High School, Villa Park, Illinois, the school's counselors have taken the initiative in developing a means of employing computers to aid students in grades seven through fourteen with vocational educational exploration and choice making. Through Project CVIS (Computer Vocational Information System), youngsters are helped to relate ability, interest, and school achievement data to job and higher education requirements. The computer sends messages on cathode ray screens and students reply via typewriter keyboard. A simulated, immediate response conversation can take place. Counselors also employ the system for information storage and retrieval, scheduling, and registration operations.

Project CVIS is especially noteworthy with respect to innovative use of computers by school personnel for a number of reasons. First, the project was initiated and developed from inside an educational institution. Second, it is functional in nature. It was developed to meet recognized and actual needs and not primarily for commercial or research purposes. Moreover, this system has shown that routine and time consuming guidance chores can be accomplished more effectively by computers. This frees counselors for personal interaction counseling duties. Fourth, CVIS indicates that educational practitioners (counselors and teachers) can provide the leadership necessary for innovation. Direction and responsibility are not the exclusive province of technology.

Computer mediated instruction

One important contribution which computers are making to education is their emphasis upon the necessity for painstaking descriptions of the behaviors expected to result from instruction. When teaching units are programmed, each step in the learning process must be identified and put in logical sequence. If progress in the program and the program's effectiveness is to be assessed, the location of each learner moving through the sequence and his ability to behave in the desired manner must be capable of determination at any time. Printouts based upon the capacity of computers to store and retrieve large amounts of data have made such an instant diagnosis possible.

Computer mediated or computer oriented programs of instruction incorporate many of the advantages of CAI without the high cost of providing instructional stations and computer programming. A Los Angeles corporation has cooperated with local elementary schools in the development of an instructional management system for teaching reading. A series of self-administered diagnostic tests along with files of remedial and developmental reading material plus computer printouts enables teachers to know what aspects of each child's reading needs development and where to go for the materials to accomplish this. Subsequent printouts provide a continuing diagnosis and indicate the effectiveness of what has been done. Each child has the opportunity to study independently and progress as far and as rapidly as his abilities permit.

A more comprehensive and more widely known example of computer mediated teaching and learning is the Individually Prescribed Instruction (IPI) program developed by University of Pittsburgh educators in conjunction with elementary schools in that area. Paraprofessionals are employed to check pupil worksheets and computers store and retrieve large amounts of information with respect to each learner. Teachers thus are able to know every youngster's position relative to a continuum of carefully specified behaviors or objectives. Information readily is available concerning any pupil's difficulties in mastering each behavior in the order specified and teachers are able to prescribe appropriate learning activities on this basis. Both youngsters and teacher not only know where they are, they know what behaviors are to be gained next and what must be done to gain them. Prerequisite learnings are facilitated and needless repetition is minimized.

To some degree, certain aspects and advantages of computer assisted instruction are provided by both the Los Angeles and the Pittsburgh methods with neither the necessity nor the expense of involving youngsters directly with computers. Furthermore, computer mediated instruction type programs well may have greater immediate application potential on a practical cost-feasible basis than the more elaborate, considerably more expensive CAI systems. Similarly, youngsters have the opportunity to progress continuously and are not pressured to keep up nor held back because of grade placement. Although not to be confused with independent study, each pupil's program does take his individual learning needs and style into account. This differs from programmed instruction in that no two pupils must follow the same path and that, in order to deal with individual difficulties and concept gaps, branching is possible. Also, learning is conceptualized as a process or as a series of behaviors to be demonstrated rather than as amounts of information to be memorized or as skills to be gained. Other advantages of CMI are that the relationship of instructional materials and techniques to desired behaviors is carefully studied in terms of the difficulty and sequence of items and feedback concerning the performance of pupils and the effectiveness of the instructional program is continuously and immediately available in the form of evaluations from paraprofessionals and computer printouts.

In comparison, no CAI program can involve youngsters for more than a fraction of the school day. Despite the attraction of the machine (computer interface), even the most sophisticated of CAI multisensory presentations can command attention for only a limited amount of time (Bundy, 1968). The need for variety and boredom will not be eliminated just because presentations are made by computers. If youngsters are placed at interface stations for too long, they probably will be unable to learn maximally from the experience.

Audio and video feedback systems

In order to develop this topic it is necessary to reemphasize some ideas which were advanced earlier and briefly to describe other concepts which subsequently will be developed more fully. These are: (1) If self-directed independent learning is to be fostered in children, the process must be exemplified by teachers. (2) Technology, and especially the programming of instructional units for teaching machines and computers, has emphasized the necessity and furnished a model for describing desired action patterns clearly in as small behavioral units as possible. It has emphasized the importance of such guidelines if development or change is to be accomplished and assessed. Although usually applied to planning learning experiences for pupils, teachers can also adopt this process for their own personal and professional development. It does not have to be other-directed in order to function. (3) The humanistic, personal interaction, affective aspects of behaving which constitute the crux of a good learning environment and effective teaching can also be described in observable and manageable units. The reduction or breaking down of behavior patterns or systems into manageable units or subsystems is characteristic of the systems analysis approach employed by management. The same process is accomplished for human behaving when it is subdivided and arranged in logical sequence through the stating of behavioral objectives. (4) In order to determine those behaviors which require changing, those behaviors which need to be developed and the extent to which this is accomplished, outside objective observation which communicates with, and feeds back to, the behaver is necessary. (5) Devices such as video and audio recordings which are capable of recording and reconstructing human interaction experiences can be of great value in this respect. Through their use it is possible for the behaver to become directly aware of the effects of his own actions. (6) Such devices provide the feedback function without which no system or subsystem can be purposefully self-regulated or directed. Consider the simple example offered by the thermostatically controlled heating system in a modern building. Here the thermostat is the feedback agent. Its function is to reintroduce or feed back into the system a part of its behavior, product, or output as a guide for changing and regulating its subsequent behaving. Human interaction systems, though much more complex, are similar in principle. A person who wishes to increase the effectiveness of the subsystem represented by his own actions and subsequently to affect the functioning of those larger interaction systems of which his behavior is a part, must arrange means of feeding back into his own system a knowledge of the reactions which his behavior produces in his associates. It can be maintained with justification that an individual can be self-directed only in proportion to his ability to recognize and to use sources of feedback (Haddan, 1970, p. 230).

Video tape recorders. One of the most effective ways of recording and recalling human experience is furnished by videotaping equipment (Adams and Biddle, 1970, p. 23). Unprecedented opportunities are provided for studying interpersonal transactions for as many times and in as much detail as desired. Audio recording cannot capture important nonverbal, body message communication which, as shown in Chapter 5, often reveals more than words. Human feedback agents also are limited by an inability to observe completely and without bias. While one may doubt with good reason another person's rendition of what has happened, he finds disagreement much more difficult when the experience can be shown to him repeatedly.

With videotape, participants in an interpersonal transaction are enabled to see themselves behaving and then can be more objective about their own actions. Feedback in terms of the effect of their behavior upon associates is there to be used. Whether or not and how this will be done, of course, is a human not a machine function. Most videotape-based feedback systems require interpretation by human agents other than participants for maximum effectiveness.

A good example of how this is accomplished exists at Michigan State University (Kagan et al., 1969). Called *Interpersonal Process Recall*, this use of video tape as a feedback agent includes an offtape observer to interrogate or assist participant behavers in examining and assessing the effects of

The teacher is videotaped in her classroom.

The teacher watches and discusses videotape, comparing her performance to her previously selected behavioral objectives. She also reviews the interaction analysis tally sheet.

151

their actions. Although the technique is primarily employed in counselor education, there is no reason why teacher training and in-service experiences cannot be conducted along similar lines.

Actually this is being done in a limited way. Teacher behavior analysis techniques developed by Flanders (1965, 1970) and termed interaction analysis (see Glossary) have been implemented with good success through the use of videotaping, playback, and outside observer feedback and critique (Hoehn, 1969). These programs operate on the premises that: The most potent single controllable variable in school-based learning is teacher behavior; feedback which functions to acquaint teachers of the differences between what they think and say they do and how they actually behave is essential if teaching behavior is to be changed; when accurate and appropriate feedback is provided in connection with a set of improvement procedures, teachers will become more able to formulate objectives for personal and professional improvement; and, as teachers gain greater knowledge of the possibilities for growth, they will tend to become more self-directed with regard to their own improvement and actively to solicit observation and feedback experiences.

Another technique which can be readily adapted for self-directed teacher improvement is *Microteaching* (Allen and Ryan, 1969). This is so called because it reduces a number of the complexities of the normal teaching encounter to manageable units. Time, class size, and scope of content, for example, are compressed as are, most importantly, the teaching or interaction behaviors to be dealt with. Practice and performance are analyzed and feedback rendered on the basis of one or two desired objectives. The time saved permits retrials with the same goals and the added insight provided by feedback in mind. Because progress can be noted, learning motivation is reinforced.

The process of describing desired behaviors, feedback, and self-analysis is far removed from the traditional concept of educational supervision. This process differs in the respect that it is teacher self-oriented, self-directed, and requested for situations in which help is desired and needed. It is not imposed or scheduled according to administrative convenience and it is not externally directed or based on goals which are not pertinent to the teacher and the situation. Most importantly, it is not evaluative in nature or intent. Teachers and behaviors are not rated or judged or labelled good or bad, right or wrong, or blameworthy or blameless. The idea is merely to describe behavior and to facilitate awareness in terms of each teacher's own performance criteria. Indeed, there is reason to believe that when evaluation is imposed, teachers rarely are able to look critically at themselves (Hoehn, 1969). Self-analysis is supplanted by administrative ratings. In-service programs for teacher improvement and innovation seldom get off the ground.

Stating personal behavior objectives

Because of the current emphasis upon stating teaching goals in behavioral terms, most educators probably have been involved in this experience. They have learned that it is considerably more difficult to describe desired behavior in terms of small, observable specifics than it is to phrase the broad, global, rather abstract objectives of a few years back. But the chances are that the behaviors they have described have been those of students anyway and that they have tended to overlook the necessity of being explicit about their own actions and inputs.

Describing desired personal behaviors. When a teacher attempts to state his own personal objectives, he faces different circumstances than he experiences when he formulates behavior descriptions for a student. While procedures for the latter (Mager, 1962; Jenkins and Deno, 1970; Kibler, Barker, and Miles, 1970) are readily available and applicable in part, few, if any, guidelines are available to the teacher who may wish to describe desired behaviors in himself. The following suggestions are offered on this basis. In the first place, a teacher stating his own objectives may be concerned largely with behavior in the human interaction, affective area, with what he himself communicates, and how well he does so. These kinds of behaviors are not so easy to describe as physical skill, information retaining, reasoning activities. Second, trying to be objective about one's self almost is to attempt the impossible. But with feedback this can be done because outside agents are engaged to furnish the perception. Feedback may be used to find where change is needed as well as to assess the effectiveness of changes made. Third, stating personal objectives is a continuous process. While a lengthy and comprehensive list often must be developed when the learning activities of others are to be directed, only one or two desired behaviors need to be kept in mind when one wishes to modify his own actions. The accomplishment of one leads to the recognition of the need for another. A teacher may be able to describe terminal behaviors for a student because the instructional relationship can be expected to end. But he cannot do so for himself because the responsibility for what he will learn will continue to be his for as long as he lives.

When stating a behavioral objective for one's self, it is important to bear in mind that one of the main reasons for doing so is to facilitate meaningful feedback. Such objectives can serve not only as guides for behaving, but they also can function to insure pertinent observation. Hence one needs to describe how he wishes to act in such a manner that the amount of conformity to his goals is easily observable and in such a manner that observations can be understandably communicated. A question properly stated is half answered and a well-defined objective may be even more than half met. If possible, such objectives should meet the following criteria.

1. *Desired behavior descriptions should be phrased in process terminology beginning with an active verb.* Suppose a teacher wishes to enlist the help of observer feedback agents in developing the ability to listen. He may start by merely stating, "Listens intently to students." Later he may wish to describe the situations in which he wants to do this and the subbehaviors which indicate it is happening, but he doesn't begin "to learn to listen," in the conventional fashion. He describes the manner in which he wishes to function.

2. *Personal behavioral objectives should describe the desired actions in such a way that empirical and consensual validation can be gained.* Whereas it is possible to see a person behaving, it often is not possible to observe such intangibles as knowing or understanding. One is limited to seeing the person act as if he knows and behave as if he understands. Informally and unsystematically, all of us make such inferences throughout our relationships with other people. What is needed here is a catalog of the

components of the desired behavior. These are the small, indicative behaviors which one needs to describe if he is to enable an observer to furnish clear and explicit feedback for him.

Just saying "Listens intently," in the example above, is not enough for an observer to provide much feedback. The kinds of actions or subbehaviors which indicate intense listening also must be described. Thus, such actions as establishing a comfortable listening distance (21 to 30 inches), keeping visual contact, and leaning toward the speaker need to be specified.

3. *Separate and distinct objectives should be stated for each behavior to be developed.* If two or more behaviors or facets of a behavior are considered together it is difficult to give explicit feedback about the effects of either. That is, it is easier to deal with one thing at a time. One would not state as an objective, "Asks questions which elicit further response and nods to show understanding." If the behaver accomplishes only one, an observer response or rating in terms of "yes" or "no" either must be qualified or is not possible.

4. *Not only the behavior but the frequency of its desired occurrence should be specified in a workable objective.* While some consistency of acting is necessary before the inference can be drawn that the actor has learned how to function in a certain way, it may be impossible or inappropriate always to act in that manner. So it often may be necessary to include such phrases as "four-fifths of the time" and "limits verbal responses to twenty words or less" with objectives which deal with listening.

5. *A behavioral objective should include a description of the conditions under which the behavior is to take place.* Listening "four-fifths of the time" may be desired only in "one-to-one interaction" or in "a counseling situation." And maintaining a listening distance of 21 to 30 inches may be not possible or natural when interactors are seated. Hence a well-stated objective might begin with, "Given a one-to-one counseling situation, limits verbal input to 20 percent," or simply, "Limits verbal input to 20 percent in a one-to-one counseling situation."

6. *Desired behaviors should be described and organized in such a way that they are capable of achievement.* Positive feedback is necessary in order that a sense of accomplishment is maintained as a reinforcement and in order that the behaver continues to be motivated. At least three condi-

155

tions are necessary for this. First, the behavior units to be learned must be arranged in a logical sequence. One cannot run before he learns to walk. Second, the learning must be described and proceed in small steps so that the learner's ability to succeed is never in question. Third, small units of time should be specified initially; it is easier to act acceptably for two minutes than to maintain the behavior for thirty.

Teacher accountability

An additional development which has its roots in technology and which bodes well to have a strong and lasting influence upon teachers and education can be found in the concept of accountability. The basic idea is that schools or, more precisely, the professional educators who operate them, are held responsible for what children learn. Each member of the educational organization is expected to accomplish certain tangible performance results and to answer to someone for producing specified outcomes. This, of course, is not really a new idea. To some extent all of us have been held responsible for what we have done or have failed to do. What is new is that, through technology, implementation is becoming possible and because of school finance difficulties, the concept is being accepted by educational leaders and school administrators to a greater degree than ever before. Indeed, Lessenger (1970, p. 217) has prophesied that the problem of engineering accountability for results will be the central educational concern of the seventies.

To an appreciable degree, however, accountability has been received by the public and by the profession in a manner similar to a number of other ideas which have been heralded as the answer to educational ills. There may be considerable difference between what proponents envision and its implementation. There is a good way to go and much to be done before the theory becomes formalized practice in many school systems. Despite improved statistical procedures and computer assistance, much remains to be done in the way of identifying the many variables which influence learning and assessing the nature and quantity of their effects. As Lopez has pointed out, "The measures of accountability so far developed have not met even minimum standards of reliability and relevancy." [4]

Still, the need to be much more explicit concerning the competencies of school personnel exists and pressure is increasing upon the schools to justify what they spend in terms of educational outcomes. A more rigorous accountability appears inevitable. Lieberman's conclusion that ". . . the underlying issue is not whether to have accountability but what kind of accountability will prevail," [5] really may leave educators with little choice. They either may participate in developing the processes by which accountability will be affected or they may be forced to apply procedures developed by less knowledgeable exterior agents.

Reasons for accountability. Beside the overriding fact of public pressure, there are other arguments, some of which also are advantages, for accountability. Teachers need to be aware of these if they are to direct and use the movement rather than to be manipulated by it.

Accountability may turn out to be a potent force for recognizing the efforts of good teachers and for professionalizing the job of teaching. The really proficient teacher, of course, has little to fear from observation and evaluation. The ambitious and growing teacher should be able to use the accountability process for gaining greater competence. In any profession the positive public image created by the capable practitioner is cancelled and dispelled by those who are not. If the dictum *improve or leave* can be implemented by accountability, the overall image and practice of education will be enhanced.

Another reason for the adoption of accountability may be that educators will be forced to look more closely at the interactive process of teaching and learning. There will be pressure—very strong pressure—to develop the process of describing desired teaching behaviors and gaining feedback on this basis. This should help teachers to become more aware of their emotional affective inputs and to teach more by design than by accident in this area.

[4] Felix M. Lopez, "Accountability in Education," *Phi Delta Kappan* 52 (December 1970): 231.
[5] Myron Lieberman, "An Overview of Accountability," *Phi Delta Kappan* 52 (December 1970): 195.

An additional reason for accountability is that it always has existed informally and always has placed most pressure on the concerned and conscientious. Providing a formal means of doing this and hence of increasing awareness and control of the process may serve to decrease frustration and psychological stress for these teachers.

Problems contingent upon accountability. While changes usually are adopted to deal with concerns and to improve conditions, they can also create or reveal other problems. Accountability may be no different in this respect. When the process is more refined and widely applied, this will become apparent. Anticipating difficulties, therefore, may indicate in advance how to use accountability best. Some of the obstacles which educators may face in implementing the concept of accountability are given.

1. Accountability may be perceived by teachers as evaluating, judging, and scapegoat identification. High threat levels and consequent defensiveness may cause them to reject the process and lead to its failure.

2. When a program for accountability is instigated by administrative decree and desired outcomes are prescribed, rather than teacher initiated and developed, feelings of being evaluated, pressured, and forced to conform are likely to be paramount in teachers. They are apt to see themselves as other-directed rather than as self-directed. Feedback will then be rejected rather than solicited.

3. Ideas for professional improvement which overlook the need for practitioner involvement in establishing patterns for self-improvement not only may fail, but may also increase teacher resistance and decrease administration-teacher cooperation and rapport. Intrinsic motivation is essential (Smith, Cohen, and Pearl, 1969, p. 138).

4. Only a fraction of the variation in educational results can be attributed to teachers. Other factors or variables such as socioeconomic status, home environment, and peer groups, which are not controlled by the school probably exert a greater influence. In addition, only a part of the school environment is directly controlled by the individual teacher. While statistical techniques permit some effects to be parcelled out and attributed to certain contributing variables, it is extremely difficult to determine which ones

and how much of each are the responsibility of any one teacher (Barro, 1970).

5. Trends toward team teaching, open space school buildings, and the use of paraprofessionals expose pupils to larger numbers of adult, teacher type influences than ever before. The relatively simple structure of the one-teacher classroom is passing. As the variables which affect pupil learning increase, the possibility of assessing the contributions of each one decreases.

6. Accountability can be expected to reemphasize the more tangible, information oriented, measurable aspects of teaching at the expense of social learning, emotional psychological, human interaction factors. Teaching pupils to pass standardized tests with high scores may be forced or at least encouraged. An increase in this type of instruction appears inevitable with accountability of this nature even though there is good reason for educators to believe that: (a) school grades and achievement are poor predictors of future success (Taylor, 1968); (b) this type of instruction better can be performed by machines (Adams and Biddle, 1970, pp. 35-36); and (c) information-based teaching inevitably must be past oriented. It is pertinent only to what has been, and with the advent of change as a fact of living, less and less pertinent to what will be (Snygg, 1966).

Pressures placed upon teachers by technology

New concepts and machines and even old ideas which have been rediscovered and made more possible by technology tend to be invested with panacealike qualities and press to be put into practice. This pressure is increasing, for public education is everybody's business. Everybody is affected by it and everybody pays for it. For these reasons, discontent and dissatisfaction are more apt to surface here than anywhere else. The voice of the taxpayer may not be heard loudly in national circles but its importance for financial support on local school levels cannot be discounted.

These things combine to make teachers and what they do more and more highly visible and more and more open to criticism. The once relatively inviolable one-room domain enjoyed by teachers is fast disappearing and their control over teaching content and process is passing. Contracts with industrial organizations to perform certain instructional functions with payment contingent upon specified pupil performance outcomes are increasing (Barro, 1970; Lessinger, 1970; "Performance Contracting," 1970). The implication is that the job can be done better and more economically by technicians.

Related social movements appear to be operating in the culture at large. In addition to the interaction analysis, microteaching trend in education, there is the systems analysis approach in industry and government, the transaction analysis approach in psychotherapy (Berne, 1964) and the metacommunication approach (See Chapter 4) for analyzing the effectiveness of communicative behaviors. In all of these, people are attempting to learn about the kind of behaviors which are effective and those which are not. In all of them, there is implicit the willingness to be accountable for actions taken and the recognition that some sort of systematic method of observation and reaction is necessary.

The alternatives available for teachers, therefore, no longer include the option of sitting tight and maintaining the status quo. The rationalization that change is impossible for whatever reason is a delusion that no longer can provide much comfort and security. Teachers will change on their own initiative or change will be imposed. But the situation is not so bleak as it appears at first glance. Technology, while furnishing the impetus and the demand for change, also has provided the tools, ideas, and changes in attitude to make change possible. To the extent that teachers are able to perceive challenge and opportunity rather than threat, technological concepts are not difficult to put into practice. No very complicated machines or talent are necessary. A willingness to risk, experiment, and reorganize and a willingness to look critically at one's own behavior inputs and the causes and effects of his relationships are the essential requirements. A teacher can start in a classroom with a single interaction with a single pupil lasting a few minutes. He can describe desired behaviors and involve feedback agents by merely thinking through how he wishes to act and asking a fellow teacher or even his pupils how they view what he does.

But a word of caution is in order. It may prove to be difficult for the majority of teachers to focus upon, and to be primarily concerned with, their own actions and inputs. After all, teaching traditionally has operated to influence the behavior of others. Even yet many professional publications fail to provide this important emphasis. The teacher who aspires to improve pupil learning first must look to his own behavior and the model which he furnishes. The less he is aware of the effects of his own actions, the more he teaches by chance and by accident and the less he really knows what it is that he teaches.

SUMMARY

Ambivalent attitudes exist in this culture toward science, technology, and the social system. While people identify with, and expect to be served by, them, they also feel competitive, distrustful, and minimized as a result.

The stimulus-response experimental approach in psychology, with its emphasis on cause and effect relationships and behavior control has come to be identified with technology by many teachers. They consider this approach mechanizing and dehumanizing and tend to be antitechnology for these reasons.

The humanistic existential system of psychology which views people as capable of choices and self-direction is often identified with the opposition to technology.

Controversy between the experimental and the humanistic points of view may have resulted in either/or attitudes and an inability to combine and apply the contributions of both in making learning and teaching more effective.

A humanistic experimentalism which employs the methodology of science to the achievement of existential goals may offer the greatest promise and advantages for teachers' personal and professional growth.

Technological aides to education include ways of thinking, attitudes, and techniques as well as machines and computers.

The use of computers in education, though not widespread, has generated ideas and techniques which can be applied to improving both formal instructional and the analysis and understanding of teacher-student interaction patterns. Many computer techniques can be used without actually involving computers in the process.

Among the important concepts which have developed with programmed learning and computer programming are the necessity for describing desired behaviors in small component, observable terms and the necessity of arranging these in a logical priority sequence.

Feedback which functions to reintroduce or play back a part of a behavior system into the awareness of the behaver is necessary not only to determine the extent of desired behaving but also to establish self-direction. The videotape recorder is an excellent device for this purpose. With it, interpersonal transactions and individual behavior inputs can be recorded and studied as many times and in as much detail as needed.

Some working examples of the use of behavioral descriptions and feedback agents for behavior improvement are the Interpersonal Process Recall (IPR) technique for developing counselors and microteaching situations used in connection with interaction analysis in teacher and in-service education.

If the process of describing desired behaviors and getting feedback is to function optimally, however, it must be managed by the teacher, not imposed by administrative decree and should not be judgmental in nature or intent.

Teacher self-direction and movement from theory to practice requires stating of behavioral objectives in order to facilitate meaningful and pertinent feedback. Such objectives should describe the behavior to be developed in such a way that its taking place can be observed and agreed upon.

Accountability, the placing of responsibility for pupil learning outcomes, appears to be a coming thing in education because of (1) the impetus furnished by technology, (2) public dissatisfaction with learning and holding power in the schools, (3) the financial burden of education on taxpayers, and (4) the successful examples furnished by industry and by some other social service areas.

Difficulties which may be encountered in implementing the concept of accountability include: (1) a rejection by teachers because of a possible scapegoat nature, (2) difficulty of attributing total responsibility for pupil performance to teachers, and (3) resulting emphasis upon tangible, information-oriented, fast recall teaching at the expense of social, human interaction type learning.

Because of accountability and the implication of performance contracting that education can be accomplished more economically and better by businesslike methods, teachers no longer can choose to do nothing. Their choice is between self-initiated and directed changes and those imposed and managed by exterior agents.

SUGGESTED ADDITIONAL READINGS

Adams, Raymond S., and Biddle, Bruce J. *Realities of Teaching Explorations With Videotape.* New York: Holt, Rinehart and Winston, Inc., 1970. This is a short, relatively inexpensive paperback which combines theory with practice. It deals with both the why and the how from an experiential research basis. Some excellent ideas concerning the use of videotaping and modifying teacher behavior are advanced.

Allen, Dwight W., and Ryan, Kevin A. *Microteaching.* Reading, Mass.: Addison-Wesley Publishing Co., 1969. Here is a book that can lay some claim to distinction among educational publications. In addition to pointing out a number of things that don't work, it suggests procedures that do. Better still, these are workable ways of teaching teachers as they teach. This book can provide real assistance for teachers and schools interested in self-improvement.

Gorman, Alfred H. *Teachers and Learners in the Interactive Process of Education.* Boston: Allyn and Bacon, Inc., 1969. Teaching is described as a mutual, two-way interaction process. The use of groups as a basic way of teaching is considered in depth and the affective emotional component of the interacting learning milieu is not ignored. The teacher who would like to gain more satisfaction from his relationships with pupils will find good suggestions in this book.

Haddon, Eugene E. *Evolving Instruction.* New York: The Macmillan Co., 1970. Many subjects of interest to today's teacher are considered here. Although it is generally humanistic in orientation, there is a good integration of the contributions of science and technology. Chapters 4 and 9 in particular contain information relevant to the present topic.

Jenkins, Joseph R., and Deno, Stanley L., "A Model for Instructional Objectives." *Educational Technology* 10 (December 1970):11–16. Anyone who has difficulty writing clear, concise, and explicit behavioral objectives will find this article helpful. Its authors divide objectives into four levels. Their descriptions of each level can do much to clear up any misunderstanding the reader has about these types of objectives.

163

Jensen, Larry C., and Young, Jon I. "Effects of Televised Instruction on Subsequent Teaching." *Journal of Educational Psychology* 63 (1972): 368–73. This article presents television in a somewhat different perspective from the usual ones on teaching and learning, i.e., its impact on teachers is investigated. Experimental student teachers, using simulated instruction, made higher scores than controls on five of six criteria of teacher effectiveness.

Mager, Robert F. *Developing Attitude Toward Learning.* Palo Alto, Calif.: Fearon Publishers, 1968. The author of this short book presents a paradigm for behavior change similar to that offered in this chapter. He covers both rationale and how to do it in an easily read and easily understood manner.

Meacham, Merle L., and Wiessen, Allen E. *Changing Classroom Behavior: A Manual for Precision Teaching.* Scranton, Pa.: International Textbook Co., 1970. This book advocates a "humanistic behaviorism" in describing what its authors are pleased to call "precision teaching." This type of instruction, they say, is concerned primarily with observable behaviors. And they make a good case for their assertion that complex human behaviors can be broken down into these kinds of specific responses.

Saturday Review of Education. May 1973. Contains a special supplement which deals with technology in education. The disparity between possibility and practice is reemphasized along with the gap which exists between the enthusiastic theorist and the conservative educator. Perhaps the reader will be surprised, as the authors were, that so little change has occurred over the past five to ten years as far as the actual use of technology in classrooms is concerned.

CHAPTER 7

Programmed Learning, Open Education, and Creativity

Programmed learning and creative teaching constitute a rather odd pairing. Here, the combination stems from the authors' belief that the maximum value of programmed learning can be achieved if the merits of teaching for creativity are simultaneously kept in mind. Open education, however, contrasts markedly with programmed study and elicits creativity from pupils and teachers.

Programmed learning has been practiced for many decades but different names have been given it. It was once assign–study–recite–review. Some "progressive" educators called it subject-matter-set-out-to-be-learned. Now, when a teacher writes his plan of study, records questions to be asked and topics to be covered, lists his behavioral objectives, and devises tests of comprehension, he is using a form of programmed learning. The addition of machine presentation or the use of a programmed text add structure to conventional methods.

The structured process has proved successful for multitudes of pupils who have profited from school and college attendance. For some learning styles, programmed learning has clear advantages and continuing research confirms the claim. Other pupils, with a different learning style, are uncomfortable with the programmed approach, and open education is a viable alternative for them.

Those pupils who do not fit the conventional mold challenge teachers to express creativity in their work. Unless used with discretion, programmed learning may stifle the creative urge that is particularly strong in some pupils, conflict with their preferred learning styles, and, alienate them altogether from the education process. Open education, on the other hand, enhances the prospects for nurturing creativity.

THE CONCEPT OF PROGRAMMED LEARNING

Programmed learning, as is often the case with educational practices (progressive education, contract method, and more recently, independent study, and open education) has varied meanings. In this section, we will deal with programmed texts.

Linear programs. A linear program presents material to each pupil in small steps, with successful completion of one step influencing succeeding steps (or frames). The steps are small so that the probability of making errors is small. The reward of success and immediate feedback on correctness or incorrectness allows reinforcement psychology to operate. Students can progress at their own comfortable rates and competition between unequals is minimized, if not eliminated. Because the steps require the student to commit himself, there is some degree of involvement. An illustrative linear program, by one of the foremost champions of programming, B. F. Skinner, can provide the reader with a test of his own reaction to programming. Read the heading at the top of Set 1 and turn the page as instructed. Record the answer at the top of page 2, turn the page to see if it is correct, read the next frame, record the answer, turn the page, continuing this procedure as far as possible (in the text itself, the program goes up to page 8). Then turn back to page 1 and make the same consecutive steps, starting on frame 1–8, until the end is again reached. The student would continue in this fashion until he has successfully worked the entire book.

SET 1	SIMPLE REFLEXES Estimated time: 23 minutes. Turn to next page and begin ➤
Stimulus *(tap on the* *knee)* 1-7	Technically speaking, a reflex involves an eliciting stimulus in a process called elicitation. A stimulus _____a response. 1-8
threshold 1-15	The fraction of a second which elapses between "brushing the eye" and "blink" is the_____of the reflex. 1-16
threshold 1-23	The greater the concentration of onion juice (stimulus), the_____the *magnitude* of the response. 1-24
elicit 1-31	In the pupillary reflex, a very bright flash of light elicits a response of greater_____than a weak flash of light. 1-32
latency 1-39	A solution of lemon juice will not elicit salivation if the stimulus is_____the threshold. 1-40
(1) magnitude *(1) potency* 1-47	Presentation of a stimulus is the "cause" of a response. The two form a(n) _____. 1-48

FIGURE 7-1. *Three frames from a typical linear programmed textbook.* (From James G. Holland and B. F. Skinner. *The Analysis of Behavior.* New York: McGraw-Hill Book Co., 1961, pp. 1–3. Reprinted by permission.)

➡	A doctor taps your knee (patellar tendon) with a rubber hammer to test your_____. 1-1
elicits 1-8	To avoid unwanted nuances of meaning in popular words, we do not say that a stimulus "triggers," "stimulates," or "causes" a response, but that it _____ a response. 1-9
latency 1-16	In the patellar-tendon reflex, a forceful tap elicits a strong kick; a tap barely above the threshold elicits a weak kick. Magnitude of response thus depends on the intensity of the_____. 1-17
greater *(higher,* *larger)* 1-24	Onion juice elicits the secretion of tears by the lachrymal gland. This causal sequence of events is a(n) _____. 1-25
magnitude *(intensity)* 1-32	A response and its eliciting stimulus comprise a(n) _____. 1-33
below *(less than,* *sub-)* 1-40	The latency of a reflex is the (1)_____ between onset of (2)_____ and_____. 1-41
reflex 1-48	The layman frequently explains behavior as the operation of "mind" or "free will." He seldom does this for reflex behavior, however, because the_____ is an adequate explanation of the response. 1-49

FIGURE 7-1, continued.

168

reflexes (reflex) 1-1	If your reflexes are normal, your leg_____to the tap on the knee with a slight kick (the so-called knee jerk). 1-2
elicits 1-9	In a reflex, the stimulus and the elicited response occur in a given temporal order; first the (1)_____, then the (2)_____. 1-10
stimulus (tap) 1-17	The magnitude of a response corresponds to (is a function of) the_____of the stimulus which elicits it. 1-18
reflex (lachrymal reflex) 1-25	When speaking technically, instead of saying onion juice "stimulates" tears; we say onion juice "_____" tears. 1-26
reflex 1-33	In a warm room, your sweat glands rapidly excrete sweat. The response is (1)_____ ; the stimulus is (2)_____; and the two together form a(n) (3)_____. 1-34

(1) time
    (interval)
(2) stimulus
    (and)
    response
1-41
	A very hot surface brought into contact with the hand, elicits arm flexion with a(n)_____latency than a less hot surface.
	
	1-42

stimulus 1-49	Because the stimulus is sufficient in accounting for the reflex response, there * * * a need to explain reflex behavior with concepts of "mind" or "free will." 1-50

FIGURE 7-1, continued

169

Branching programs. Another manner of programming texts is called branching. Multiple-choice questions are used in dealing with larger units of instruction than are found in linear programs. If the student makes a correct choice, he proceeds normally. If he makes an error, he is shifted from the main line of progress onto a branch where he gets additional instruction and the specific error is clarified. Still another wrong response directs him to supplementary material in which that specific error is clarified.

If the student responds correctly to a number of questions, he may be directed to skip a certain number of exercises so the material to be studied will be somewhat more difficult and challenging. The following example is a branching program devised by one of its leading proponents, Norman A. Crowder:

Lesson 1 The Power of Numbers

A modern electronic computer performs complicated mathematical calculations in a matter of seconds. Inside the computer, electrical impulses are translated into a number system which differs considerably from the one commonly used in pencil-and-paper mathematics.

To understand how a computer uses its unique system of numbers to perform such amazing feats, we will have to spend some time dissecting and examining more closely the number system we already know.

Our familiar number system uses ten different numbers: 0, 1, 2, 3, 4, 5, 6, 7, 8, and 9. Each single numeral is called a digit. Because the system uses ten different numerals or digits it is called the *decimal* system (Latin *decem* = ten). The arithmetic we learned in school is decimal arithmetic.

We are so familiar with the decimal system and decimal arithmetic that the decimal system may seem to us the "natural" system. Actually it is only one of many systems of writing numbers.

Now here is a question on the material you have just read. Select what you believe to be the correct answer and turn to the page number indicated to the right of the answer you choose.

Would you say that the two numbers 492 and .29 are both written in the decimal system?

Answer

Both 492 and .29 are written in the decimal system. page 4

Only .29 is written in the decimal system. page 8

If the student says 492 and .29 are written in the decimal system, he turns to page 4, which tells him:

Your Answer: Both 492 and .29 are written in the decimal system.

You are correct. The word "decimal" refers simply to the fact that our common number system uses only ten different numerals, or digits. With these ten single digits (0, 1, 2 . . . 9), we can count up to 9. Beyond 9 we must use combinations of these numerals, such as 1 and 0 for ten (10), and 1 and 1 for eleven (11), etc.

Do you know, or have you ever heard of, a number system for representing quantities other than our familiar 10-digit decimal system?

Answer

Yes. page 14.

No. page XIV.

I'm not sure. page 1111

If the student's answer is "Only .29 is written in the decimal system," he then goes to page 8, where he gets some "remedial" information:

Your Answer: Only .29 is written in the decimal system.

Well, let's see.

You once learned that

$$.29 = {}^{29}\!/_{100}$$

and

$$.4 = {}^{4}\!/_{10}$$

and

$$.333 = {}^{333}\!/_{1000}$$

Fractional quantities such as .29, .4, and .333, written with the aid of the "decimal" point, are called "decimal" fractions. You probably were thinking about this use of the word "decimal" when you decided that the decimal fraction .29 is written in the decimal system and the whole number 492 is not.

The fact that no decimal point is shown does not exclude the number 492 from the decimal system. The word "decimal" means "ten." The decimal system is a number system which uses ten different digits. Both whole and fractional numbers may be written with decimal system digits.

The number 492 and the number .29 are both written in the decimal system because they both use the decimal system digits—which are 0, 1, 2, 3, 4, 5, 6, 7, 8, and 9.

Please return to Page 1 and choose another answer.[1]

Psychological rationale

Programmed learning moves away from the long-standing custom of expecting all pupils to finish a given piece of work in the same time period. It moves away from some ideas that have had, and still have, rather tight hold on classroom practice: punishment or threat of punishment as a valid source of school motivation; school tasks must be difficult in order to take big steps; one learns effectively by making mistakes. Sharply contrasting views are taken by the supporter of programmed learning. The urge to grow, to learn, is sufficient motivation if reinforced by a reward like success. Reward need not always be a good grade or a piece of candy or the like. Success is a spur to further success.

A programmed text calls for the learner to commit himself and to be active in the learning process. Many authorities— Dewey, Guthrie, Hull, Skinner, Thorndike—have tried to convince teachers that mere sitting, listening, or reading are ineffective in learning unless there is pupil interest and involvement.

Skinner (1958) objected to the kind of program that used multiple-choice questions because the wrong alternate response could be learned and therefore confuse the learning situation. He deemed it important instead for the learner to

[1] Norman A. Crowder and Grace C. Martin, *The Arithmetic of Computers* (New York: Doubleday and Co., 1960), pp. 1, 4, 8. Copyright © 1960 by U.S. Industries, Inc. Reprinted by permission of Doubleday and Company, Inc.

"compose" the answer. He emphasized the fact that the program does not teach; it is merely a means of presenting material. The effectiveness of programming depends on the care with which the program is constructed. Textbooks are typically not much help in building a program because they are not written with the step-by-step logical sequence that is required in a program.

Skinner indicated that one big advantage of a program is that it is unnecessary to make assumptions regarding its success. A trial run immediately identifies the frames that are inaccurate or inappropriate. No such feedback is available to the lecturer, textbook writer, or filmmaker. There can be no gaps in programmed material.

A big factor in defense of programming is that it replaces the punitive, aversive approach to motivation with the reward of success. Skinner (1971) believes that the large dependence teachers have placed on punishment and failure is a major factor in the current criticism of education.

Results of programmed learning

Immediate and positive feedback provided in programmed learning results in subject mastery and is liked by students. Holland (1959), reporting on the use of the programmed text shown in Figure 7-1, found that over four-fifths of users felt they would have gotten less out of the course without the program. The majority of pupils report liking the programs. Most of the many reports on performance contracting, in which programming is heavily used, claim positive and gratifying results. Students can achieve one, two, or three years' growth in a given subject in one academic year (Elam, 1970). These gratifying results have resulted in the increasing popularity of performance contracting. In the day of scarce educational monies, we are hearing about accountability and measurement of tangible results (Holland, 1968).

Some procedures that contribute to the success of programmed learning raise serious questions among concerned educators. One is the matter of quantification in evaluation (Edmonds et al., 1973). The skeptic is asking if finishing a program or showing a year's gain on an arithmetic achievement test is the issue at stake. The performance contractors

GOALS, ESPECIALLY TO THE YOUNG, ARE LESS IMPORTANT THAN DOING!

The process of learning often is more important than its measurable, achievement-type products.

and the program enthusiasts answer, "Yes. At least you know what has been done." The critics respond, "There is no fundamental polarity between ego development and measured achievement, but such achievement must not be allowed to assume priority." Some persons are genuinely concerned that a pupil would be given green stamps in proportion to his achievement or that a child would receive a transistor radio for gaining 2.8 grade levels in math between October and March. And they can show that this does something for the ego concept. The "go-slow" believers are asking if the fact that the teacher-pupil interrelationship cannot be quantified—in contrast to the completion of a program—means that teacher-pupil interrelationships are unimportant.

Computer-aided instruction, behavior modification techniques, and sophisticated machine-aided methods of evaluation are streamlining a once-cumbersome, unwieldy conception of schooling. In attempting to streamline education, however, we cannot afford to assume that a student's most significant insights can be objectively measured, that the ritual of scientism can explain the meaning of existence, that the totality of the human being lends itself to definitive quantification.[2]

STYLES OF LEARNING

Life styles

Recent studies in child development have begun to focus more pointedly on the fact that neonates reveal distinctive patterns of behavior. These different and unique patterns are consistent and persistent. They are not attributable to prenatal nourishment, psychological or physiological condition of the pregnant woman, conditions of birth, traumatic experiences, body build, and the like. Regardless of source, these distinctive patterns of behavior have implications for cognitive development, which in turn influences how and what a child perceives (Koerner 1971). Koerner also asserts that differences in neurological makeup help to shape the different ways in which mothers respond to their infants. Freud (1950) stated his belief that each individual ego is initially endowed with its own predispositions and tendencies. Children and adolescents may have strong and persistent tendencies to react in a reactive expressive or a retractive inhibitive style (Honzik, 1964). Longitudinal studies show that some children consistently respond quickly and impulsively to problem situations (Kagan, 1967). Others as consistently and tenaciously respond to problems in a cognitive style marked by reflectiveness and caution.

The challenge to innovative teachers

Despite long-standing talk among educators about individual differences, very little has been done to effect a consistent

[2] Michael B. McMahon, "Positivism and the Public Schools," *Phi Delta Kappan* 51 (June 1970): 517.

175

recognition of them. Programmed learning, for instance, is a way to implement recognition of differences in learning style and speed but as soon as it becomes *the* method, the differences of some pupils are submerged. As long as it is thought that any one practice can universally meet the needs and styles of all pupils, the differences of some are violated. If we hope to use a pupil's learning and strengths as an induction into the more widely popular style (academic approaches), we will fail with those pupils whose learning styles are persistently different. Let it be repeated for the sake of those who do not believe that critics of classroom education (Coleman, 1972; Dennison, 1969; Friedenberg, 1969; Holt, 1964; Leonard, 1968) have *the* answers in their open schools, sidewalk academies, "any experience is educative" persuasion—many pupils like and profit from the structure and achievement standards already prevalent in most schools.

There is also the challenge of the "Yes, but . . ." practical teacher, "These things are possible if you have a class load of ten pupils." The answer is simply, "That which thirty, well-behaved, conforming pupils do learn is not necessarily in conformity with teacher objectives, the lesson plan, and the behavioral outcomes specified." Some pupils have learned that they cannot learn, that they hate the establishment, that learning is done for someone else. In short, there is no alternative: Pupils will learn because they must learn in some degree of accord with their unique learning style. Some have the potential to learn how to use many styles, but some, despite all that is done, will continue to learn only through their unique styles.

A prime motivating power behind innovative practices in education is the hope that a multitude of ways to facilitate the processes of learning will be found. Efforts to find *a practice* that will appeal to all learners have been, and will be, futile. Pupils will not, because they cannot, learn the same thing, in the same way, at the same pace. The futility of this is inferred in Chapter 8 in the suggestion that nongraded classrooms work, if for no other reason, because graded classrooms cannot work. The ungraded classroom may be somewhat better than the graded classroom because of adaptations to differences in learning speed, and speed seems to be a major difference in style that has been, theoretically at least, given some attention.

Speed, however, is only one of a myriad of learning styles. There are those who learn by talking; there are those who learn by listening: When such pupils get to the eighth grade with a second grade reading level, teachers are discouraged and wonder how the system has gone wrong to allow the pupil to get so far. If individuality of learning style can be respected, so too should such a nonreading pupil be respected because he has proven that he can move ahead by using his own, almost private, access route—listening, observing, doing.

Below, as a stimulus to the continued search for more varied educational approaches, a number of learning styles are presented. There are not sufficient current research data to describe these styles in detail. In fact, the matter is largely speculative. The purpose of the speculation is more to engender respect for pupil differences than to provide definitive programs that will capitalize on idiosyncratic styles.

Riessman (1966) was among the first to designate some specifics in the matter of learning style, postulating that some pupils learn best by reading, others by listening, and still others by physical action. Some clarify, organize, and apply conceptual materials by talking. A given style may be used in various ways. Some pupils employ a leisurely pace and others work best under pressure. Some like to pace the floor but others do their best thinking when quietly isolated in a corner chair. Some pupils prefer quiet, order, and routine but others work well in the midst of noise, turmoil, and physical freedom.

Nations (1967) conceptualized learning styles as various combinations of modes. The "sensory mode" describes whether visual, auditory, or tactile contact is the learner's favorite means of perception. Sensory orientation influences whether the pupil sees, hears, or feels the stimuli that provide information and perceptual stimulation. The "responsive mode" determines whether one works best alone or in a group. Active participation, observation, or standing outside the activity show the responsive mode. Responsive mode describes those pupils who tend to depend on teachers as contrasted to those who act autonomously. This mode describes whether one tends to ignore, accept, support, or challenge an assignment or suggestion. A "thinking pattern" refers to whether one learns best by getting many details first and then organizing them into a pattern or if he begins with a comprehensive gestalt and then gathers information to support the hunch. Thinking patterns refer to whether one utilizes a deliberate, methodical gathering of information or whether he is comfortable making giant intuitive leaps.

Guilford (1967, pp. 138, 171) and others speak of convergent and divergent thinking. The convergent thinker uses logic and seeks to find a known answer to a problem; he tries to obtain the "right" answer. The divergent thinker moves away from facts and known solutions to processing novel and unknown products. Divergent thought patterns are revealed in fluency, flexibility, and elaboration in thinking. In group activities these contrasting styles identify the building, encouraging, harmonizing roles from the roles of aggressor, standard-setter, and challenger.

Students in one of the author's classes administered a questionnaire regarding how seventh graders and high school juniors best liked to approach school work. Results showed that there were seven categories of preferred learning styles: seeing, hearing, reflecting, speaking, writing, doing, and testing-predicting.

The mechanical and the academic mind

The myth. One popular myth, not only in the public mind but also in the minds of many professional teachers, is that there are pupils with academic abilities and those with mechanical talents. The "proof" of this is that pupils who are failing the struggle with language, literature, and mathematical concepts are shunted into shopwork and there do entirely acceptable jobs.

The difficulty with the myth that there are mechanical and academic minds is that there is some truth in the concept. *Some* people can learn by verbal description while others get vivid and durable mental pictures of objects. But there are some shop teachers who resent having their facilities used as an intellectual trash barrel; and the pupil soon discovers that he is no better off working with his hands and with machines than he was when assigned tasks dealing with the abstract and ideational.

The reality. The reality of the school world is such that the concept of the academic *vs.* the mechanical mind cannot be summarily dismissed. This difference may be as natural and as congenital as is eye color. Minds are different to some extent, but how much different is a great mystery. Drawing from what is known about the psychology of learning, some academic or mechanical mindedness is learned. Many shop teachers use methods that are much different from those of the academic teacher. A shop teacher may, for instance, have his pupils work on projects that are scaled to the pupils' present level of skills. Book ends are simpler than a mortise and tenon joint in a chest of drawers and thus more suited to a beginner. The shop teacher may be more interested in knowing that his pupils understand more about using a chisel than in being able to recite the number of threads per inch in a machine vs. a carriage bolt.[3] The shop teacher may not be so bound to a lock-step speed of progress as the academic teacher. Because pupils are engaged in different projects, have different time allotments, and are using different tools, grades need not be bound to the ego deflating evaluation process of comparative competitive grading. The process of evaluation for the shop teacher is the individual product. Somehow or other the biology teacher has more difficulty thinking of a butterfly collection as a process than as a product; and the English teacher is too frequently concerned about spelling, punctuation, and grammar than he is about a story as an end in itself.[4]

It is being postulated that part of the distinction between the academic and the mechanical mind is a response to the way pupil effort has been evaluated. Those teachers who have used comparative competitive methods have suppressed the blossoming of academic potential in some pupils. The positive feedback essential to a child's continued pursuit of planned learning is provided by the shop teacher who evaluates in terms of individual product. Such a teacher provides a milieu where the myth of mechanical mindedness takes root and so flourishes that it serves to perpetuate the fallacy.

---

[3] One shop teacher made a survey of his classes and found that they were quite creative spellers; there were twenty-three different ways to spell chisel. This may have some devious relationship to learning styles.

[4] Natalie Cole, *The Arts in the Classroom* (New York: The John Day Co., 1940), and Herbert Kohl, *Teaching the Unteachable* (New York: The New York Review, 1967), provide examples of the fact that the process of grading the product instead of letting the result be the culmination does not have to be the case.

Conformity and divergency

An area which merits considerable study by classroom teachers is that of conformity and divergency. We tend to hold the conformist in contempt and talk with disdain of the "man in the grey flannel suit," and the organization man, of lock-step methods in education, and "ticky-tacky houses." We hardly dare look at our own lives to see the extent to which conformity dominates our dress, living accommodations, activities, and esthetic preferences. Conformity, despite our verbally expressed contempt for it, is preferred in our students. Those who digress from the subject at hand, who would prefer not to write a term paper, who protest the teacher's viewpoint are, more often than not, discouraged from their pursuit. Sometimes, as an educational innovation in and of itself, divergency is made a specific assignment. For example, a geometry teacher made an assignment each term that a particular unit was to be reported on in any form but pencil and paper. Reports came in the form of mobiles, zoological and botanical specimens, old wagon wheel rims, bizarre bits of clothing, and complicated contraptions for achieving some simple act.[5] Typically, even in arts and crafts work, and especially in the lower grades, it is difficult to encourage pupils not to copy the basket-making, mat-weaving, bottle-cutting, flower-painting activities of a classmate.

Implications of the mechanical *vs.* academic mind fallacy

The foregoing is not intended to suggest that the only difference between the academically and mechanically inclined minds is learned. There probably are different predispositions that merit encouragement and cultivation. At Benson High School in Portland, Oregon, the emphasis is on technology, mechanics, and science. But by using the boys' interests in these subjects, Benson has maintained a reputation for the highest academic achievements in the city in all subjects including literature and the humanities. Unfortunately (in the opinion of the authors) not all this reputation is based on

---

[5] A fishing reel and line, attached to a bicycle wheel, was used in lowering a box containing a piece of chalk.

utilizing the strengths of boys. In part, Benson has perpetuated the worst in the academic world—the ego-deflating use of comparative competitive grading. The faculty rationalize this antediluvian practice with the claim that their reputation must be maintained among employers.

Mechanical interests, mechanical experience, and a mechanical culture can be used advantageously as a point of departure in formal education. They should not, in terms of present knowledge, be used as a rationalization for the exclusion of involvement in that which is called academic. Rather, the task is to parallel latent academic proclivities with some of the positive feedback that, in our society, rewards mechanical pursuits and whose efficacy is revealed in programmed learning.

Styles of life and styles of learning

It is unnecessary here to decide if these styles of life are dictated by methods of child rearing, characteristics of mental activity, or, as some have suggested, are products of birth order. Nor is there any advantage in deciding that an ascendent person is any more effective than one who is submissive, unless, of course, either of these styles becomes so extreme that it interferes with individual and social effectiveness.

Terrence, as a fourth grader, was often seen working by himself. He would join other pupils when called but after a few minutes would again pursue his self-appointed chores.

In the sixth grade his teacher noted that he played baseball considerably better than the typical boy his age but still did not become interested. When his teammates urged him to practice, he would do so with marked competence. But when it came time for the next game he would have to be pulled away from his perusal of bookshelves and his study of certain volumes.

When he was in high school his mother reported that he would spend hours in a big chair *studying* the dictionary. Occasionally he would spontaneously join a conversation of peers or older persons but more typically would have to be invited.

As a college freshman his score on the Inglis Test of

English Vocabulary was equivalent to the norms for high level executives and college professors. Once in a while, during college, he would go out with a pal or a group of boys but spent most of his time studying, often not on assignments but in a succession of unrelated topics of his own choosing. Near the end of the term he would cram to pass the courses for which he was registered. This approach netted only mediocre records of academic achievement but he did get a degree in history.

Upon being graduated Terrence took a job in the welfare department of a large city government. He would listen to people—supervisors, peers, friends—with apparent interest. He sometimes asked a question that had been answered earlier or on another occasion, thus indicating his detachment from the affairs of others. He did learn his job and within surprisingly few years was one of the top officers in his department. At home he watched the development of his sons and daughters with obvious pride but was not demonstrative in his affections. If they wished, they could share his interest in music and reading but it was their choice rather than his persuasion.

The history of Terrence shows that the trait of reticence is not, contrary to widespread belief, necessarily handicapping. This judgment would be very different if the reticence were accompanied by job failure, alienation, and personal unhappiness.

Observation suggests that learning may be influenced by relationships with others. Some people, such as Terrence, like to be and study alone. Before they can concentrate they seem to need a degree of solitude. Others just as surely need the proximity of another person—a whisper to provide feedback that he is on the right track, a query on some point of puzzlement, a chance to test out some hastily achieved insight. Yet classrooms have, until recent years, demanded silence and virtual social isolation. Some classrooms, e.g., college lecture halls, even yet deny the social relationship aspect of learning style.

Even when teachers do recognize the social interaction component of learning style, it may be a source of discomfort or even of outright irritation. Some pupils learn by agreeing; they are by nature, apparently, yes-men. Others are contributors and supplementers. They do not initiate action but when it is started by another they supply variations on the theme. The unpleasant ones are those whose chronic approach is disagreement. They wait until there has been some discussion, or even consensus and then "level their guns" for a demolition of whatever has been concluded.

Group studies with control classes will not prove that children learn arithmetic better in small groups or individually. However, studies of individuals do show that some pupils learn better in groups and that others are wasting their time (as far as arithmetic is concerned) by working in groups, even those groups that the teacher has formed by means of sociometric analysis.

OPEN EDUCATION

The very phrase "open classroom" connotes much greater scope for individuality and freedom than in a conventional classroom and rouses certain expectations among educators and parents. As is the case with many other educational plans and techniques, open education has varied interpretations. It does frequently mean that walls and rooms are minimized. Large rooms and open space invite freedom of movement. Openness is suggested by virtue of having a wider age range, somewhat like a family with parents, older, and younger siblings. This age range inhibits unison teaching so that some have completed an assignment before others discover the answer to what page they are on. Self-governance is encouraged and assistance is given in its practice. The teacher, after reviewing skills and routine study, sketches what he expects during the free-flow part of the period. The pupil might be expected to spend some time at a math activity center, or at a language center, or at a reading center. There is a little bit of chaos (Gross and Gross, 1970) but there is also some structure (Perrone, 1972).

Open education in action

In Hartford, Connecticut, the concept of open education has been evolved under the leadership of Randazzo, who is concerned with the development of children who have difficulty keeping quiet at desks and those who learn at a "comparatively slow" rate (Randazzo and Arnold, 1972). Children are allowed to follow their own interests in selecting materials and activities but it is expected that time will be spent in the subareas where materials are concentrated for language, literature, art, science, and mathematics. It is freedom but not license. It is freedom for pupils to choose from a number of options, to discover the type of materials that interest them, and to learn at their unique individual pace. Both freedom and adult direction are regarded as being essential. This is in entire accord with Maslow's (1970) opinion that the safety needs of a child tend to be satisfied by rules, regulations, and routines. Maslow's "three Rs" become inhibitory when they are exercised in an authoritarian, not an authoritative, manner. When exercised judiciously, decreasing as the child grows older, the "Rs" promote growth. Order and routine contribute to a feeling of safety that encourages one to exercise his heterostatic urges.

Open education works at Hartford because of involved leadership, because of parental consultation and participation, and because teachers learn and grow with the program (Rogers, 1972). The program is a big one, comprising 10,000 pupils, 350 classrooms, 1000 teachers and aides, and a permanent teacher learning center. In the teachers' center materials, books, and ideas are pooled. Each primary teacher and each aide spends three weeks, full-time, being trained or retrained to use the materials and concepts. Plans call for open education throughout the entire elementary school system within the next few years. The plan does not work for all. Some teachers remain unconvinced and unchanged.

Randazzo (1972) singles out several prominent items in Hartford's auspicious start on open education:

Pupils appraise themselves with emphasis on the future.
Learning processes are examined in terms of individual children.
Open education emphasizes the centrality of the teacher rather than depending on teacher-proof packages.
Teachers are retooled by a three-week, process orientated, in-service program.
Community involvement depends largely on teacher aides who study with the teachers.

When teachers leave the training program, they are helped and encouraged by on-the-job consultants.
Curriculum change is constant as teachers perceive unique pupil needs.

It is suggested that the reader consult the summary list of propositions on pages 46–47 and answer for himself the questions: Does open education promise support of Proposition I, Proposition II, and so on through Proposition XV?

CREATIVITY IN TEACHING

The encouragement of creativity in pupils presents three challenges to classroom teachers. The first of these is to provide a milieu that will stimulate the emergence of some creative potential in all pupils. The second is the encouragement of the teacher's own creative potential, especially as it relates to his being an innovative teacher. The third challenge is to provide the structure needed to encourage the convergent conforming pupil without stultifying the creative bent of the divergent exploring pupil.

The concept of creativity

The word creativity is one of those that seems to mean just whatever the user has in mind when he uses it. Kilpatrick (1935, p. 4) says that learning itself is creative, that when one faces a problem and works his way out he has created a novel response. The ability to create, he says, is found in the lowest and earliest instances of learning (p. 15). All persons are creative—some in low degree, some in high degree. Others are agreed that all persons are creative in some degree; but they like to give the word some specificity by calling a person creative when his product or idea is clearly beyond the ordinary. Torrance (1962, p. 76) describes the creative child as one who tends to give unconventional responses, expresses wild and fanciful ideas, and moves "off the beaten track" in combining thoughts and objects. Being creative is not the same as having high intelligence; one may be bright and convergent or bright and divergent. The incidence of creativity is relatively

185

greater in the higher ranges of intelligence. Gallagher (1964) also emphasizes the unusual, the original, and the divergent as being characteristic of the intelligent creative individual.

Convergent-divergent thinking

Guilford (1959, 1967), in conceptualizing the structure of intelligence, makes a clear distinction between convergent and divergent thinking, citing these two dimensions as having influence on many remaining dimensions of intellectual activity. Divergent responses are varied, flexible, fluent. He illustrates by using a test item which asks how a brick may be used. One responds: build a wall, school, barn, sidewalk, chimney, barbecue. Another says: build a house, drown a cat, make a red powder, drive a nail, throw it at a dog: and thus shows both flexibility and fluency. The convergent thinkers are deductive, they seek categories and formulate classifications. The world needs both the convergent and the divergent citizen; it needs both the creative and the conservative individual. Progress in technology and life requires both the creative, inventive, idea-maker and the practical, steadfast worker who keeps the machinery running.

Typically, educational methods have tended to discourage latent talent, incipient divergence, and idiosyncratic thinking. The consequence has been that some pupils are forced to leave school by the pressure to conform. Their own drive toward creativity and divergence is so great that it cannot be suppressed. On the other hand, some pupils have suppressed their creative urges and the potential for divergence atrophies. Some pupils have little of the creative urge and that which potentially exists literally "dies in borning." Such violations of children's life and learning styles should not be allowed to occur. It is assumed that a fully functioning person is one who develops and preserves his uniqueness (Torrance, 1962). The task is to recognize and utilize the divergent nature of individuality.

Perceiving creative potential

Three out of four people in the United States prefer to depend on objective evidence (sense perception); one out of four prefers to depend on his individual interpretation of what he sees (intuitive perception). Among creative writers, mathematicians, research scientists, and architects, the preference for intuitive perception runs from 90 to 100 percent (MacKinnon, 1971). Because it is a natural, normal, comfortable feeling to be with those of one's own kind, those traits that place one in a minority group tend to produce discomfort, i.e., creativity and divergence. It is not easy to change a cultural norm. Conant (1959) and Coleman (1965) have noted that adolescent boys sometimes dislike being known as an "egg head" and girls frequently want to avoid the shame of being a "brain," for superior intelligence is often viewed with suspicion.

Taylor (1968) suggests that a start toward recognizing individuality be made by using aptitude tests that probe for many different kinds of intelligence—and such are available. Instead of seeking one global intelligence score (IQ or MA), tests should make it possible to identify many kinds of intellectual talents. If school personnel were to test for ten talents (and it is possible to test for over eighty of the 120 facets of intelligence that Guilford postulates) there would be a greatly increased number of pupils at the head of the list *in some area*. Thus, in Figure 7-2, pupil A heads the list in test 1 but pupil F makes the top score in test 2. Taylor says that there will be some slippage (pupil A may be at the top of two lists). He has not found that, given enough tests, every child will be at the top in some talent, but all children, he postulates, will be above average in something. By using many tests, many children will be in the topmost 10 percent in some category. His enthusiasm for what such a talent detecting program could do for the ego concept of children, and the expectancy hypotheses of teachers, is expressed in such terms as "beautiful phenomenon," "promising picture," "sunrise for education," "heartening," and "rewarding."

The fact that the top 10 percent of a group of children will differ in composition is common knowledge, but the idea has often failed to enter our day-to-day thinking. Not only do children differ from each other but they differ from themselves. This is exactly what we seek to know through the use of such tests as the SCAT (School and College Ability Test) and the DAT (Differential Aptitude Test). These and other tests, however, sometimes have boomeranged. When a young-

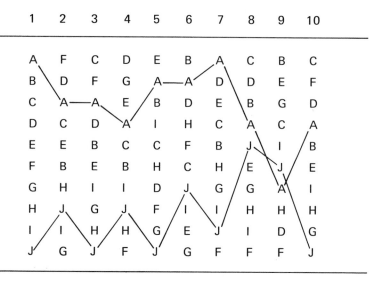

FIGURE 7-2. *Scores of ten pupils on ten tests of talent. Profiles of two pupils are indicated.* (Adapted from Calvin W. Taylor, "Cultivating New Talents: A Way to Reach the Educationally Deprived," *Journal of Creative Behavior* 2 (1968): 83–90.)

ster scores well in some areas but does poorly in others, he immediately is marked as a candidate for remedial work. Because remediation is accentuated, he tends to internalize a concept of an inadequate self. The good intention is to bring him "up to average." For the class as a whole such an objective is self-defeating because it is a statistical impossibility. If the child is brought up to average, he raises the class average and someone else must slip below. The "sunrise for educaton," of which Taylor speaks, will be that day when it is the pupils' strengths that get attention, when emphasis is placed on development of talent instead of stressing weakness and developing mediocrity. This emphasis does not mean neglecting the weakness but that the weakness is approached (or exercised) through the area of strength. For example, the slow reading boy who has marked artistic talent will get to spend more time at the easel, clay pot, or drawing board and he is given special books on art history, biographies of artists, use of brushes, chisels, and mallets, and the preparation of oil and water colors.

All evidence and demonstrations to date show strongly that a largely new group will be found to be most gifted as we either test or train in the classroom for each new type of giftedness. Classroom searches and development of talent also show that those who are seen as academically deprived will move upward as each type of giftedness becomes the focus of attention in classroom activities. In turn a different subgroup of people slip downward to the bottom of the talent ladder for that particular type of giftedness.

The challenge, then, is to devise and initiate various educational programs focused on developing creative and other new talents, for the sake of both the educationally deprived and the unrecognized, underdeveloped gifted persons.

This entire approach is a very healthy one indeed and should make our school systems much more efficient in identifying and developing the nation's important human resources for the overall benefit of the individuals, and communities, the nation, and the world.[6]

Conditions of creativity

It often seems as though one either has, or does not have, creative talent and that, if he does not, there is nothing he can do about it. Creativity can arise under stress and adversity. It may appear in an emergency. But peace and serenity also, and freedom from stress, appear to be essential conditions. Hence it seems to be a matter of individual potential with circumstances lending little. There are some clues, however, that are generally applicable, but the clues must be tested on individuals to see what response is generated in each.

Creativity demands background, experience, data, study, and information. It requires discipline and conformity (one does not paint simultaneously in oils and water colors); a plan must be followed. This is the phase of preparation. There is also the phase of incubation, the period in which one mulls

[6] Calvin W. Taylor, "Cultivating New Talents: A Way to Reach the Educationally Deprived," *Journal of Creative Behavior* 2 (1968): 89–90.

over his data and objectives, both idly and purposefully dreaming and plotting alternatives and possibilities. It takes time to be creative in problem solving, artistic productions, and scientific research. There is the point, actually a span of time, when the new combination of ideas that have been incubating, assume a novel gestalt, referred to as illumination. Torrance, in relating the conditions of creativity to teaching, recognizes these preparatory, laborious, elaborative phases:

> . . . It does indeed seem possible to teach children to think creatively. The most successful approaches seem to be those that involve both cognitive and emotional functioning, provide adequate structure and motivation, and give opportunities for involvement, practice, and interaction with teachers and other children. Motivation and facilitating conditions certainly make a difference in creative functioning but differences seem to be greatest and most predictable when deliberate teaching is involved.[7]

It has been postulated, and Skinner has so argued, that there is no basic conflict between creativity and programmed learning. If a person is to be truly creative, especially in science, business, or architecture, he needs facts, data, and information for background and base. The Wallas-Patrick analysis of creative thought consists of these stages: preparation, incubation, illumination, and verification (or generalization). Many naive enthusiasts for creativity ignore the preparation aspect, although study, research, practice, and dreary repetition are essential even in the pictorial and graphic arts. The biographies of Charles Schreyvogel and Malvina Hoffman tell the stories of this arduous, time-consuming, basic work. The fictional account of Michelangelo's struggle to master many crafts and arts is also illustrative.[8]

Programmed study can only make a contribution to creativity when the pupil sees the pursuit of a program as pertinent to his goals. He can then treat the program as a quick way to get past a boring detail and can experience choice in the selection of the program.

[7] E. Paul Torrance, "Can We Teach Children to Think Creatively?" *Journal of Creative Behavior* 6 (1972): 132–33.
[8] James D. Horan, *The Life and Art of Charles Schreyvogel*, New York: Crown Publishers, Inc., 1969; Malvina Hoffman, *Heads and Tales*, Garden City, N.Y.: Garden City Publishing Co., 1936; and Irving Stone, *The Agony and the Ecstasy*, New York: Doubleday and Co., 1961.

There are programs, such as the Osborn-Parnes Creative Problem Solving and the Purdue Creativity Program, designed to promote creative thinking. Communication, creative arts, reading, motivation, reward, and a deemphasis on testing are characteristically features of a milieu that fosters creativity.

Creativity demands both—freedom and hard work!

Encouraging creative potential

Those who have been concerned with the development of creative talent have implied, but not often directly stated, that encouragement is not a matter of technique but of teacher personality (Getzels and Jackson, 1962; MacKinnon, 1971; Torrance, 1962). The teacher must grit his teeth (and that means he can stand it for only a brief period) or relax and smile (and he can then endure a little longer) and live with the ambiguity. A chance to kid oneself about it later in an interpersonal process group may help.

Gifted, creative, children are unpredictable. They give off-beat answers, make sly jokes, pick flaws in synthesizing processes, and themselves combine ideas into odd combinations, thus making the structure-oriented teacher uncomfortable. Some pupils are interested in one specific area but others are going off in a dozen directions all at once.

A teacher may use programmed material to enhance creativity, but in addition, it is possible to check methods

191

against Joan Brunswick's (1971) ten commandments for creative teaching. These include not accepting answers without saying, "How do you know?" "Really?" "Are you sure?" Brunswick would hesitate to settle pupil arguments, hesitate to say, "Not now. Later," hesitate to follow the rigid curriculum. She would listen, observe pupils' varied interests, depend less on the clock, and use more words and pats of encouragement.

Research indicates that pressure to conform, authoritarian attitudes, ridicule, overemphasis on grades and rewards, a teacher's desire for answers, hostility toward the divergent child, and intolerance for playful attitudes must be avoided if creativity, indeed all learning, is not to be inhibited. Success in stimulating creativity becomes more likely when teachers:

provide for self-initiated activities and self-evaluation,
develop a nonauthoritarian attitude,
encourage overlearning,
defer judgment,
make efforts to become a more sensitive person, and
provide freedom and opportunity to handle material, ideas, tools, and programs.

In our school visits, we were impressed by the quality and variety of pupils' art in certain schools. Upon postvisit analysis, we saw that those schools most impressive in terms of zestful innovation were also the ones in which the delightful art was seen. We wished we had had the idea earlier so we could have looked for confirmation or denial, but we were able to form the hypothesis: In those schools in which variety and freedom are ways of life, the pupils' art work is of high quality and stimulating variety; in schools where structure and conformity prevail, there is less interest, and less art work of lower quality. Of course, the possibility exists that the number of schools visited would not constitute a reliable sample so the difference might have been one of chance. Perhaps the "halo effect" was in operation. It could be that schools have competent pupil artists when they are fortunate enough to have a staff member who is both teacher and artist. The issue is further complicated by the possibility that professionals who are both teachers and artists seek and accept jobs in those schools where freedom and autonomy are in the air.

Much more certain is the general thesis that there are

varying degrees of pupil appreciation of structure or opportunity for autonomy. Much less speculative, as far as reaching pupils is concerned, is the thesis that what teachers do (including use of programmed material) and are, is more important than any gadget or teaching method used.

SUMMARY

The prominent characteristics of programmed learning are small steps, immediate feedback, satisfaction deriving from task completion, and pupil self-pacing. Linear programs capitalize on small, easy steps so that failure is highly unlikely. Branching programs use somewhat larger units and may veer off to supplementary or basic materials if errors are made or the user may skip a number of exercises if the material is too easy. Research evaluations show that programmed studies do get positive results, and in substantial preponderance.

It is suggested that programmed learning gets the results it does because most pupils have a sense perception cognitive style and fewer (about one out of four) have an intuitive perception cognitive style. Success of programmed learning, or any other innovative approach, probably depends to a great extent on the individual pupil's learning style. Some need structure, some need to exercise autonomy, some tend to be convergent and deductive thinkers while others are divergent and intuitive thinkers. Some pupils learn best by reading while others learn by more active modes. Some learn in the midst of turmoil, others in quiet solitude. People are born with different preferences for cognitive style as surely as they are born with potentials for varied learning speeds. The challenge to educators is to use pupils' strengths to change a weakness into a strength. If the weakness rather than the strength is emphasized, one's ego is injured.

Open education contrasts markedly with programmed study and tends to elicit creativity from pupils and teachers. There is some structure but there is also much freedom. Open education is facilitated by physical structure but the key resides in teachers who are creative. Being creative, they enhance the prospects for nurturing creativity in pupils. Open education tends to implement the propositions on learning that are set forth in Chapter 2.

193

Teaching for creativity is contrasted to the presentation of learning material by programs to show how different cognitive styles influence the goals and methods of instruction. Creativity demands mastery of fundamentals, abundant data, and varied experience, and it is conceivable that programmed learning is a means by which a creative pupil can use a program and then get on with his major concern.

A starting point for a teacher's evaluation of programmed study, recognition of learning styles, and possible encouragement of creativity is to look at himself and his learning style. His learning style should be congruent with his teaching style and, with help from others, any contrast probably can be lessened.

SUGGESTED ADDITIONAL READINGS

Berberich, John P. "Do the Child's Responses Shape the Teaching Behavior of Adults?" *Journal of Experimental Research in Personality* 5 (1971): 92–97. What children do is, for the most part, attributed to the behavior of adults. The author presents data showing that the behavior of children clearly helps to shape the input of the adults.

Coleman, James S. "The Children Have Outgrown the Schools." *Psychology Today* 5 (February 1972): 72–82. The author of *Equal Educational Opportunity*, a federally sponsored study, concludes that classrooms for the dispensing of information are obsolete. He proposes no alternative, but says the challenge of education is to find new purposes.

Mecklenberger, James A. "Epilogue: The Performance Contract in Gary." *Phi Delta Kappan* 54 (1973): 562–63. A three-year contract with business to teach pupils or not be paid has been cancelled. Many factors enter the cancellation but there was pupil improvement. The author concludes that innovation may produce results but is not liked because it creates "waves" and forces teachers to change.

Ojemann, Ralph H. "Self-Guidance as an Educational Goal and the Selection of Objectives." *Elementary School Journal* 72 (February 1972): 247–57. The development of a self-guiding individual requires that a person gradually take over the formulation of his purposes in life. This requires a teacher who is neither permissive or dictatorial but one who is developmental.

Torrance, E. Paul. "Can We Teach Children to Think Creatively?" *Journal of Creative Behavior* 6 (1972): 114–43. Torrance's answer to the question, supported by a review of 142 studies, is "Yes." Helpful conditions are structure, motivation, involvement, practice, and interaction with teachers and other children.

CHAPTER 8

Nongraded Schools and Continuous Progress

One acknowledged difficulty of mass education is how to deal effectively with the large pupil differences which are found within a class group. No matter how classes are composed— by age, sex, intelligence test results, social maturity, years in school, subject matter achievement, skin color, or whatever— differences in some important aspect of development set some pupils apart from the group. The problem of pupil differences has not been, and will not be, solved as long as educators insist on classifying pupils. Although individualism is a valued concept in our national and educational ideology, human differences in school practice become a source of discomfort. Conformity and sameness seem to result in teacher approval. However, differences may be so treated that they become a source of personal satisfaction and social approbation.

Many of the plans devised to accommodate individual differences have had some distinctly deleterious effects. Ability grouping, retention in grade, special classes, and special schools all have perplexing side effects. The harmful aspects have resulted from an emphasis on certain differences and ignoring the existence of others. For example, IQ has been glorified to the detriment of creativity; academic achievement has been exalted at the expense of social competence; and egocentric activities have been emphasized to the neglect of group identity.

Nongraded schools and open education place value on pupil differences without making such variations a focal and competitive point. In the graded school, where passing from grade to grade is dependent upon achieving certain norms, some pupils feel superior and others inferior. Nongraded schools can use the same curricula and secure at least similar academic gains, but no more emphasis is placed on making one grade of academic gain in one school year than is placed on height, apparel, or hair color. In the nongraded school, the child is a member of the group despite his different rate of academic progress; and because he is one with the group his ego is strengthened—or at least it is not deflated.

BASIC CONCEPTS

Nongraded schools

Differences are everywhere, not only among pupils but in the definitions of education, in the purposes of education, and ways for teachers to be "traditional" or "progressive."

Similarly, there is no consensus regarding the meaning of nongraded schools. McLoughlin (1968), in a study of over 300 schools and 400 bibliographical references, found that homogeneous grouping, departmentalization in reading, and "no fail" policies were all regarded as essentials of nongraded education. Focal concerns in nongradedness are time and content. Whereas conventional education keeps time constant and attempts to measure learning in terms of amount ("A" equals a great deal, "B" quite a bit, "C" average), the nongraded concept construes time as the variable and amount of learning as the constant. Each pupil reaches a certain level of competency. It may take one semester, two semesters, or four or five, but all pupils learn to function effectively before moving forward.

One way to conceptualize the more widely accepted meaning of nongraded education is to plot it in terms of levels instead of grades (see Figure 8-1). The basic idea is that different pupils take varying lengths of time to develop required competencies and to achieve readiness for subsequent learning experiences. The conventional school period—preschool through high school—is composed of four levels instead of the customary twelve grades; these are primary, intermediate, junior high school, and senior high school levels. Each of these conventionally consists of three grades. Instead of speaking of grades 1, 2, and 3, we are encouraged to think of the primary level and of one pupil's taking two years to complete the work, another requiring three years, and yet another possibly taking as many as four (see Figure 8-2).

The controlling idea is that curricular requirements can be compressed or stretched to suit the learning pace of individuals. The controlling hope is that pupils, by accepting whatever their learning pace is, can utilize whatever talents they have to better advantage. The thing which is automatically eliminated, if nongrading is to mean more than some ploy to make the grade system work, is nonpromotion. The emphasis is upon adjusting the school to the needs and developmental patterns of the individual. It eliminates curricular requirements as a sort of antiquated Procrustean Bed.[1]

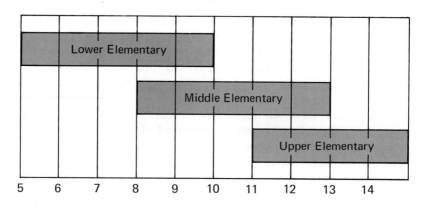

FIGURE 8-1. *Ages of pupils in nongraded school. Note the overlapping of ages: Pupils can take from two to four years to complete a level. Those whose pace is deliberate would take about four years while speedsters could take about two years to a level.*

[1] We are well aware that pupils are required to fit the eight- or four-year curriculum. If classroom exams are too easy, test questions on footnotes and bibliographical references may be used to keep the student from being too comfortable!

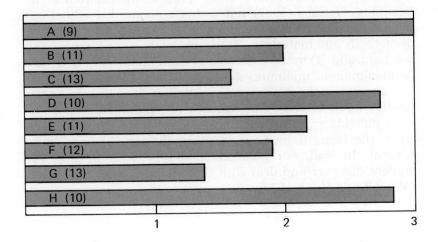

FIGURE 8-2. *Subject Matter Mastery. Eight pupils after two years in the intermediate level of a nongraded school (composite grade equivalent). Age of pupil at the end of two years is in parentheses.*

Nongradedness should and does make possible (1) recognition of differences in learning rates, (2) development of new subject matter sequences, and (3) the implementation of continuous pupil progress. For example, the University of California at Los Angeles Elementary School uses overlapping ages to form instructional groups.

Ages	Designation
9, 10, 11, 12	Upper Elementary
7, 8, 9, 10	Middle Elementary
5, 6, 7, 8	Lower Elementary
3, 4, 5, 6	Early Childhood

Within each designation, there is a large group and a small group. Those in the small group need, or can use, more individual help from the teacher. The larger group may be broken into small groups for specific instructional purposes or kept as a large group when this is expedient. A pupil may take two or three years to go through any one of the designated levels.

The attractive feature of nongraded organization is its flexibility. Nations (1967) stated that a nongraded school has flexibility in (1) individual educational goals, (2) the selection of methods and materials, (3) the organization of learners and teachers, and (4) in the processes of evaluation, since there are no maximum or minimum standards.

There are those who point out that concern about the relative merit of graded as opposed to nongraded schools, or even individualized instruction, is a rather specious concern when the focus is on time spent on mastery of curriculum content. Instead, our concern should be with helping the student discover and deal with that which is relevant to him (Metcalf and Hunt, 1970).

Continuous progress

The great value of nongradedness and continuous progress resides not so much in organization as in ways of looking at pupils. Continuous progress consists, psychologically and philosophically, in ways of thinking about, attitudes toward, and action with, humans rather than managing pupils as "things." Whatever the learning content, the emphasis must be on what teachers do to realize pupil potential rather than on some curricular or organizational form (Tanner, 1970). No matter what the form, the function of nongraded schools is to implement the concept of continuous progress.

The unique feature of continuous progress is that it does not stigmatize the slow learner or the one with a different background. It emphasizes accepting all pupils and making appropriate provisions for each one (Anderson, 1973). Continuous progress has special advantages for education of culturally different pupils (Heathers, 1966). Another way of voicing this is to say that no pupil has to continue to practice and do exercises to cover again material that he already knows. There are probably many pupils who share the attitude which the primary school boy is alleged to have expressed, "I already know more about penguins than I want to know." Conversely, no child must continue to flounder in subject matter areas which he does not understand, or to read books which he does not comprehend.

However, merely eliminating conventional grade designations; and grouping children by developmental age, achievement, or ability rather than by chronological age does not fulfill the purpose of a nongraded instructional program. In order for the organizational device to have significance for the child that it serves, the flexibility that it provides must be used to chart for each child a path of individual progress suited to his needs. The essence of nongrading is continual progress and continuity of progress—each child has the opportunity to progress as rapidly as he is able; he is neither held back nor pushed ahead by an organizational system based upon the implicit assumption that children of similar chronological age are similar in all other respects.[2]

Continuous progress is an alternative to the distressing dilemma presented when success is tied to mastery of one established body of content. There are questions about just how much of graded content is essential to competency in our culture. Goodman (1968) believed that the process of learning is the important thing and that, with guidance, whatever a child learns, at least until about age twelve, can be highly educative. But we cannot ignore the claim that curriculum content is also necessary. Basic skill in computation is a frequently cited example. However, there must be different ways of teaching these essentials if recognition of individual differences is to be a reality. Individualized instruction and continuous progress are impossible when expectations are based on sources extrinsic to the pupil (Strom, 1969).

It has been postulated that a child would have a great deal of difficulty learning his mother tongue if it were taught as other subjects were taught in school: programmed bit by bit, blocked out in units, fed in uniform daily doses, etc. Out of school the learner tries, he experiments, he makes mistakes in grammar and choice of words. He is corrected, he is helped, but long theoretical discussions of his errors are not typical (Brown and Bellugi, 1972). Eventually, he learns to speak just

---

[2] Dorothy Bromage, *The Oakmont Nongraded Primary Program*, Claremont, Calif.: Claremont Unified School District, 1967.

about in the way others around him speak, with their grammar, emphasis, inflection, and even tonal quality. We may, with Bruner (1968), Goodlad (1968), Hart (1969), Roberts (1970), Ellison (1972), and others question the "mastery of content" orientation.

While the concept of curriculum content may have been justifiable historically, the notion today is disturbingly questionable, in view of the continuous knowledge explosion. Without underestimating the value of the *tools of learning*, we must entertain the proposition that the process of learning rather than its products must receive major emphasis (Bernard, 1973, p. 311). We cannot prepare pupils to deal with concepts which do not yet exist on the premise of curriculum mastery. Half the pupils now in elementary schools will be occupationally engaged in jobs which are nonexistent today (McCully, 1969).

The aims of education today might well be:

1. Learning to enjoy the process of education, i.e., learning to love learning,
2. Evolving a concept of self which permits the pupil to say, "I am a worthy person quite capable of learning those things which the events of today and tomorrow demand," and
3. Mastering the tools of knowledge (reading, writing, talking, and computation) by using them in the daily events of school living.

Few persons are ready to abandon subject matter content. Most will admit that some knowledges are more significant than others, but, while we can cite extremes, many areas are less readily colored black or white. If it really does not make any difference what the pupil learns, then there need be no hurry about discontinuing present content, provided content is not used to place the child on the rack or cut him to pieces. Continuous progress may be the device by which transition from the tradition of content to the urgency of process may be effected. Thus continuous progress makes a contribution to the recognition of differences by its emphasis on tackling tasks which are developmentally appropriate in terms of where one was at the beginning of the learning period. It also has the potential of serving a transitional function to innovations still in various stages of formulation.

The ultimate [of what the nongraded situation may be] might be realized when each child is intrinsically motivated to work to his full capacity and is faced with problem-solving situations at his level of competence and capacity. It is necessary to deal with group situations in our massively populated school systems. Some framework for capitalizing on this child's commitment to his ultimate development must be thought out. The organization could be one in which collections of these youngsters, each of whom is a group unto himself, are set up so that these clusters are taught at the same time. They would be at nearly the same problem-solving level, in a particular substantive area relative to their ability, their desire, their intents, and their skill in learning. Any teacher will agree that this is devoutly to be wished and represents the ideal. This remains the ultimate nongrading ideal, however. Immediate nongrading of a different sort can be a practical reality. It can open ways for teachers so that steps toward the ideal come more readily and easily.[3]

Innovative packages

The authors have noted that schools in which there is pupil, teacher, and parent enthusiasm about the educational approach, there are likely to be several innovations occurring simultaneously. This is the "innovative package" which combines various concepts such as team teaching, flexible scheduling, and independent study (Petrequin, 1968). South Brunswick, New Jersey, created a school system so attractive that parents from neighboring districts were willing to pay extra tuition to have their children attend its schools. This was done by combining learning centers, continuous progress, individualized instruction, independent study, and classes in human relations for teacher, administrators, and pupils (Harrison, 1970).

[3] Maurice Hillson, "The Nongraded School: A Dynamic Concept," in David W. Beggs, III, and Edward G. Buffie (eds.), *Nongraded Schools in Action*, Bloomington, Ind.: Indiana University Press, 1967, p. 34.

NONGRADED SCHOOLS IN ACTION

Joseph G. Wilson Elementary School

A school in The Dalles, Oregon, provides an example of the continuous progress concept. The building in which the program is housed is the oldest in the city and thus demonstrates that implementation need not necessarily wait upon equipment and facilities. The staff has shown that continuous progress is an idea rather than a thing.

Premise for Continuous Progress Education
at Joseph G. Wilson Elementary

1. The continuous progress school is not an overwhelming kind of organization which requires months and years of a staff's time to study, create, and launch. It is not a highly structured program requiring a complex framework. It is really not a thing at all, but a *process,* a spirit. A school does not actually have to organize anything in order to embrace and encourage the continuous progress concept. The continuous progress way of school life is quite simple and natural and extremely essential. It is compelling not complex.
2. There really is no such thing as a "grade." Yet we proceed in the traditional elementary school as though we do have a precise and definitive identification. As we hold on to the myth, we injure and handicap boys and girls emotionally. Why have we for so long continued this practice?
3. The best way to start a continuous progress school is to stop a number of practices. The moment these things are stopped, right then, with nothing else being done to create it, the continuous progress school begins! What should be stopped?
    a. Rigid ability grouping. Instruction needs to be personalized and this can best be done within the confines and social structure of the heterogeneous classroom.
    b. Passing and failing children. Knowing the harm failure and flunking children does, supported by research which identifies the harm of being branded a failure, we must stop this terrible practice!
    c. Forcing children on to new learning before they

204

have the present one conquered. Stop this throughout our school, and we have taken a major step toward continuous progress.

d. *Timing* children's learning. We expect so much learning by a certain time, i.e., 3.9 by the end of third grade, and the like.

e. Prepackaging of education. This is the organizing of a certain body of knowledge and skills into a "grade's worth" as, in fourth grade, *this* is what we will learn.

f. Ignoring all the things we know about child growth and development. We know that:
   1. Children learn at different rates and in unique ways.
   2. Learning should be a satisfying process.
   3. Children learn in lags and spurts.
   4. Learning should be related to the maturity of the learner.
   5. Learning is best served when the learner has appropriate motivation.

g. Reporting on children! Destroy the report card and one of the great enemies of the continuous progress (or schools of any kind) has been eliminated![4]

h. Stop all practices (and we have quite a few!) which in any way degrade a child, steal from him his self-respect, cause him to weaken his self-esteem, or say to him, inferentially, "You aren't much good."

i. Labeling children. Phrases such as "slow learner," "immature," and "gifted" can only restrict the child's development.

j. Giving the same assignment to every child and then judging all children's work with one standard.

4. If we want a continuous progress school, the following condition will prevail in our school at all times: *Every child is constantly kept in a learning milieu—in assignments, activities, enterprises, and endeavors in which he is being successful or has a reasonable chance of being successful.*

---

[4] The reader is reminded that the technique or instrument is far less important than the persons using the tools. Blaming grades and report cards may reduce the guilt of some teachers who should examine the things they do to diminish the pupil's sense of worth. See point 6.

5. Destroy the concept in your minds and in the minds of our parents that an elementary school education consists of *six* magical years. It should never be less than six, but for many children it should be seven and for some even eight.[5] For, as long as a child is taking in learning which is essential to an elementary school program, why force him into a junior high school without that learning, knowing full well he will not succeed?

6. In the continuous progress concept, there is no place for "remedial" reading or remedial anything. If we truly proceed in a continuous progress manner, no child could possibly need remediation, for he will never be in trouble! He will never be forced into learning for which he is not prepared and thus become a remedial candidate.

7. In the continuous progress school, the individual child's potential and selfness is let out like a kite—it takes the "wind" when needed or slacks off when that is necessary.

8. It is a great thrill for principals and teachers to be able to say, "Every child in this school is reading successfully!" And this situation is so very possible and essential.

9. If we have continuous progress in reading alone, we will provide our elementary pupils with so many more chances of learning to read well. Take all of the time necessary to teach reading and the related language arts!

10. The parent-teacher conference, with the weaknesses it does have, is the most satisfactory way of reporting pupil progress. Let's remove any existing barriers involved with our present parent-teacher conferences in order that they truly project a better form of communication to parents concerning their child's school progress.

11. In the continuous progress school, such terms as "grade level," "below grade level," "falling behind," "my slow group," "making little progress," and "problem reader" are taboo; they have no meaning now and are considered "swear words" to a continuous progress staff.

---

[5] Research does not support the assertion that elementary schools should consist of a minimum number of years. Acceleration has, in fact, more arguments in its favor than there are against it.

12. No child will be taught anything today he already knows!
(Philosophy Credit to Dr. Marshall Jameson).

The principal of the Wilson Elementary School, Darryl Corey, had been intending for some years to implement changes but decided after a short workshop in continuous progress that the time was *now*. Teachers were called back early in the fall and the concepts were presented, discussed, and evaluated. One teacher said, "I'll go along if I don't have to give grades." Another was concerned about having time for individual and small group activities. It was decided that the teacher aide program should be stepped up. Thousands of hours of help were provided by junior and senior high school students and by volunteer parents before the end of the school year. It should also be noted that at the end of the year many teachers reported that they found a surprising number of pupils quite capable of independent study.

Corey responded to the author's questions as follows:

Q: What are the first few days of school like?
A: It used to be that teachers insisted on having all their books on hand so they could get a "vigorous start." Now the first few days are spent giving tests to determine status, listening to pupils discover their interests, talking with pupils to determine what personal concerns might impede learning. Then teachers send aides to various libraries to get first grade readers, third grade social studies books, fifth grade arithmetics, etc., so pupils and small groups can have appropriate materials. If the third grade teacher steals subject matter from the fifth grade teacher then that is the latter's problem. Initially there was confusion but pupils settled down. Historically pupils settled down and then confusion accelerated as varying speeds and statuses became evident and tensions mounted.

Q: Do parents object to having no grades?
A: The results surprised me. Among the parents of our 800 plus pupils, one mother wanted grades. I told her that we would either grade the child or enroll him in another school next year. She said, "Let it ride for now," and last week she enrolled her son for the next school year.

Q: What would you consider the biggest change which was made?
A: Actually there were many. The one I think of right now is removing the "finishing tape." I mean that we do not expect children to end the third grade with test scores which average 3.9. We are still concerned with progress. We still use standardized tests. We still have subject matter—we just take away the finishing tape—the expectation standard. Nothing is changed as far as learning is concerned. Differences still exist. Some pupils are at, some are beyond, and some are below grade standards. But each pupil is successful in doing as well as he can. The finish line as an objective is removed, hence the feeling that one is a failure or that he can coast is less likely to be aroused.

Q: What about those who still dislike school?
A: They are still with us. We help some who would dislike schools under the graded system. We are still studying others. We have a little more hope than formerly that fewer will find the dissatisfaction in school that is an accompaniment of failure. Continuous progress is not a panacea. It probably does more for how teachers view children than it does to make learning enthusiasts of all children.

Nongraded high schools

High schools in which the nongraded concept is used also accept the premise that students do not develop at an equal pace in all academic areas. Bright individuals are not forced to wait at grade barriers (see Figure 8.3) and deliberate learners are not frustrated by striving to maintain what for them is an impossible pace. The organizational aspect of the nongraded high school consists of breaking up one year of this or that into a much larger number of units. In Middletown, Rhode Island, for instance, instead of six years of social studies, there are over 300 social studies concepts. At Nova High School in Fort Lauderdale, Florida, there are sixty units or steps in each subject field which could span six years. At Miami Springs, Florida, any given subject, geometry for example, may be studied in any of several phases, such as:

Phase 1—Courses at this level are designed to help students who are quite deficient in basic skills and

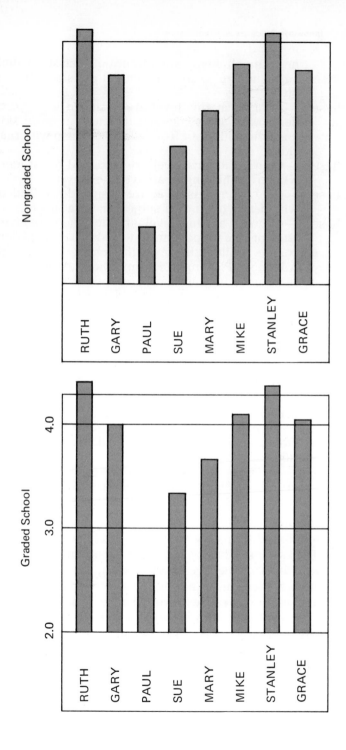

FIGURE 8-3. *Pupil achievement in the third grade. Taking away the "finishing tape" of grade expectation.*

need much help and attention. Classes will be small in size so that individual assistance can be given.

Phase 2—Courses at this level are designed to help students who are somewhat deficient in basic skills and who will profit from additional help with these skills.

Phase 3—Courses at this level are designed for students who are achieving in an average way.

Phase 4—Courses at this level are designed for students who desire to study a subject in great depth.

Phase 5—Courses at this level are designed to give a student the opportunity to take a college-level course while still in high school through the Advanced Placement Examination program.

Phase 6—Courses at this level are special seminars for selected students who have demonstrated an ability to work well on their own course of study with the help of an instructor.

Phase Q—Courses at this level are labeled QUEST and are open to students who have demonstrated outstanding ability in a given area and who possess high motivation for working primarily alone for extended periods of time. (SPECIAL REQUIREMENTS FOR ADMISSION TO THIS PROGRAM)

Phase S—Courses at this level require special criteria which are noted in the specific course descriptions.

Phase X—Courses at this level are open to all students. No criteria have been established to predict success at this level. [Crafts, chorus, band, team sports].[6]

While Corey (1970) asserts that a child may spend more than, but not less than, six years in the elementary school, Brown (1963) seems to have no concern for minimum time in a high school. In a space age, says Brown, the criterion for placement is achievement, not IQ or age. If one can speed through high school and speed through college, he is then more likely to pursue the graduate work which is coming to be increasingly popular and increasingly demanded by employers. Brown, as does Corey, uses the race track simile: Something is done for the students who can "run a faster mile." [7]

[6] Miami Springs Senior High School. *Schedule of Classes.* Fall 1967—Spring 1968.

[7] B. Frank Brown, "The Nongraded High School," *Phi Delta Kappan* 44 (1963): 209. In this connection, it is pertinent to note that Shannon, in surveying and

Major points of difference between the conventional and ungraded high school are:

Classes vary greatly in size, from 125 in typing, a sort of mechanical encounter for students, to fifteen in deficiency levels of reading.

There are no study halls in the ungraded schools; students are expected to take responsibility for their own study.[8]

Considerable emphasis is placed on "discovery" in the ungraded school. This, in its simplest form, means curiosity linked to action.

Some pupils in the tenth grade begin college level work in their Quest and advanced placement programs.

The concepts of freedom and responsibility are exercised frequently in the ungraded school.

Ungraded high schools require bountiful academic fare—dozens of courses rather than one—and consequently place heavy demands on teachers for participation, often with pupils, in curriculum planning. The need for variety is indicated by the above description of phases.

As was the case with Joseph G. Wilson Elementary School, Miami Springs Senior High School in Florida emphasizes that nongradedness is a point of view, a process, and a spirit rather than a thing:

Philosophy and Objectives

Miami Springs Senior High School is dedicated to the individual and his pursuit of excellence. We are committed to a belief in the worth and uniqueness of the individual. In order to foster each individual's potentialities, the educational milieu should offer varied opportunities for successful learning and growth.

We affirm the value of differences within and among human beings; we strive to encourage variability and to

---

summarizing the studies made on acceleration, found that none of the alleged advantages of taking a year for each grade are based on fact. Younger and more able students when in college win more scholarship honors, take part in more activities (including football), and are elected to more offices, and on graduation become nationally known in greater proportions. Dan C. Shannon, "What Research Says About Acceleration," *Phi Delta Kappan* 39 (1957): 70–73.

[8] When the authors visited Nova High School, they learned that some students rode bikes for several miles to school because they had projects which occupied them until five-thirty or six. Riding the bus would have entailed leaving school at three or three-thirty.

recognize social responsibility within the framework of our democratic ideals. Realizing that learning involves many dimensions of intellect as well as the senses and emotions, we seek to develop and utilize the awareness of inherent human processes in order to cultivate knowledge, attitudes, emotions, and skills. We recognize man's propensity for exploration and learning. Therefore, we strive toward the following objectives:

1. To place the student into an intelligent environment in which he might thrive and grow in relationship to the ideas, problems, and accomplishments of mankind.
2. To provide a program which aims toward an increasing acceptance of responsibility by the student.
3. To encourage each student to discover and develop his potentialities.
4. To develop an understanding, respect, and love of self in order that meaningful and compassionate relationships with others may evolve.
5. To protect and encourage free inquiry and to stress the heuristics of the disciplines. Therefore, the teacher-student relationship should promote, not stifle, individual styles of learning.
6. To promote freedom of choice and to guide the student toward an understanding of the responsibilities of freedom.
7. To assist the student to interpret, evaluate, and *synthesize* knowledge in order to discover its meaning and uses in new situations.
8. To facilitate insight into the interrelatedness of the disciplines.

An operational definition

A nongraded program as presently in practice at Miami Springs Senior High School is defined as follows:

1. Students are scheduled into courses required for graduation on criteria other than chronological age.
2. The curriculum is organized so that five appropriate learning environments are represented in each academic discipline.
3. Students are able to move from one learning environment to another in each required course at any time during the year when their performance indicates that the move would be salutary to their academic progress.

4. Success or failure for the student is under his own control.
5. Students are individually scheduled across subject offerings commensurate with a functional level in each subject, as predicted by derived success indices.
6. Each teacher has the freedom to schedule class meetings the way he sees fit.
7. Some students are free to work independently of a class for varying lengths of time.

THE IMPACT OF THE NONGRADED CONCEPT

Effect on pupil achievement

Test results of nongraded organization have provided little assurance for the adherents of the plan (McLoughlin, 1968). Such surveys as have been conducted, to put it most optimistically, indicate that there is no loss in pupil achievement as a result of nongradedness. This, to those whose educational philosophy includes concern for the whole child—his mental health, his self-concept, his social adjustment, his individuality, and creativity—is a major victory. All such areas of development have increased chances for realization at no cost to academic achievement. Even for those who view the function of the school as the acquisition of factual information, the test data suggest that there is no need to become alarmed over changes which produce no practical or demonstrable subject matter loss.

If research on continuous progress is to be most pertinent, however, it is probable that measures different from the conventional achievement and ability tests should be used (Edmonds et al., 1973). The point is heightened by Jensen's assertion that compensatory education of the past few years apparently has failed because it did not raise the IQ or academic achievement of disadvantaged children. He then wrote, *in a footnote,* that medical disabilities were detected and remedied in certain compensatory programs (Jensen, 1969, p. 3). Head Start programs, he observed, had favorable effects on children's self-confidence, their motivation, and their attitudes toward school. Hence it appears that, when devices to evaluate freedom of inquiry, self-concepts, and compassion in human relations are constructed, research can provide better assessments of educational innovation.

213

Studies are not available to prove that pupils learn any more or better when they are involved in nongraded schools, have access to programmed learning, use computer aided instruction, or are taught by teams of teachers (Heathers, 1966). Research has not been built into the "bloodstream" of American education; schools are probably the only large-scale institutions in the United States that do not systematically update the skills of employees (Goodlad, 1962, 1969). Research data are lacking also because (1) there is little consensus on what is meant by a particular innovation, (2) there is no functional agreement as to whether the school is made for the child or whether the child's role is to contribute to achievement statistics, and (3) there is lack of agreement on whether the outcomes of education should be expressed in terms of academic knowledge or whether attitudes, values, self-concepts, and socialization are of equal merit. Because there are no adequate instruments to measure the latter, they too often are regarded as intangibles not worth evaluation (Guba and Horvat, 1970).

Visits to a number of ungraded schools, interviews, and a sampling of the literature on continuous progress reveal that there are great gaps between the theory espoused by a particular school and the practices which occur in the classroom. These are not necessarily deficiencies to be remedied so much as they are conditions to be assessed. Another consideration, and one that merits study, is that any novel practice in education has not really had a fair trial until teachers have been *pre*pared through involvement and are themselves factors in the consideration and implementation of the innovation.

Effect on pupil behavior

The effect of nongradedness on pupil achievement is less important than the effect on the pupil's emotional responses. The eagerness with which pupils react to continuous progress is exhilarating to the observer. It seems to suggest that, when the pupil is treated a little differently from others in the room, he begins to feel the excitement of autonomy. When he perceives that he has a role in his own educational plans, this tends to produce involvement. His role may be limited to determining pace only, and not content, but even that is an improvement over being told what to study and how fast one is to achieve. When he sees the purposeful activity of a roomful of "continuous progress pupils," the observer is tempted to hypothesize that the lack of results cited in the foregoing section must be a function of inadequate research design and instruments, that researchers have placed undue emphasis on knowledge at the expense of personality factors.

Pupil response is indicated by the low dropout rates of ungraded schools. Middletown, Rhode Island, for example, reported a dropout rate of 1 percent as compared to the national average of about 30 percent. It is claimed that pupils put forth greater effort in ungraded than they do in graded schools (Rollins, 1969). This does not agree with McLoughlin's statements that there is scant evidence of superior student adjustment in ungraded schools and that the contribution of nongraded schools to social and emotional development is marginal. He observes, however, that there are many variations of the interpretation of the meaning of nongraded schools. He concludes that nongraded schools are defensible only because graded schools are indefensible.

The effect of nongradedness on teachers

Just as there are styles of learning, so too are there styles of teaching. If it is ineffective to require that all pupils should learn through the verbal symbolic methods of reading, it may also be ineffective to require that all teachers use the continuous progress approach. Huxley (1956) long ago observed that the major issue is that the learner must be induced to expend some effort. A teacher who wants and needs the structure of grades, firm schedules, and standards for promotion will be uncomfortable in the nongraded school. However, as with styles of learning, where pupils are led to develop through capitalizing on strengths, teachers also can evolve new skills by varying their teaching emphases.

If teachers are not in agreement with the shift to nongradedness, they will continue to teach as they always have even though an official shift is made. This is the reason the involvement of teachers in the innovative package is emphasized. If teachers are not interested in any innovation, two alternatives are available:

215

(1) They can be required, by administrative pressure, to participate in interpersonal process groups. There, an attempt may be made to get them to face themselves and evaluate their impact on others. Because facilitators of interpersonal process groups have so much trouble with recalcitrant persons, however, and because resisters can so readily impede the progress of others, such pressure to participate is of questionable value.

(2) Help can be given those who are willing, in the hope that teachers favoring unexamined adherence to conventional methods may be either caught up in the current or forced out. Innovators may be able to create a milieu which will attract the recalcitrants. Adherence to conventional methods after examination is quite different from adherence without openminded evaluation.

A factor that should be noted about new programs in education is that aging occurs immediately and inevitably, and that obsolescence may occur simultaneously with aging. Plans once effective and exciting tend to become routine and boring. Many ideas in education—the Dalton Plan, the Winnetka Plan, progressive education, the comprehensive high˜school, the sixteen Carnegie units—were once hailed with enthusiasm. Unfortunately, high expectations promoted disillusion and contributed to their being discarded. Moreover, most named above dealt with administrative organization and structure; needed changes in teacher and administrator attitudes were not stressed. The need for continuous teacher and pupil involvement in the process of change was not emphasized. These omissions, rather than flaws in underlying theory, in part were responsible for the demise of these programs.

Newness of a program—the Hawthorne Effect—is a factor in the success of new programs. Variety is an antidote for boredom. Both are ingredients of enthusiasm. The fact that pupils are in a new grade with a new teacher is not, it seems, enough to sustain the zest which accompanies novelty. The constant revision of a plan, its evaluation by teachers and pupils, and its involvement of all concerned—teachers, pupils, and parents—is the essential aspect of innovative impact.

A society whose maturing consists simply of acquiring more firmly established ways of doing things is headed for the graveyard—even if it learns to do these things with greater and greater skill. *In the ever-renewing society what matures is a system or framework within which continuous innovation, renewal and rebirth can occur.*[9]

The effect of nongradedness on "intangibles"

There are questions about innovative impact which tend to be ignored because techniques for their evaluation have not yet been devised. We are convinced that continuous progress has really significant impact on (1) the pupil's self-regarding attitudes, and (2) the development of a love for, and the habit of, independent and autonomous learning. For teachers, the important effect may be in terms of the excitement which teaching has as a way of life. Does the teacher's zest for an innovation lure persons to teaching who might otherwise go to other activities? Does the teacher's *elan* infect the pupil's enthusiasm, not just for the academic but for life? Are youngsters better prepared for processes of continuous change by innovative practices than they were formerly?

The main value of innovation, however, well may reside in the process of looking for, and implementing, new and better ways of teaching. In this way other improvements in education may be conceptualized and developed. Unless this occurs, nongradedness will not long remain innovative. If it or any of its accompaniments can give impetus to the search for further improvement, they have a justification for being. If their development can make educators comfortable with the process of change or uncomfortable with monotony, much has been accomplished.

Meanwhile, materials which lend themselves to individualized study must be developed and made available. These can, in part, be prepared beforehand, especially when working with young people. They can also be developed as the program matures. As with other aspects of the program, materials should be subject to continuous evaluation and revision. Starting small with manageable units (one subject or one class at a time) should provide the school staff with adequate "learning by doing" opportunities. Unless there is a variety of learning activity packets and unless these can be adapted to a

[9] John W. Gardner, *Self-Renewal* (New York: Harper and Row, Publishers, Inc., 1964), p. 5.

wide range of pupil differences, teachers will encounter difficulties in serving as educational consultants to their pupils.

PSYCHOLOGICAL VALUES AND CONTINUOUS PROGRESS

Educational orientation

If one subscribes to the conventional belief that the acquisition of knowledge and the development of skills is the proper purpose of education, then measurement of outcomes can be the criterion of successful education. Such a position implies that there are predictable conditions with which one can be prepared to cope in advance of actually meeting with them. Either the carrot before or the stick behind, if they produce effort, is justifiable. Short of cruelty, there are many who feel that coercive discipline has a quite proper place in school. Neale (1969), for instance, shows that some pupil resistance to formal learning is more effectively counteracted by punishment than by persuasion. Conversely, Breslaw (1973) reported gratifying results, even at the college level, when all threats and punitive measures were eliminated and bonuses, credits, and achievements were substituted for the conventional grades, passing, and absences were noted.

If one is swayed by the argument that change is taking place so rapidly that one cannot prepare in advance to meet unknown exigencies, then the function of learning assumes a different quality. The goals of learning with this orientation are (1) to use every legitimate means possible to build a robust, durable, and positive self-concept and (2) to provide such success and challenge in daily activities that the pursuit of school tasks is enjoyable and learning and self-renewal become established habits.

Keeping the latter in mind, but not necessarily excluding the former, a prognostication is presented of what might happen to pupils in the ungraded school.[10]

The natural curiosity and innate urge to grow and become, which is characteristic of healthy children, will be recognized and encouraged when lock-step programs and prescribed time schedules are replaced by continuous progress.

[10] The theses which follow are illustrated and explained in more detail in Chapter 2 as "Propositions for the Facilitation of Learning."

Continuous progress will enhance the teacher's opportunities to consider not only pupils' different growth rates but also their different motivations. Such recognition will enhance the pupils' self-concepts while interpersonal comparisons serve to endanger it.

The small groups which are a part of continuous progress will make it possible for teachers to do more about recognizing unique learning styles as well as different speeds of learning.

Each pupil's self-regard will be enhanced by recognition and acceptance of his idiosyncratic speed and style of learning.

When teachers are not faced with the necessity of getting every pupil over the hurdles in a prescribed time interval, they will not be so likely to be irritated by the deviant learner (either fast or slow, intuitive or deliberate), which will result in the pupil's seeing a more acceptable image of himself.

The pupil's self-image will be bolstered not only because others view him favorably, but also because he will gain confidence by having dealt with appropriate tasks and challenges successfully.

Because continuous progress places much emphasis on the processes of learning, pupils will be prepared better for subsequent life changes. The processes of learning will have greater likelihood of becoming habitual when invidious interpersonal comparisons are not a built-in feature of education.

Because innovation is typically a source of enthusiasm on the part of teachers, pupils (because of the phenomenon of contagion) also will be more likely to become learning enthusiasts. And the enthusiasm of pupils reciprocally will reinfect teachers.

Because there are multiple causes of any human behavior, continuous progress will not be a panacea for all educational ailments; it will not meet all pupils' needs; it will not make all teachers comfortable. It is probable, though, that continuous progress possesses points of superiority over graded organization.

SUMMARY

Nongraded schools make it feasible to implement the concept of continuous progress. There is no one organizational plan which is called nongraded, but whatever the nuances, the basic ideas are to eliminate thinking and acting in terms of grade levels and to reduce the temptation to evaluate pupils negatively because of different speeds and styles of learning. The design is to adjust pace and curriculum to the needs of the pupil. If educators should decide that process has more merit than mastery of content, continuous progress may constitute a transitional medium.

Nongraded schools and continuous progress will have maximum impact when they are combined with other innovations, for example, team teaching, independent study, computer assisted instruction, which thus constitute an innovative package. The innovative package has additional value when, in addition to various educational plans, it includes teacher involvement in planning and assessment. An illustrative nongraded school in The Dalles, Oregon, emphasizes that the pupil does not repeat materials he already knows, is not being pushed ahead when he is not prepared, and is not graded competitively. More rather than fewer tests are given, but with the purpose of finding a place to start rather than determining comparative rank or passing or failing. At the high school level, continuous progress involves breaking subject matter units into numerous concepts, stressing mastery of those concepts without regard to time limitations.

All in all, nongradedness and continuous progress are matters of spirit and process rather than tangibles. Research has not proven that continuous progress is superior to other plans as far as academic achievement is concerned. Some hope remains, however, at least in terms of humanistic psychology, that the spirit of continuous progress may be reflected in an elevated esprit de corps for the school and in strengthened ego concepts for individuals. The promise seems to reside as much in effects on teacher personality and on teacher-student transactions as it does in organization.

SUGGESTED ADDITIONAL READINGS

Beggs, David W., III, and Buffie, Edward G. eds. *Nongraded Schools in Action.* Bloomington, Ind.: Indiana University Press, 1967. Various chapters describe the philosophy, problems, and procedures used in different nongraded schools, with examples drawn from both elementary and secondary nongraded schools.

Fantini, Mario D. "The Reform of Teacher Education: A Proposal for New York State." *Phi Delta Kappan* 53 (1972): 476–79. Reforms in education go beyond the classroom to social and political considerations. One prospect is to reform teacher education, including visitation and participation of teachers-to-be in various schools, and another is to reeducate teacher educators.

Mitzel, Harold E. "The Impending Instruction Revolution." *Phi Delta Kappan* 51 (April 1970): 434–39. Self-determined pace, beginning learning at an individually appropriate point, wealth of instructional material, revision of evaluation procedures, and, of course, individualized programs are among the elements in the education revolution. Much of the discussion is highly pertinent to continuous progress.

Robinson, Donald W. "Alternative Schools: Do They Promise System Reform?" *Phi Delta Kappan* 54 (1973): 433, 443. The current innovation is alternative schools. In introducing this issue of *Phi Delta Kappan*, with several articles on alternative education, Robinson says the theme is the same as it was in the 1960's— acknowledging life styles and learning styles of pupils. The answer is the same—the quality and behavior of individual teachers.

CHAPTER 9

Independent Study

Words such as freedom, choice, responsibility, accountability, and independence flow freely from the mouths of educators, but the words have varied meanings. Freedom, to one person may mean doing just what he likes; to another, the privilege of doing what one wishes if he observes the rights and privileges of others, the kind of freedom referred to in Article I of the Bill of Rights. Or it may mean freedom to do what one wishes as long as the action is approved by an authority, whether premier, president, parent, or pedagogue (Schrag, 1972).

Independent study, as is the case with other words, has several definitions. Some of these varied meanings will be discussed in this chapter. The purpose of this discussion is not so much to settle on a meaning as it is to create awareness of alternative concepts. Like other educational ideas, the more each is studied, the less likely it seems that simple definitions are satisfactory. It may be less important to decide on definitions than it is to provide a basis for dialogue. The really important matter is to devise teaching-learning situations that will be more effective than current practices in meeting educational objectives.

BASIC CONCEPTS

Self-paced learning. There are three conceptualizations of the meaning of independence in educational circles. One of these

222

refers to self-pacing, another to individual programs, and the third to self-selection of activities. Learning activity packets (LAP; see Glossary) can serve as self-pacers. Each packet may consist of an outline, together with suggested readings, activities to be performed, and a set of questions, the answers to which will determine whether the pupil should restudy or go on to another learning activity. Packets often are arranged in sequence, and completion of one entitles the pupil to have access to the next. A packet in arithmetic may consist of problems dealing with division of four digit numbers by two digit numbers. When a prescribed number of problems has been answered correctly, the pupil may tackle division by three digit numbers. Whatever the contents of the LAP (language, social studies, or science projects), the variable is time. Some students may take three or four days while others may take two weeks to complete a packet. In high school, LAPs usually require more time, at least several weeks but typically less than a semester. The use of learning activity packets decreases the chances that harmful interpersonal comparisons will be made, but does not eliminate them. Some teachers may still evaluate more highly the pupil who uses the least time. If quality of work is the criterion, it will be less necessary for the slow learner to leave the field with the words, "I don't care," because he must salvage his ego by not wanting that which is unavailable. Flexible time intervals make it understandable and acceptable to proceed at varied rates.[1]

Such technological aids as tape recorders, reading accelerators, and language laboratories may be employed as LAP components. Depending on how these are used, such technological aids may also be part of individual programs.

Individual programs. Theoretically, at least, individual programs refer to various ways to achieve similar goals. Instead of a single channel, simple learning presentation, there are attempts to adjust the channel of approach to each pupil's style of learning. Such approaches call for the development of

---

[1] One criticism on the matter of time might be noted: variable times may lead to the phenomenon of "race-horsing." Some students rush through learning packets in a perfunctory fashion. Their concern seems to be getting credit for having completed the packet. They show little interest in content, forget the topic immediately upon completion, and follow-up testing reveals inadequate mastery.

various resource units, many texts instead of one, and multi-media activities. Pupil contracts, individual projects, discovery, and creative endeavors are examples and aspects of individual programs.

The nongraded school with its emphasis on continuous progress (see Chapter 8) is a whole school approach to individual programs. Recent and vivid examples of individual programs include use of many technological teaching aids. Some of those which promote individual programs include devices that may go into an individual learning carrel, such as tapes, records, film strips, 35 mm. slides. Talking typewriters, language laboratories (depending on how they are used), autotutors, computer assisted instruction, and reading accelerators also are technological aids which facilitate individualization.

Independent study. Independent study, according to the *Dictionary of Education,* is carried on with a minimum or a complete absence of external guidance. In the school setting, there is probably always a "minimum" of guidance but the meaning of minimum calls for examination. In one situation it may mean that the pupil is released from a physical setting to carry out an assigned task; in another it may mean that he chooses what, as well as where, to study. Another interpretation of independent study relates to pace; pupils study an assigned task in the classroom, but finish at different times. It is felt that there is a significant difference between guidance and assignment or prescription, even prescription on an individual basis. Either independent study or individually prescribed instruction may be read into the following definitions:

For example, independent study is regarded as . . . learning activity largely motivated by the learner's own aims to learn and largely rewarded in terms of its intrinsic values. Such activity as carried on under the auspices of secondary schools is somewhat independent of the class or other group organization dominant in the past and present secondary school instructional practices, and it utilizes the services of teacher and other professional personnel primarily as resources for the learner.[2]

. . . a learning situation within the school day which allows a student to develop personal competencies through experiences as an individual but in interaction with others when needed. It is characterized by freedom from constant supervision. Students read, write, contemplate, listen to records and tapes, view, record, memorize, create, build, practice, exercise, experiment, examine, analyze, investigate, question, discover, and converse. Independent study emphasizes the individual's role in learning. It implies that all students possess potentialities for self-initiative, self discipline, resourcefulness, productivity, and self-evaluation.[3]

of this chapter is akin to that used in Syosset (New York) High School (Plunkett, 1969). Students are allowed to select, with faculty approval, and pursue, under guidance, topics of their own choosing. They select the time, place, pace, and nature of the independent learning.

A RATIONALE FOR INDEPENDENT STUDY

The need for continuous learning

Of the many innovations designed to motivate and facilitate learning, it would be difficult to find any more important than independent study, especially in terms of an individual's becoming a lifelong learner. At any time it is an aim of education to produce an individual who knows enough and has sufficient skill that he no longer needs a teacher or parent. In times of rapid change this need for independence in learning becomes greater. The McGraw-Hill Book Company, in a recent advertisement, congratulated young men who were beginning their college freshman year as engineering students, noting at

[2] W. M. Alexander and V. A. Hines, *Independent Study in Secondary Schools,* Cooperative Research Project No. 2669, (Gainesville, Fla.: University of Florida, 1966), p. 67.
[3] David W. Beggs, III, and Edward G. Buffie, *Independent Study: Bold New Venture* (Bloomington, Ind.: Indiana University Press, 1965), p. 2.

the same time that a large portion of what the students learned in that year would be obsolete by the time they were graduated. This suggests that the student must learn how to study independently, and acquire a taste for it, if he is to survive in his future professional world. Continuous progress, computer assisted instruction, team teaching, modular scheduling, and other innovations must capitalize on the opportunities provided in the independent study concept.

Rapid technological change and the knowledge explosion tend to render the goals of subject matter mastery obsolete. If, however, the process of learning, learning how to learn, and the enjoyment of learning are taken into account, subject matter mastery may be a source of satisfaction. There is evidence that rigorous and relevant learning experiences make subsequent learning easier.

The need for relevance

Even young children are known to utter the criticism (in their own terminology) that schools lack relevancy. One sixth grade girl at Kalakawa School in Honolulu, during a summer school, said, "They should let us talk sometimes about things that are important to us." The word "sometimes" includes more wisdom than educational critics occasionally reveal. Some of the pupils at Kalakawa School who were "culturally different" *wanted* to study arithmetic and grammar. A fifth grade boy, in response to the question, "What do you think of school this summer?" said, "I wish they wouldn't play around so much. I'd like to have more arithmetic. I'm good at that." It seems that relevance, in part, is a matter of what teaching approaches do to the ego. These "disadvantaged children" suggest that relevance is not a matter of either/or but one of "sometimes I'd like to be recognized."

The need for independent study at the high school level may be somewhat greater than in the elementary school. The plea for relevancy has behind it a degree of sophistication. Pupils can document their interest in contemporary issues, those concerns of the day they read about, discuss, and view on television. They are closer to the reality of getting a job and deciding what to do about military service. In addition, the pressure of peer groups becomes greater as their maturity parallels increasing social contacts. They are being weaned away from home and they are less inclined to accept adult prescription.

No decisions need be made here about what the course of study should include.[4] Teachers should, however, examine such questions as the relation of school curriculum to the daily lives of pupils. News media, for example, are a part of the lives of pupils and merit evaluation in terms of the relative worth of sources, reliability of facts, the propriety of reporter's opinions, the impossibility of obtaining all the data, the impact of emotions on the part of reporters and receivers, and the role of profit making (Langer, 1970).

The need for independence

In addition to the matters of relevance and contemporaneity, there are matters of (1) being mature enough to be self-directive and responsible, (2) having a voice in decisions that affect one's life, and (3) the apparent rejection of the culture of the old and concern for youth culture. Each of these intensifies the need for taking advantage of the opportunities which rest in independent study.

It is possible for pupils even in the primary grades to work constructively, cooperatively, and independently. The authors observed, at the Corte Madera Schools in California, primary children working in groups of three to seven, *by themselves*, in rooms clustered about a large learning center. The teachers were able to see into each of the several rooms surrounding the learning center but might not, for an hour or so, actually enter the room where the children were. It seems possible that some of the inability of young pupils to exercise independence results from the teacher's inability to allow for it.

The desire to be self-directed and responsible is cited as one of the traits of adolescence (Erikson, 1968). Yet excessive direction by teachers is likely to result in apathetic conformity, defiance, or an attempt to escape. The opportunity to plan and

[4] The authors have resisted the recommendation that this book include suggestions for curricular content. Aside from endorsing acquisition of the tools of learning, we feel that would detract from our emphasis on process. While we would endorse content in professional education, we are not at all sure that there is *a* content for general education. Again, love for, and skill in, learning is the concern we wish to highlight.

DO I HAVE TO DO JUST WHAT I WANT TO DO?

be selective quite frequently results in wholehearted pupil participation (Howard, 1969). The need to have a voice in decisions which affect one's own life is a persistent human characteristic. This urge toward self-assertion shows up, for example, when youths reject their parents' advice, or demands, on matters of dress and grooming. Given a choice, they behave in ways which adults consider quite responsible. In school, many youths would not choose subjects much different from those offered in conventional curricula. A few would choose different subjects and unusual projects but many would be content simply with having a choice (Plunkett, 1969). In either case, it is likely that the pupil's motivation to achieve would be stronger than under conditions of compulsion.

The attack of youth on "the system" could become a legitimate area of scholarly investigation by high school students. Metcalf and Hunt recommend that such issues as the following become a part of the high school curriculum:

Liberal-reformist tradition
Means *versus* ends
The place of intuitive, involved thinking *versus* reason and
   persuasion
The nature, worth, and necessity of violence.

Metcalf and Hunt propose that relevance and the bringing of
the generation gap be approached via curricular provisions.

> Finally, what has been said about the use of relevant
> utopias in social analysis and prescription also applies to
> personal development and self-analysis. The significant
> questions are: What kind of person am I now? What kind
> will I become if present habits and trends persist? What
> kind of person would I like to become? What can be done
> now about tendencies and preferences that conflict? This
> approach to the problem of identity is more promising
> than some of the programs offered these days in the name
> of black studies, black history, and black pride. Historical
> and cultural studies have maximal relevance when they
> help us to predict the future or to make transition.[5]

The curricular approach has merit but faculty philosophy
and psychological orientation are at least as important as
academic outlines. If teachers must reach conclusions about
what black studies should accomplish or what kind of persons
youth should become, the matter of relevance will be academic
in the derogatory sense. The teacher's role is to orchestrate the
learning rather than to write the score by which the tune is
played.

If the faculty believes that soon the students will have to
get along without them, then they will encourage pupils to
reach their own conclusions (which the students will do in any
case, covertly or openly). If the faculty believes that motivation should be primarily internal rather than external, then
compulsion and rewards will become subordinate to the
psychology of task completion and success (Lee, 1973). The
faculty must develop the viewpoint that it is most successful
when it renders itself superfluous. At least one teacher required therapeutic intervention to achieve this orientation.
Jersild and Lazar (1962, p. 115) describe a teacher who took

[5] Lawrence E. Metcalf and Maurice P. Hunt, "Relevance and the Curriculum,"
Phi Delta Kappan 51 (March 1970): 361.

229

pride in pupils' crying on the last day of school because they loved her so much. During therapy she learned that she was exploiting her pupils to secure admiration and affection. Later she rejoiced in seeing her pupils depart with smiles of confidence.

The need for variety

Independent study in the form of honors courses, senior tutorials, and early entrance have been tried with and for bright, gifted, and creative college students for many years. The sporadic record of successes has been so characteristic that no great faculty enthusiasm has developed. However, the occasional successes have fostered the idea that honors, tutorials, and other forms of independent study need not be restricted to bright or unusually able students. Hatch and Bennet have concluded that:

1. Grade points were not necessarily good indicators of students' ability to profit from such programs.
2. Not every superior student, as identified by his grade points, was interested in honors work.
3. Students electing honors programs as upperclassmen were poorly prepared for such work because their previous training lacked the necessary depth and/or breadth.
4. The passive role engendered by the conventional lecture, laboratory, and conference methods to which honor students were exposed as freshmen and sophomores made honors work difficult, irksome, or distasteful.[6]

The above observations bear some resemblance to observations about convergent and divergent thinkers. There are some persons whose intelligence consists in bringing together the distillation of knowledge gleaned from the systematic pursuit of established studies. Others are disposed to wild flights of fancy and are willing and able to persist in the pursuit of one of those flights. Thus, one bright student may appreciate the order and regularity of classes, schedules, and established curriculum, and without such structure he may become bewil-

[6] Winslow R. Hatch and Ann Bennet, *Independent Study*, New Dimensions in Higher Education, No. 1 (Washington, D.C.: United States Department of Health, Education and Welfare, 1962), p. 5.

dered, frustrated, and even hostile. Conversely, a second bright student may profit from the freedom to investigate his own intuitive conclusions and delight in finding them to be correct or incorrect, as long as he does it himself. *His* source of bewilderment, frustration, and hostility may be coercion, direction, and the confinement of prescribed studies. Moreover, the creative, intuitive, independent student does not necessarily have to have above average intelligence (Torrance, 1962, p. 54). In fact, one's need for structure or freedom in learning probably is learned. Hence a part of what pupils are taught should be how to find out on their own. These lessons should begin early and, as maturity is achieved, prescriptive aspects should be markedly diminished. Creative behavior is learned—and it can be taught (Reese and Parnes, 1970).

A sixth grade girl who was an indifferent, somewhat apathetic, pupil approached her teacher with a question about geology with more than her typical enthusiasm. The teacher was pleased on two counts—she could answer the question and the girl's interest was gratifying. The teacher dealt with the question in considerable detail and suggested some additional investigations. However, the girl returned to her place and resumed the indifferent attitude. A few days later the girl asked another question but this time the teacher had no answer; she did suggest some references where answers might be found. The girl pursued the search vigorously and immediately asked another question. Again the teacher had an answer but said, "I know just a little about it but I'd like to know more. Will you see what you can find and report to me and the class?" And again the girl went seriously to work. The teacher's conclusion was that the girl did not want to spend her time looking for answers that someone already had.

A college instructor emphasized to his class in "Personality Theory" that there were many fine references on the subject. He provided a list of authors and books and articles. There was also a syllabus of "Suggested Topics and Readings." He remarked that systematic and specific observation of personality orientations would also be in order. Moreover, students could pursue their study by reading novels, biographies, related texts or by other means which the students could determine in conference with the professor. A few days later one of the students, a

girl with an enviably high academic record, after expressing some resentment in class, asked for a conference.
- During the conference she expressed considerable anger
with the professor's inefficiency. He had listed a second
edition of a text in connection with a topic. It turned out
that the discussion in the text was not related to the topic.
The fact was that the topic was related to the chapter cited
in the first edition. "I have read every chapter cited in all
the books for each chapter; and I wasted an hour reading
the wrong chapter."

The fact that pupils differ in their preferred styles of
learning does not alter the need, stated earlier, for independence in the continuous pursuit of knowledge. The most
important contribution a college can make to its students is to
develop in them a capacity to continue their education
throughout their lives. Although some may find independence
irksome, others find it inspirational and should be encouraged.
It is not a matter of either-or, but one of prompting all
students, especially the conformist and structure-seeking, to
cultivate a style that will be useful at a later time. It becomes a
matter of leading from one's strengths, not one of neglecting
weaknesses. The college girl described above needs to be
understood but also needs encouragement in the exercise of
independence.

INDEPENDENT STUDY IN ACTION

Role of the pupil

It has been indicated, in the preceding discussion, that independent study can provide a means by which pupil differences
in learning style and pace may be recognized and implemented. It can be used as a means of recognizing variations in
the meaning of relevance. It enables the school to promote the
habit and skill of continuous learning. There are other advantages to the pupil ascribed to independent study.

Competition. There are some young people who thrive on
competition while others seek to escape confrontations. For
the latter, independent study may be a valuable source of

motivation. There is an aspect of motivation that stems from exploration, activity, and mastery of the environment as distinct from competition (Gagné, 1970, p. 287). Independent study provides pupils with an opportunity to exercise hetero-static tendencies without testing themselves against others.

Interest and choice. The industry with which people pursue their hobbies suggests that interest and choice tend to promote persistent effort. In the classroom, freedom of choice may supplement individual recognition as a motivating power. Independent study may perform the valued service of helping transform the pupil from a computer number to that of an identifiable person.

Self-pacing. This concept is closely related to the matter of competition but the emphasis is on time rather than quality. In self-pacing the individuals face the same task (learning to spell a certain group of words or doing a number of arithmetic problems involving a given process), but are allowed to do the task in their own time. Feedback comes from task achievement rather than rate of work. The advantage resides in letting able students achieve their maximum without stress or pressure while permitting others to proceed at their own pace without frustration or humiliation (DeVault and Kriewall, 1970).

Role of the teacher

The image of the teacher as imparter of knowledge, as informant, as all-knowing is deeply imbedded in the tradition of formal education. Transformation to the role of educational consultant and counselor for independent study may prove to be difficult.

Trust. The way a teacher views his pupils is probably the key factor in the degree to which independent study is accomplished. There is a wide gap between individually prescribed instruction and independent study as defined in the first part of this chapter. IPI implies low trust, or lack of faith, in pupils. There is an implicit attitude that, unless he is doing what the teacher had envisaged for him, the pupil is wasting his time.

233

Independent study may also suffer from this, as revealed in the widely extant attitude that a pupil will be granted the privilege of independent study when he is sufficiently mature, i.e., does in his "independent" time what the teacher has envisaged for him. If there is a genuine trust in pupils and a deep faith in their capacity for development and self-direction, then a teacher can permit the exercise of independence up to and including the privilege of failing. One teacher reported his experience as follows:

> For the most part, independent study worked very well—surprisingly well. My seventh graders did develop their own projects and pursued them with varying degrees of success and enthusiasm. I knew better than to hope that all would be enthusiastic, but I hoped anyway. But George just sat. I talked with him, I made suggestions, I offered to work with him, I threatened him with the uncertainty of the future. But George just sat. I asked him if he would get up and join the others at recess or go to the library, or shoot baskets. He was pleasant but said he preferred to sit. There was really nothing in school for him; he was going to be a wheat rancher, just like his father, and on the same ranch. He did not mind the work at home but came to school because he could just sit. Fortunately for my own peace of mind, I had given over only two hours a day to independent study. George perfunctorily did some work during the rest of the day but during the independent period he just sat.

The difficult question to be resolved is whether or not independence can be learned in the absence of opportunity to practice it. If one can be "independent" only in approved ways, does he really have the privilege of exercising independence? Is the basic question one of teacher development or of pupil development?

Variability of pupil product. Despite much discussion about individualizing instruction, it is not clear that we really mean it. One of the traditional functions of education was to meld people of widely variant cultural backgrounds into one society (DeVault and Kriewall, 1970). With the emphasis on the culturally different pupil and the reduction of school dropouts, this function continues to be operative. This melding process presents a dilemma to those who espouse variety in the school product. It is not expected that the question can be resolved by faculty members but discussion of the polarities may result in some tenable compromises.

Creativity. Much of the research on the encouragement of creativity is of an equivocal nature. A particular method (e.g., discovery vs. systematic presentation) may result in improvement of scores on a test of creativity in one pupil but lower the score of other pupils. Moreover, it has been found that it is very difficult for teachers to distinguish between and use, voluntarily, an openminded, freewheeling questioning approach.

Impact of independence on pupils

The results of teaching for creativity are equivocal (Torrance, 1972). However, those things that bolster self-confidence and persistence—pursuit of personal interests, more success than failure, autonomy, and acceptance—are unlikely to discourage nascent creativity and independence.

Some cultures and some families provide what Christie (1970) calls *unilateral* environments, ones in which parents provide determined standards. Great emphasis is placed on conformity, mothers are dominant, and there is an orientation toward tradition. In contrast, there are child rearing milieus that are *interdependent,* in which parents are interested but allow the child, even at a very early age, much opportunity for autonomy. Feedback is in terms of giving information and the process is mutual; parents also expect feedback from children. Pupils from an interdependent environment score highly on tests of diversity of thinking and behavior, they develop realistic perspectives, and can tolerate ambiguity. Pupils from unilateral environments are restricted in these kinds of learning.

Yamamoto (1963) found no significant differences between the classroom behaviors of teachers who scored low or high on tests of creativity. There were, furthermore, no typical differences in the personal adjustment patterns of their pupils or in reading achievement scores. Arithmetic scores, on the other hand, were highest when there was a combination of low

235

teacher creativity and low pupil creativity; low teacher creativity combined with high pupil creativity characterized low achievement in arithmetic. Rippey (1965) also found that there was no difference in achievement in grammar, punctuation, and English usage when structured versus unstructured approaches were compared.

One of the apprehensions regarding instructional technology—one approach to the individualization of instruction—is that it will dehumanize the process of education. The danger is real, but because of the persons involved rather than the hardware.

> In one school, highly reputed for its leadership in IPI, this dehumanization was highly apparent. Pupils went to the file for learning activity packets on the subject concerned. If one of them had a question, he went to the teacher. Help from the teacher was available when difficulty was encountered while working on the package. When the package was completed the work was taken to a teacher aide—who with no remark (she had been told that she was *not* the teacher), checked the answers according to the key. If there were a satisfactory minimum of checked errors the pupil took a mimeographed test from the aide—with no comments. Again if a satisfactory minimum score were obtained the proper entries were made on his record and another package was selected—with no comments. It is extreme—it may be unbelievable—but there was, in this version of IPI, a minimum of humanity expressed.

Impact on teachers

Even if one concludes that what teachers do with pupils in terms of giving freedom and responsibility makes little difference in academic achievement, the same cannot be said with respect to what teachers are. Whether teachers want and use structure or encourage creativity and independence, all teachers get better results in achievement and growth of pupil autonomy when they are warm, nurturing, and accepting. Moore and Moore (1972), in a critique of early childhood education, point out that research continues to endorse children's need for warmth, continuity of adult contact, and security. The implications of such statements are sobering, if not staggering. The data mean that effective instruction is dependent upon a complex mixture of (1) academic and professional knowledge, (2) professional skill, and (3) artistry in teaching. On the cheerful side, teachers who risk innovative thrusts are investing in their own personal growth. Their awakened enthusiasm for life and work, their renewed faith in developmental processes, and their satisfaction from new experiences redound to their personal benefit as well as to professional growth and teaching competency.

Resort to independent study will not make an ineffective teacher into an effective one. No adoption of a method will do that. It does appear that investigation of independent study, experimentation with some of the underlying assumptions, and examination of one's philosophy of education outlook on human nature may help to improve the kind of person one is by involving him in the process of becoming.

SUMMARY

Independent study has no uniform or widely agreed upon meaning. Interpretations range from individually prescribed instruction to "quest" activities which the student pursues with only minimum guidance. The need for independent study of the latter type mounts with the phenomenon of rapid change. It is needed because it makes possible the achievement of relevance despite different pupil orientations. A further justification for independent study resides in pupil variation in levels of development, interests, and vocational and avocational orientations. It is worthwhile also in terms of the commendable urges that young people have to grow, be independent, and be depended upon.

Independent study in action provides pupils with opportunities to practice skills that will have lifetime significance. It makes it unnecessary to compete with unequals. It helps them develop their own interests, pursue their own choices, proceed at their own pace, and capitalize on their unique learning styles.

Independent study changes the role of teachers from instructors and coaches to that of facilitators and assistants in the process of learning. However, it demands that teachers develop trust in pupils and learn to tolerate the unconventionality of creativity and divergence. The demands that independent study make on teachers may call for close self-examination and sometimes the help of small group discussion so one may learn how he "comes across" to others.

Most, but not all, of the postulations on learning that are emphasized in this book are satisfied by independent study.

SUGGESTED ADDITIONAL READINGS

Bauer, David H., and Yamamoto, Kaoru. "Designing Instructional Settings for Children Labeled *Retarded*: Some Reflections." *Elementary School Review* 72 (April 1972): 343–50. Teaching retarded children highlights two pervasive factors: (1) pupils behave as teachers and society expect them to, and; (2) the medical tradition of individual prescription and treatment is central.

Broudy, Harry S. "Educational Alternatives—Why Not? Why *Not?*" *Phi Delta Kappan* 54 (1973): 438–40. Some alternative education models merely suggest change for the sake of change. Others are meritorious because they (1) promote freedom, (2) encourage intelligent and responsible choice, (3) provide for pupil differences, and (4) foster creativity. Independent study, with the guidance of concerned teachers, would score high on Broudy's criteria.

Goodale, Robert A. "Methods of Encouraging Creativity in the Classroom." *Journal of Creative Behavior* 4 (Spring 1970): 91–102. The practical suggestions for encouraging creativity may also serve as guiding principles for teachers who wish to make independent study more effective.

Parnes, Sidney J. "Creativity: Developing Human Potential." *Journal of Creative Behavior* 5 (Winter 1971): 19–36. Fostering creativity demands sensitivity, synergy, and serendipity. The author tells what these are and describes the human climate that promotes their occurrence.

Plunkett, William T. "Independent Study at Syosset High School." *Phi Delta Kappan* 50 (1969): 350–52. Experience shows that students respond well to independent study but do need guidance in topic selection and the availability of resources. Wise independence is learned by progressive experience.

PART III

Organizing for Innovation
and Change

CHAPTER 10

The Team Approach to
Learning

Theory can best be converted into practice and purposeful self-direction, and personal and professional growth best can be accomplished, through the two step process of describing desired behaviors in observable terms and gaining feedback concerning the degree to which this desired behavior is being accomplished. Fortunately for the development of this process and for education and those involved in it, the relative isolation of teachers in the self-contained classroom appears to be giving way to arrangements that combine school personnel in cooperative activities. Classrooms are less and less considered the domain and sole responsibility of any one teacher.[1] Rather, such tools as team teaching, open space buildings, and the use of parent aides, paraprofessionals, and student tutors are bringing those individuals most concerned with the teaching and learning relationship—teachers, students, and parents— into closer interaction than ever before. Two-way, peer type relationships in which communication can take place on an equal-to-equal rather than a superior-to-subordinate basis are becoming more and more common.

[1] Opinions differ here, however, and Colman and Budahl (1973, p. 41) state their belief that, despite dramatic growth, team teaching as yet poses no real threat to the one teacher classroom.

In Chapter 3, communication was described as not only a prime requisite for the teaching and learning process, but as an essential in dealing with social environments and in developing and maintaining an adequate self-image. People maintain contact and direction and gain support through the process of communicating. When anything interferes with good communications, in a school or elsewhere, feelings of insecurity, doubt, distrust, and loneliness develop and feed on themselves. Knoblock and Goldstein (1971) found these feelings to be pervasive in the teachers whom they studied and further assumed that many, if not all teachers experience such feelings in varying degrees. They observed a physical and psychological isolation and a resultant need for meaningful communication which was not met by interacting with students but that required contact and transactions with adult peers. Colman and Budahl indicated that "Team teaching offers the educator unique and challenging opportunities that would otherwise be denied him in the self-contained classroom." [2] As a case in point, one teacher of the authors' acquaintance often maintained that she had spent so much time with first graders she had forgotten how to talk with adults and felt inadequate and inferior around anyone over twelve years of age. She had come to see herself as inept in social situations, and did not initiate contacts with, or tended to withdraw from, other adults.

Providing the conditions for effective communication cannot ensure that this will happen. Accessibility and physical proximity, as we have seen, do not, of and by themselves, foment understanding, sharing, problem solving or the free interchange of feelings and ideas that stimulates creative and innovative thinking. Loneliness is not a matter of physical space. Loneliness is a matter of poor communication. As long as combinations of individuals are used mostly as administrative arrangements, and interactive communication processes are not stressed or facilitated, improvement in the way of self-direction may not occur.

Educational and psychological role of feedback

The process of receiving feedback as a basis for self-direction,

[2] Clyde H. Colman and Leon Budahl, "Necessary Ingredients for Good Team Teaching," *National Association of Secondary School Principals Bulletin* 57 (January 1973): 41–46.

Loneliness is not a matter of physical space. Loneliness is a matter of poor communication.

even when aided by clearly stated behavioral descriptions, is much easier to talk about than it is to practice.

Even though feedback can help behavior systems become more effective and more capable of self-regulation, the cultural proscription, "If you can't say something nice don't say anything," often operates to restrict its expression. At the same time the tendency to feel threatened, to become defensive, and to counterattack inhibits its reception and use. Clearly, the gaining of feedback as a basis for self-direction is a technique that requires learning and for which social contact and communication with others is necessary. As Gorman emphasizes, "The high school of the future will give more thought to an organizational design giving teachers more encouragement and more opportunity to stimulate themselves and each other." [3]

Growth as a person and as an educator depends upon the opportunity and the ability to interact effectively with people.

[3] Burton W. Gorman, "Change in the Secondary School: Why and How?" *Phi Delta Kappan* 54 (May 1972): 567.

Our belief and experience lead us to suggest strongly that, of the current new ideas in education, team teaching and the interpersonal process group experience best can be utilized and combined to provide this. The first can be used to bring teachers together in a cooperative peer interaction relationship. The latter can be operated to teach and to practice effective communication interaction skills in order that this relationship can be maximally productive. We envision a teaching and learning team composed of teachers, teacher aides, paraprofessionals, counselors, psychologists, and supervisors that, on regular occasions, could declare a teaching moratorium and deal with its own communication interaction difficulties. That is, it could take time to metacommunicate.

THE TEAM TEACHING CONCEPT

Team teaching may be adopted by schools as an administrative arrangement; it may be adopted for the purpose of facilitating contact and communication among school personnel or it may be instigated to gain the advantages of both. For whatever reason, it represents a concept that is becoming increasingly common in education (Shaplin and Olds, 1964; Sterns, 1972; Tyler, 1968). Since 1960, its adoption in one form or another has been so widespread that the term "educational practice" now may be a more acceptable label for descriptive purposes than "innovation." Varieties of such programs in expanding numbers have come into use in elementary and secondary schools and even in colleges and universities throughout the country.

Definition and status

Because of this popularity, team teaching has been conceptualized and defined in a number of ways. Commonly included aspects in such definitions are:

(1) Two or more teachers work together.
(2) Responsibility is placed and accepted for instruction in specific subjects, combinations of subjects, or grade levels.

(3) This responsibility extends over a substantial period of time.
(4) The pupils served comprise a distinct group or unit.
(5) Members conceptualize and implement a mutually helpful, sharing cooperative role as contrasted with merely taking turns or dividing work and responsibility.

All of these characteristics are not exhibited by all teaching teams and there are differences in the degree to which any one of them is shown. So it is difficult to say how many and how much of each a school or a combination of teachers must have in order to be said to be doing team teaching. Because of its popularity, prestige, and bandwagon appeal, it is probable that more schools claim to be doing team teaching than actually implement it. Cass, in pointing out that it is easy to accept the forms of innovation while losing the substance, remarked:

> . . . it is quite possible to initiate team teaching in large open classrooms with 100 students and four teachers— only to find that each teacher has put her desk in one corner, arranged 25 students in front of the desk, and continued business as usual. The only thing that has changed is the rhetoric in the teacher's lounge.[4]

Team teaching may represent a process of change, adaptation, and reassessment of policies and techniques or it may have lost much of its novelty and capacity to involve school personnel. In some schools, it may continue as a dynamic force for the involvement of staff after several years of implementation. In others, an attitude of tedium may replace initial enthusiasm within a few months. Noteworthy in this respect are the figures quoted by Cawelti (1967). He found that 41.0 percent of the 7,237 high schools that he surveyed were using team teaching and an additional 310, or 4.3 percent, had tried and abandoned it. He hinted that inadequate planning and initiating procedures may have been responsible. It also may be significant that, during visits to innovative schools and discussions with teachers and students, the authors found none who wished to return to traditional methods. By way of comparison Sterns (1972) indicated that around 30 percent of

---

[4] James Cass, "Are There Really Any Alternatives?" *Phi Delta Kappan* 54 (March 1973): 452.

the nation's elementary schools were utilizing some form of cooperative teaching. Here again, responses from teachers, student teachers, and students were enthusiastic. No one wanted to return to their previous form of teaching and learning.

Organization for team teaching

Teaching teams also vary with regard to the manner in which they are organized. In terms of administration and lines of authority, there are several possibilities. Teams may be democratic and collegial in structure and all members may share equally in planning and decision making. They may be organized more in an autocratic hierarchical manner with a master teacher or supervisor in charge who bears most of the responsibility for the way in which the teams function. Or authority may shift from member to member depending upon the nature of the team's concern and the assumption of member responsibility. There often is a good deal of flexibility and the teams may present any number of gradations between the collegial and hierarchical extremes.

In terms of instructional responsibilities, teams may function either vertically or horizontally. That is, they may operate within a single discipline or academic area or they may have the responsibility for teaching a number of subjects to a specific group of students.

Teaching teams may therefore be classified as:

(1)   Hierarchical vertical, with leaders and lines of authority specified and instruct in one academic area
(2)   Hierarchical horizontal, with authority designated and instructional duties covering several subjects
(3)   Collegial vertical, with democratic procedures and equal authority for members and instruction in one area
(4)   Collegial horizontal,[5] with democratic organization and the responsibility for teaching several subjects.

[5] This type of organization is termed "interdisciplinary" by DiVirgilio, who feels that it especially is necessary and proper for middle schools. James DiVirgilio, "Guidelines for Effective Interdisciplinary Teams," *The Clearing House* 47 (December 1972): 209.

246

These organizational patterns may be specified by the school administration, by curriculum committees, by the team itself. Within these limits, the composition of teaching teams may differ widely. While some may be made up of teachers of relatively equal status, experience, and expertise, others may be composed of one or two expert teachers plus beginners, novices, and interns. In some instances, paraprofessionals, clerical and library assistants, and equipment technicians may be included as team members and share in the planning of team functions. Students, however, especially on the elementary and high school levels, are seldom included or consulted by most teams in planning for instruction as much as they should be.

It is easy to see that many possibilities exist under the rubric of team teaching. Teams may vary within school systems and school systems may differ in the manner in which they conceptualize and structure for teaming. As Shaplin indicated: ". . . it is hardly an exaggeration to say that there are as many different types of team teaching as there are different school systems that have undertaken projects." [6] Direct comparisons between teams in any but general terms are not possible. Like any other innovative practice in education, the variables that can effect the processes and products of team teaching are so great in number that it is difficult, if not impossible, to say with conviction that team teaching, of and by itself, will produce certain expected results. Perhaps because of this, research which either substantiates or denies its effectiveness is limited and the relative advantages of the possible organizational classifications have not been determined. Although team teaching probably can make desirable educational procedures more possible, it cannot guarantee that they will happen. This remains the function and the responsibility of those who put the idea into practice.

Evaluation of team teaching

There is a gap between theory and practice with team teaching as well as with other innovative educational practices. It is as

[6] Judson T. Shaplin, "Description and Definition of Team Teaching," in Judson T. Shaplin and Henry F. Olds, Jr., eds., *Team Teaching* (New York: Harper and Row, Publishers, Inc., 1964), p. 5.

prone as any other innovation to be oversold by enthusiasts and as often adopted without essential ground work and planning (Colman and Budahl, 1973; Shaplin, 1964). Despite its relatively long period of implementation, it remains difficult to differentiate an actuality from a claim. What proponents say could happen may not be what does happen. Both possibilities are discussed in the following commonly claimed advantages for team teaching.

ADVANTAGES CLAIMED FOR TEAM TEACHING

Specialties and talents of teachers are better utilized

Each team member has a chance to do what he does best and to concentrate on the development of a particular competence. Individual teacher differences have a better chance of being utilized to improve instruction (Darling, 1965). Better feelings and relationships are generated because people are working in areas where success is both possible and recognized. Pupils benefit because the most knowledgeable and best qualified teachers usually are the ones to present materials. Cawelti's study of innovations in the high schools led him to conclude: "If your purpose is to extend the teaching of a first-rate person to more students and to integrate knowledge, the answer is 'yes.' Team teaching can do this." [7]

Although specialization may result in better instruction and although teacher satisfaction may be higher when this is possible, it also may prove to be no blessing in disguise for either pupil or instructor. Specialization and well-rounded professional growth may be counter claims. A teacher's functioning on one specific team in a specific subject assignment may not fit him to operate as a member of another team or in another setting with different requirements. A sort of academic tunnel vision may be promoted in which overenthusiasm for one aspect of the curriculum may lead to a lack of support for another. Vars, for example, thinks that specialization, as the "inevitable concomitant of team teaching . . . tends to pull the organization apart and split the central unity

[7] Gordon Cawelti, "Innovative Practices in High Schools," *Nations Schools* (April 1967).

248

of the teaching process." [8] Sartain (1968) also sees a danger that specialization might lead to the impersonalism and lack of interest in individual children characteristic of departmentalism if teaching teams and class sizes are too large. This position, however, does not appear to be widely held. Other observers (Shaplin, 1964; Sterns, 1972) see team teaching as a way of individualizing instruction and a way of teachers getting to know more about the personal and learning problems of their pupils. Probably the variable that makes the difference is not in the manner of organizing teachers but in the attitudes and interests of the personnel involved.

Variety in presentation and learning activities

When asked whether or not they would prefer to return to self-contained classroom methods of instruction, youngsters consistently give "variety" as a reason for favoring team teaching. Teachers concur. Both tend to characterize the more traditional structure as monotonous and boring. Teachers believe they can be more creative and challenging with occasional presentations than when the pressure to interest and motivate continues through several classes everyday. There is more time to plan and prepare and a greater opportunity to use instructional aids such as audiovisual materials and outside speakers. Less emphasis is necessary upon textbooks, workbooks, assignments and homework as time fillers. Pupils appreciate the extra effort on the part of their instructors and they value the opportunity for discussion and involvement provided by the small-group meetings which often follow and supplement presentations (Casey, 1964). As one youngster phrased it, "There is something new going on every day."

Perhaps educators underestimate the potential that variety has for holding interest and combating boredom. When something different is happening and opportunities for involvement and participation are provided, learning is facilitated (Gorman, 1972). When an innovation forces the process of examination, evaluation, and change, adjustment and further innovation become necessary for coping with the different

[8] Gordon F. Vars, "Can Team Teaching Save the Core Curriculum?" *Phi Delta Kappan* 47 (January 1966): 261–62.

situations presented. People must adapt and participate. When, and if, equilibrium is allowed to be reestablished, it may be necessary to reactivate the process with something else which is accepted as innovative. With respect to people, and they are what matters in education, the innovative process well may be more important than the innovative package. The package may be "old hat" tomorrow, the process may be generated at any time.

Costs are decreased by team teaching

The prospect of offering instruction to members of large groups at the same time and the expectation that equipment and teacher effort will not be duplicated as in the self-contained classroom organization leads to the supposition, and sometimes to the claim, that team teaching will substantially reduce educational expenses. If presentation could be assumed to equal learning, this might be true. Because it cannot, it is misleading to urge the adoption of team teaching on this basis. On the contrary, the increase in teacher contacts, communication, and planning fostered by team teaching generally highlights program deficiencies. This results in demands for increases in clerical help, equipment, room and schedule changes, library expansion and teaching materials (Anderson, 1964; Colman and Budahl, 1973). It probably is true, however, that with respect to use and results per unit of equipment and per person employed, taxpayers may get a greater return for their money. But this cannot be said for sure. The more tangible results of team teaching in terms of information gained have not been significantly higher (Heathers, 1964; Olivero, 1964; Sterns, 1972). The ability of individuals taught in this manner to live more effectively has yet to be measured.

Teachers also often find that a greater commitment is required. Even though some time may be gained by combining several classroom-size groups for academic presentations, the amount demanded for such activities as planning, coordinating, small group interaction, and pupil conferences more than makes up the difference (Shaplin, 1964). Olson cited this as one of the reasons for the failure of teaching teams, saying "Team teaching is not a labor saving device. In many, many ways team teaching requires more effort and sacrifice on the part of teachers than teaching in the self-contained classroom."[9] Often, however, the extra time tends to be freely given (Glenn, 1967). The feelings of involvement, the high esprit de corps, and the sense of doing a better job that frequently are generated by team teaching lead teachers to be unconcerned about the extra hours (Lortie, 1964).

Team teaching does tend to involve teachers and to make them conscious of the shortcomings and needed improvements in school programs. As a result, increased requests for facilities, equipment, and time can be expected from them. Unless a school system is prepared to view such requests with favor, it probably ought not to consider organizing teachers into teams. Without administrative, community, and financial support, the demands that team teaching generates may be more likely to lead to dissatisfaction and frustration on the part of teachers than to improve teaching and learning (Goldstein, 1967).

Closer and more meaningful teacher-pupil relationships

Three implicit assumptions made in the literature dealing with team teaching are that:

(1) Large group instruction will furnish teachers with more time for small group and individual contacts;
(2) Teachers will use this time to interact warmly and personally with pupils; and
(3) Pupils will be motivated and assisted to study individually and independently as a result (DiVirgilio, 1972).

Association with the several teachers of a teaching team provides youngsters with a choice of adult models. And further, at least one teacher of the team will be compatible to the personality of a given pupil and will be able to furnish the understanding and guidance needed. No pupil will be forced to stay with a teacher with whom he is personally incompatible (Vars, 1966).

Once again the gap between theory and practice becomes manifest. The provision of opportunity does not insure its happening. Much of the time provided by large group instruc-

[9] Carl O. Olson, Jr.," Why Teaching Teams Fail," *Peabody Journal of Education* 45 (July 1967): 17.

tion may be used up in team planning and coordination. Even if it is not, there can be no assurance that teachers who did not interact effectively in the self-contained classroom will suddenly know how to contact pupils and establish meaningful relationships when organized into teams. Unless training in establishing and maintaining effective interpersonal transactions is provided, team teachers are no more able than anyone else to relate meaningfully to youngsters. There is little evidence, either from visitation or the literature, that the guidance possibilities of small groups are exploited in schools organized for team teaching (Vars, 1966). School counselors rarely are included as team members. Group discussions generally are organized for the traditional information approach rather than for concern with the personal and unique learning experiences of the individual.

Instances of independent study, in the sense that it is self-initiated and controlled, are rare despite assertions that team teaching promotes this (Olson, 1967). Individualized study in which pupils complete externally imposed assignments or learning activity packets on their own are far more common. Frequently the distinction is not made and schools claim to be implementing independent study when the satisfaction of teacher prescriptions really is the major activity. There is a vast difference between learning to follow directions and learning in terms of one's own questions and areas of curiosity, between learning by desire and learning by prescription.

The exposure to several teachers and other adult models provided by team teaching probably does have some advantages over a long-term exposure to one teacher or to several teachers operating separately (Anderson, 1964; DiVirgilio, 1972). A better understanding of youngsters and a more realistic evaluation of their efforts appears possible when the observations of several teachers can be shared (Bair and Woodward, 1964; Grannis, 1964). It is also probable that close teacher-pupil relationships can no more be assumed to take place with teaching teams than in self-contained classrooms. Finley (1964) felt that the traditional "mother hen" role is unnecessary, even with younger pupils, and that children are positively affected by the feeling that many teachers are helping with their education.

Team teaching does appreciably extend the number of child-adult contacts. Despite a lack of statistical proof, one must grant statements of pupils and teachers involved in team teaching considerable validity. Teachers do feel that relationships are improved over those which they maintained in self-contained situations. Most youngsters do feel that they can identify with, and relate to, at least one teacher on the teams to which they are exposed. There is much potential yet to be realized in team teaching in terms of pupil-teacher relationships.

Organization

Team teaching divides instruction and personnel into administratively manageable units (Anderson, 1964; Shaplin, 1964). There seems to be little reason either to doubt or endorse this statement. If management and control are the primary concerns, however, the traditional department and classroom structure has been quite effective. From the point of view of administration, team teaching, if allowed to develop, probably does apportion responsibility even without the necessity of delegating it. Decisions such as the presentation of subject matter, the development of curriculum units, and the coordination, integration, and evaluation of instruction tend to become the responsibility of teaching teams (Vars, 1966). It may be that much of the need to motivate, supervise, and evaluate teachers by the administration can be eliminated through team teaching. Administration may come to consist of the apparatus for creating a favorable climate and not meddling too much in the control of everything that happens in a school.

The use of systems analysis techniques to study and improve teacher interaction patterns should be facilitated by team teaching. Advantages would seem to be that:

(1) observable and comprehensible subsystems can be identified;
(2) nonthreatening feedback agents in the person of other team members are available; and
(3) internal evaluation and modification of behavior from within a close-knit, supportive group is likely to be more effective than when imposed from outside sources.

Improvement of teaching

Superior opportunities for teacher training and improving instruction are provided by team teaching (Bair and Woodward, 1964; Sterns, 1972). The idea is that neophyte and interning teachers can work with, and learn from, their more expert colleagues. And further, that the experienced and effective teacher will be spurred to examine and improve his own techniques by the presence of beginners and the responsibility of passing his skills on to them. Beginning teachers can assume heavier teaching loads as they feel that they can handle them effectively. Responsibilities for controlling and instructing youngsters usually are shared, not placed upon the shoulders of beginners all at once (Shaplin, 1964). Lowe (1973) also emphasized the mutual support factor and the security of knowing that help, friendly and professional, is readily available from fellow team members.

Cooperative and supportive supervision potential, as opposed to the critical judgmental type, is built into a teaching team (Anderson, 1964). Most teacher functioning is under the observation of colleagues. If channels of communication and good personal relationships can be maintained among team members, then feedback will be constantly available and utilized to analyze pupil-teacher interactions and instruction. The "if" here is a big one and it is crucial. Teams probably must work well internally before they can be very effective externally. They must be able to deal with their own interpersonal transactions before their primary concern will be focused upon pupils (Colman and Budahl, 1973).

In order to prepare teachers for team teaching, a far greater emphasis upon working cooperatively with colleagues must be included in teacher training programs (Sterns, 1972). As Heathers indicated, ". . . members of teaching teams, in common with teachers generally, need a fundamentally different program of teacher education than is presently being offered." [10] The rise of team teaching may complicate such programs considerably. Teachers prepared for team teaching may not fit or be satisfied in the self-contained classroom,

---

[10] Glen Heathers, "Team Teaching and the Educational Reform Movement," in Judson T. Shaplin and Henry F. Olds, eds., *Team Teaching* (New York: Harper and Row, Publishers, Inc., 1964), p. 363.

while conventionally educated teachers may lack the interpersonal skills necessary to operate successfully as a team member.

Certainly, any change in teacher role as sweeping as that developed by team teaching should command a consequent adaptation by teacher educating institutions. The problem would not be great if preparation programs were to shift from the informing aspects of teaching to include the development of interpersonal competence. Education pertinent to teaching in both types of structure could be furnished. The same cooperative qualities and skills for interacting with others which make a teacher effective in one setting also make for effectiveness in the other (Heller, 1964).

Teacher satisfaction and more effective instruction

Education's preoccupation with doing something to, and for, children too often has led to a failure to recognize the importance of favorable attitudes and emotional well-being in teachers. They, as well as youngsters, need a feeling of belonging, acceptance, and involvement in order to function effectively (Kowitz, 1967; Silverman and Stone, 1972). Such a feeling appears considerably more possible when teachers are organized into teams than when they are limited to the relative isolation of the self-contained classroom (Colman and Budahl, 1973). The provision of opportunities to teachers for sharing thoughts and feelings with peers well may be the salient contribution of team teaching. Then new ideas can be developed and tested. Each person has a chance to contribute to the improvement of team function through cooperative planning and each comes to feel a part of the process of growing and becoming better. This is dynamic. Casey (1964, p. 177) spoke of ". . . the fellowship and contagion of enthusiasm which can weld together an entire faculty." And Glenn (1967, p. 36) observed, "Teacher enthusiasm seems to be an obvious product of the team teaching process." This can be felt and verified by observation in some schools. The enthusiasm of teachers is communicated to pupils who respond more positively. This favorable feedback is further stimulating for teachers. A self-reinforcing process is established, a favorable psychological climate is fomented, and positive learning environments are created.

It would be ideal, and education could move a big step forward, if such a process was introduced in all of the schools which organize for team teaching. Yet, it is possible to observe similarly organized schools in which neither teacher nor pupil enthusiasm is manifest. Variables other than team teaching itself make, or at least contribute substantially to, the difference. Identifying and dealing with these variables is considerably more difficult, especially if educators persist in ignoring the affective, conative aspects of learning and functioning.

Teachers who experience difficulty in managing their interpersonal relationships with others are probably more disruptive in team teaching than in self-contained classroom situations (Goldstein, 1967). At least their colleagues are less tolerant and long-suffering than their pupils and the inadequacy tends to surface more quickly. Such an early recognition of these ineffective teacher behaviors can be valuable. Help in dealing with the defeating actions or in seeking other employment then is possible for the teacher before the attitudes of youngsters toward learning and education become conditioned in a negative fashion. The authors agree with Heller (1964, p. 146), "Teachers who are contributing team members and helpful to students are those who demonstrate basic personal security." Positive feelings about self well may be more important for teachers than for pupils. Their influence is more pervasive. Probably one is not maximally possible without the other.

Happily, no one need be unalterably victimized by his own self-defeating actions. If properly conducted, teaching teams can be combined with small interpersonal process groups to provide real help to members in examining, reconstructing, and validating their behaviors (Jersild, 1965; Knoblock and Goldstein, 1971). Hopefully educators may come to recognize this as a necessary function and as a possible major contribution of team teaching.

Teacher participation in policy making

More effective staff and administration relationships are promoted by including teachers in policy and decision making through cooperative team planning. This statement is based on the supposition that this actually is allowed to happen. There is

Help . . . could be provided for the teacher before the attitudes of youngsters . . . become conditioned in a negative fashion. (© 1970 United Features Syndicate, Inc.)

no point in team planning if decisions must always be "cleared through the office" and can be countermanded without consultation by the school administration. The double message that says on the one hand, "Teams are free to decide," and demonstrates on the other, "But you'd better not rock the boat or oppose established policy," is more frustrating, and in the long run more limiting, than frankly authoritarian administration. All kinds and combinations of administrative attitudes and practices (democratic, permissive, double message, and authoritarian) exist in schools that claim to be team teaching. Observation strongly suggests that a high degree of teacher involvement occurs only when the administration solicits and implements decisions by teaching teams. As Shaplin (1964, p. 213) has indicated, "Probably the greatest single factor in a team's success is the principal who is in charge of the school."

The mechanism of external control inevitably places responsibility with outside sources. Personnel are free to blame the system for malfunctions and to overlook their part in the operation. When one is controlled, he tends not to feel a part of, or an identity with, the controlling agency. He often experiences resentment and opposition. The "Coleman Report" pinpointed the feeling of having some control over what happens as an essential pupil attitude factor. The same feeling is necessary for teachers. Without it, one of the strong points of team teaching is likely to go unrealized.

When teachers are organized into teams, greater pressure for change and innovation will be exerted upon the school's administration (Tomcheck, 1964). The "don't-muddy-the-water" administrator who conceives his role as "running a tight ship" or thinks he must keep everything "under his thumb" may find that team teaching provides him with more headaches than answers. He, in turn, may be unable to furnish the type of leadership required to make team teaching work. This does not mean that administration must abdicate. It does mean that decisions regarding the instructional program, pupil grouping, the use of facilities, and activities and teacher assignments must be made by, or in consultation with, teaching teams (Trusty, 1964). For the principal who can delegate responsibility, team teaching offers a way of involving teachers, improving cooperation, and initiating a practice of examination and evaluation of school operations. Unless he really means to pay more than lip service to the process of change and innovation, however, he is apt to be more threatened than challenged by the chain of events that team teaching can set in motion in his school.

An impetus for change within a school

Team teaching will act as an impetus for change within a school if teachers:

(1) are in meaningful contact and sharing new ideas with other staff members;
(2) feel that they exercise some power within the system; and
(3) can explore interpersonal processes and relationships and their effect upon school functions (Chesler and Fox, 1967).

As Chesler and Fox indicate, "Our research suggests that when teachers as a group feel powerless, isolated, uninvolved, and dissatisfied with their roles, they are not likely to instigate change." Furthermore, they may resist anything that is different and upsets the habitual and the routine.

When teachers feel free to examine their own behavior and the functions of the school, they engage in a sort of informal systems analysis. They become aware of effective and ineffective operations and behaviors and they begin to make suggestions for improvement. The procedures of feedback, describing desired behaviors, evaluation, and change become continuous and self-sustaining. Theory begins to change into practice and becomes the "innovative process," producing new ideas and innovations. When these are combined, as they often are because they are supplementary, one has the so-called innovative package. For example, Bair and Woodward point out:

As team teaching promotes nongradedness within the school, so does nongradedness promote team teaching. The theory of continuous progress is basic to most team teaching programs . . . flexible scheduling practices . . . are characteristic of many team teaching programs.[11]

[11] Medill Bair and Richard G. Woodward, *Team Teaching in Action* (Boston: Houghton Mifflin Co., 1964), pp. 32–33.

259

Other observers concur (Anderson, 1964; Glenn, 1967). This "innovative process" which involves teachers and that communicates enthusiasm to youngsters must be nurtured carefully. The authors agree with Goldstein:

> . . . if a school commits itself to a system, in this case team teaching, it must also commit itself to supporting systems since imagination, when unbuttressed, is quickly frustrated and ultimately dissolves into mediocrity.[12]

Because these innovations tend to be concomitant or to form a package, statements concerning the impact of any one are difficult to make. It does appear, however, that team teaching has great potential for involving teachers and starting the innovative process from the inside. Probably it best develops this way through the personal commitment of those affected. It can be decreed with only superficial results. One can order a package. A process must be developed.

Team teaching results in better education and more learning for youngsters

In the long run better education must be the basic criterion by which any innovation is judged. An evaluation of team teaching, however, is no less difficult than the measurement of the results of any other educational practice. This is true for a number of reasons: First, team teaching varies from school to school. What is evaluated in one institution may be something quite different from what is evaluated in another. Second, many variables affect learning. Which one really makes the difference generally is a matter of conjecture. We do not, as a matter of fact, have sufficient knowledge about the learning process to say with certainty whether any educational practice facilitates or inhibits. Ebel (1967, p. 82) quotes Professor Lee Cronback in this respect, ". . . We professionals do not know enough about learning and instruction to design the desired reform." Third, the traditional testing for the retention of information tells us little about the real effectiveness of pupils. High grades and achievement test scores have a surprisingly low correlation with future success (Taylor, 1968).

---

[12] William Goldstein, "Problems in Team Teaching," *The Clearing House* 42 (October 1967): 85.

. Despite difficulties in the identification of variables, the measurement of learning and the tendency of educators to project success into new educational ventures (Olson, 1967, p. 18), some statements of an evaluative nature can be made concerning team teaching. For the most part they are qualitative rather than quantitative and hence open to the interpretation of the reader. They do reflect the feelings and opinion of the authors.

(1)   In terms of the type of achievement indicated by school grades and measured by standardized tests, there is little evidence that team teaching results in significant gains (Olivero, 1964). On the other hand, neither is there evidence that team teaching works less well than traditional methods of instruction.

(2)   Generally speaking, both teachers and students believe team teaching to be more effective than self-contained classroom instruction. Few pupils or teachers would go back to the older method if they had the choice.

(3)   Teachers feel that well-motivated youngsters with average or above ability tend to become more self-reliant and more intellectually curious as a result of team teaching. Although they make no such claim for the remainder of the student body, they are inclined to believe that pupils here are no worse off than they were under self-contained methods of classroom instruction.

(4)   If more effective teachers do a better job of instructing and relating to youngsters, then team teaching, when properly implemented, justifies the extra time and expense it requires. Improvement is indirect (Colman and Budahl, 1973). But this may be as it should be. In any interpersonal relationship, one makes a difference to the degree that he controls the variable which he represents. If we really plan to improve learning for youngsters, perhaps we had better start with teachers.

INTERPERSONAL PROCESS GROUPS

Depending upon the point of view, the interactive group experience can be described as: (1) one of the most significant social inventions of the century (Rogers, 1968), offering much hope for the resolution of human difficulties; (2) "the most potent current learning experience . . . [and] force on the side of personal sanity, interpersonal satisfaction, and social decency," (Kagan, 1970, p. 43); or (3) brainwashing, a communist plan for manipulating people's thoughts and gaining world control (Rarick, 1970). Significantly, these views all ascribe a great deal of power to the various types of group interaction. We agree. It is for this reason that feelings, endorsements as well as condemnations, are strong. It is for this reason that the potential is high for affecting people and for generating growth and change.

Like stimulus-response psychological techniques and the principle of rewarding desired behavior, groups have been around and have influenced the actions of men for a long time. The issue is not so much whether groups will affect people, but a question of how this will be done. The ethics involved concern study, research, and systematic employment on the one hand and a continued lack of awareness of effects, unregulated use, and perhaps exploitation, on the other. Here, as with other predictions and fears concerning control over human beings, an awareness of process and dynamics is the best defense against such a possibility. This awareness, we think, can help educators profit by the group movement rather than to be used or exploited by it.

Types and definitions

There are many ways of referring to and characterizing group experiences. From the most common, such as training groups (T-groups), sensitivity training, and therapy groups, one can move to more specific terms as encounter groups, awareness experiences, personal growth laboratories, confrontation groups, intensive group experiences, and the like. It is estimated that hundreds of thousands of individuals are involved in the various types of group experiences every year under the auspices of such a wide range of sponsors as churches, industries, schools, businesses, police departments, and various professional organizations (Rakstis, 1970). Despite the extent of this participation, no clear and common understanding of differences appears to exist. The average person probably lumps most approaches under the heading of sensitivity training and pictures what takes place within such groups as somewhere between brainbending black magic, and a cure-all for anything from emotional turmoil to low factory production.

Rather arbitrarily we have designated four general classifications which seem to us to encompass most of the ways in which groups dealing with human relationships are used. The first of these is the *teaching and learning* group which is conducted to help participants find out about themselves and about their interactions with others. The aim of this type of group is to assist individuals to develop new and more effective interpersonal skills. Emotions constitute an important area of concern, but generating feelings and providing excitement for participants is not the primary reason for functioning. This type of group will be discussed in greater detail later.

The second broad area under which groups may be classified includes those groups conducted for *therapeutic* purposes. Although in its most inclusive sense therapy may include anything that helps people, this grouping is reserved for those interactions involving people seeking relief from psychological distress (Scanlan, 1971). Its primary function is to cure or alleviate an existing condition rather than to help a reasonably effective person to become more effective.

A third type of group interaction tends to be carried on and engaged in for purposes which best may be characterized as *psychological thrills*. Participants and leaders appear more interested in becoming "turned on" or in what might be termed "instant intimacy" or the "acidless trip." For these groups the experience is usually an end in itself. There may be almost religious conversions on the part of participants and messiah-like aspirations on the part of group leaders.

A fourth category that may aid in describing and understanding groups includes those *programmed, parlor-game-playing experiences* that may be conducted without a leader. This is the textbook, do-it-yourself approach and includes such games as "sensitivity" and "group therapy." Generally, the absence of leadership, supervision, and established objectives combine to render this type of group activity similar to that categorized above as psychological thrills. There are, of course, instances in which experiences of this nature are suggested and supervised by group facilitators or leaders supplemental to counseling or other group learning interactions.

But every group is unique and it is as difficult to classify any one of them as entirely of one type or another as it is to fit people into personality types. Most likely any group at some time or another will exhibit more than one of the above characteristics. An interaction may be therapeutic at the same time that it is a learning experience and it may simultaneously possess elements of psychological thrills and intimacy. The determining factor appears to rest with the reasons for forming the group and with the specified objectives or lack of them held by its members. One of the determining points used by the authors is whether the group is operated for the purpose of developing more effective behaviors and serves as a means to an end or whether it is considered to be an end in itself. We think that each participant should have clearly in mind those desired behaviors which he intends to use the group to help develop. As with other learning experiences, it is not enough to aspire to such broad generalities as awareness and sensitivity. Specific descriptions are in order. A group cannot provide experiences nor can the individual seek them effectively unless he knows what he wants and what to look for.

We acknowledge that there are plenty of experiences to be had in groups. But we contend that learning, especially in the communicative, interpersonal transaction, affective areas, should be purposive rather than accidental. We believe that the development of self-directed learners should be a primary goal of education. Each person should become an active agent in his own development. Any orientation, therefore, which sees people as losing control, being opened up, and experiencing psychological pain and disorganization is not, in our opinion, appropriate for educational purposes.

Teachers' attitudes toward groups

Despite the widespread popularity of groups and the recent disposition to include some version of group interaction on the agenda of many institutes and conventions, educators are among professionals showing greater resistance to change than any other institutional group (Rogers, 1968). The suggestion that teachers find involvement in intensive group interaction difficult is substantiated by the experiences of the authors and others (Knoblock and Goldstein, 1971). Their observation is that in general teachers do indeed find it harder to share feelings and to verbalize emotional concerns than business employees and housewives. Also, and again in general, older teachers have less facility on the affective level than their younger associates. Experienced teachers usually are less likely than those with under five years in the classroom to risk very much in groups. High school teachers tend not to interact so easily as those on the more elementary levels and women are often more open about themselves and their emotional concerns than men.

Reasons for teacher reticence in groups

A condition usually can be observed with less difficulty than the reasons or causes for it can be determined. This is the case with the movement toward the use of groups with and by teachers. Because of it, the following points are advanced as possibilities and tentative explanations. They are not expected to hold true for all groups and for all participants. Their purpose will have been served if they encourage readers to look critically at those groups with which they have contact and their own attitude and performance in relation to them.

One reason why teachers tend to look askance at intensive group interaction is that this has been inadequately and erroneously described in many instances (Lakin, 1969; Odiorne, 1970). There are descriptions which promise joy and ecstasy (Schultz, 1967), descriptions which stress transparency, self-disclosure, and vulnerability (Culbert, 1970; Jourard, 1964), and descriptions which point to more effective organizational and marital relationships (Golembiewski, 1970). Also there is some tendency on the part of teachers and the general public to associate group experiences with the hippie, love-in, flower child approach to human relations. For these reasons, many teachers think groups are outside the province of education and more properly the business of psychologists and psychotherapists. Apparently group processes have not been conceptualized as learning activities by large numbers of teachers or as avenues to increased personal and professional competence.

A second reason for teacher caution about interpersonal transaction groups may lie, strangely enough, with their popularity (Birnbaum, 1969). Enthusiasm has outstripped knowledge and expertise, and poorly conceived sensitivity experiences with professionally incompetent leaders have been included in far too many institutes, workshops, and conventions without adequate consideration of the objectives these experiences were expected to meet. Too often workshop, institute, or convention participants find themselves scheduled into such groups without having the chance to refuse. At best, some of these short-term one- or two-session groups have had little or no effect. Some may have provided members with psychological titillation and may have caused them to be emotionally more touchy and scared than sensitive. At the worst, they may have been responsible for triggering emotional upsets severe enough to necessitate psychiatric treatment.[13]

A third and closely related reason for educator distrust of groups arises because of the large numbers of self-styled and incompetent trainers and facilitators. Individuals with a yen to exert psychological power, a need to manipulate, and an overdeveloped messiah complex appear to have found a fertile field in the group movement. A good deal of seductive advertising is put out and in many cases the fees named are substantial. There can be little doubt that conducting groups is financially as well as psychologically gratifying.

Considerable agreement exists among those who have studied the trend toward groups that one of the big dangers lies with the incompetence of leaders (Lakin, 1969; Rakstis, 1970; Scanlan, 1971; Shostrom, 1969). In marked contrast with individual counseling and therapy, no training standards, certification authority, or licensing procedures exist that exert control over the person representing himself to be a group

---

[13] National Training Laboratories (NTL) estimate that less than one percent of those who have been in their sessions have been psychologically damaged and that most of these already had emotional problems (Seashore, 1970, p. 17). Only a fraction of the group experiences offered, however, are controlled by NTL. Research involving a variety of approaches and leaders with seventeen different groups indicated the much higher figure of nine percent (Lieberman, Yalom and Miles, 1973, p. 74). The experience of the authors leads them to an estimate somewhere between these extremes—around four to seven percent. But bear in mind that all kinds of people lead groups and no standards of competence are enforced. These figures include the good as well as the bad. When the large numbers of poorly prepared facilitators are considered, these percentages seem to us to be surprisingly low.

trainer unless he is a member of a recognized professional organization.[14] It is a matter of professional ethics, for example, that a psychologist should not establish a therapeutic interaction unless he possesses the competence to deal with it and that he should not terminate such a relationship until his clients' concerns have been ameliorated. It is a sobering thought that no such proscriptions have been stated or enforced for those who lead groups (Whiteley, 1970). A trainer may conduct a two-day session, encourage the surfacing of a number of psychological concerns, and then blithely bid goodbye without assuming further responsibility for the feelings and psychological condition of participants.

The fourth reason, and perhaps most basic for teacher resistance to group involvement, may be that by and large educators tend to feel threatened by this type of interaction. According to the "Teacher's Code," to ask for help is to admit failure (MacDonald, 1971). Good teachers do not require assistance. They can handle the job with no more than cursory attention from supervisors and administrators. If feelings are admitted and help is requested for either personal or professional problems, there is, according to the "Code," a tacit admission of inadequacy. Paradoxically and unfortunately, it probably is true that those who feel most lacking find it most difficult to ask for and accept assistance. Those who are most inflexible, who communicate most poorly, and who have successfully hidden unacceptable feelings even from themselves are most likely to resist the opportunities for dealing with these things provided by a group interaction experience. The following statement comes from a teacher who participated in a group facilitated by one of the authors. It describes the conflict and threat and the consequent thoughts and behaviors which frequently take place for teachers as a result of group interaction.

I have been doing some deep thinking about myself and why I have not become more involved in the group. Taking an active part can be a frightening as well as a releasing experience. I have become aware of four fears.

[14] Examples of these are The American Psychological Association, The American Personnel and Guidance Association, The American Psychiatric Association, and the National Association of Social Workers.

(1) The fear of being known. Most people spend a lot of time dressing up to impress others, to be well thought of, to be accepted. Few of us like ourselves as we are and hardly expect that others will. I am one of these. Along with many others, I do not want to look foolish or ignorant. A real fear of mine and others is that people will see us as we are.

(2) The fear of disappointment. Does the group have the insight to help me with my problems? If I do not feel that it does, I am not likely to unburden myself. And if I do decide to gamble and begin to reveal a deep need in my life but am not taken seriously—either by being given too quick, too pat answers before they have heard me out, or by having the subject changed—I will clam up and retreat from further disclosures.

(3) The fear of change. If interaction within a group is serious and honest, a person may reach the stage where he knows that changes are required of him. Most of us, self [sic] included, are resistant to change, especially if it demands that we initiate and carry through courageous new plans of action.

(4) The fear of failure. Coupled with the fear of change is the fear that having taken a new step I may "fall flat on my face," and to do so may be more embarrassing than not to take a step at all. I rationalize that since I don't want to do anything unless I can do it well, it is best not to begin.

I need to realize that when I fail and want to hide from people, that this is the time when I need people most. I need also to realize that all persons make mistakes.

I need to understand that each individual must be accepted as unique. He must be allowed to make his own decisions, choose his own direction, and move at his own pace. He must not be made to conform, but be loved and supported even when he seems to be marking time or going in the wrong direction.

If I can learn this, then I will not look at mistakes as failures but as stepping stones in the growing process.

Faced with at least three of these fears (1–3–4), I see three courses of action that might be taken. I could withdraw into a shell and try to "go it alone"—not let anyone know about my struggles.

Or I could associate with superficial, comfortable people where there is no real challenge. I could drift along in the mediocrity and conformity which characterizes so much of modern society.

I don't think either of these courses of action would be right for me. I would like to choose a third alternative, a course of interdependence. I would like to learn to be myself and have an honest relationship with others who have learned to be themselves.

PRINCIPLES OF EFFECTIVE INTERPERSONAL PROCESS GROUP OPERATION

In order to minimize teacher reluctance and to keep what takes place in school sponsored groups socially and educationally defensible, it is important to plan carefully. The authors' experience with groups involving educational personnel has led us to the development of certain principles that we have found to be successful in fostering personal involvement, learning, and growth for participants.

Group members must be kept informed

There should be no hidden agendas. The reasons and hopes which the institution and its administration have for the experience always should be explicit. Further, process and interaction patterns should be discussed.[15] As nearly as possible, all participants should know what is going on. A common vocabulary and a means of metacommunicating or verbalizing for dealing with and understanding the interaction process is essential. Harris' (1969) description of transactional analysis can furnish a model for assessing communication effectiveness (see also Chapter 3). Probably the means used for describing and interpreting is less important than the mutual understanding that is gained when participants can communicate about, share, and learn from what is happening.

[15] Carl Rogers (1967) describes a series of stages which he has observed taking place as groups function over a considerable period of time. Although not all groups exhibit all the characteristics mentioned, Rogers' descriptions furnish a means of understanding what is happening and what to expect and work toward.

   Bruce Tuckman (1965) also discusses the stages of development and the accompanying task activities that take place in groups. The "Johari Window" cited by Luft (1963) and Culbert (1968) provides a perspective for talking about the sharing process.

269

The personal control ability of each member should be emphasized

The interpersonal process group should not take the direction or control of self away from participants. On the contrary, it should be pointed out continuously that only the individual can really know his own feelings and situation and only he can determine his best course of action. Actually, the complete opposite of group control and domination of individuals can and does happen. One individual has the power, and may use it without being aware that he does so, to disrupt interaction and to interfere with the consideration of any topic. Thus it probably is as true to say that a group is at the mercy of its individual participants as it is to say that individuals are at the mercy of the group.

In groups it is well for both facilitators and members to remember that, just as love that is demanded loses meaning and the capacity to meet human needs, so behavior that is coerced cannot be trusted. Such behavior tells us little about the performer beyond the fact that he conforms and is easily influenced. He is merely a reflection of the expectations of others or, as one member put it, "a vegetable in somebody else's garden." Only when actions are freely taken because the actors feel that is the way they wish to do, can people and their relationships be really trusting and meaningful. Berdyaev (1957, p. 70) caught the essence of the idea with the statement, ". . . obligatory goodness ceases to be goodness by the fact of its constraint."

Interpersonal process groups, as we have said, function as communication laboratories in which participants can use the opinions of others as a means of assessing and improving their own effectiveness with people. Gaining, not relinquishing, control and self-direction is a primary reason for member participation. Hence this type of group interaction is not necessarily expected to curtail defensive reactions. Rather, participants are encouraged to consider the use of the various ego defenses as normal. The idea is that, as a person becomes more adept at protecting and defending himself, there is less tendency for him to feel attacked and vulnerable, less need to feel threatened and to act defensively. As one becomes capable at defending himself, he no longer needs to do so.

Behavior that is coerced cannot be trusted.

Sensitivity may therefore be a misleading name for this type of process group. Individuals who can manage and function effectively with others are not sensitive or easily hurt. They do not take offense easily. Because they have little to prove, it is not necessary for them to engage in competitive, one-up transactions. It probably is just as appropriate to say that participants can be desensitized as much as they are sensitized by a group experience. Certainly, situations that are perceived as threatening tend to orient a person's concern and sensitivity toward self rather than toward an other. In interpersonal transaction situations, the point deserves continued emphasis and reemphasis—one must deal with those things which threaten him if he is to be able to listen to, understand, and be sensitive to his associates. And this, of course, includes his pupils and students.

A certain amount of desensitization, as far as perceived threat to self is concerned, appears essential for the self-directed teacher for a number of reasons. First, feedback cannot be requested and used effectively if one is overly sensitive to self. Second, as we have indicated, one's sensitivity to others probably diminishes in direct proportion to his concern with his own psychological safety. Third, teachers today are more highly visible than at any time previously and they will, and should, become more so. The authors' visits to innovative schools have convinced them that it is possible for teaching and learning to go on with little decrease in effectiveness, with many observers looking on. When one becomes accustomed (desensitized) to being observed, the threat it once generated no longer controls his actions. He can control and use observers for feedback and the attainment of personal objective purposes.

The right of each participant to limit his own visibility must be recognized

This type of control is basic for effective behaving. When anything that is shared inside the group is discussed with nonmembers, this control is usurped. If one always must reveal or if he always must withhold, choice and the ability to control visibility do not exist.

Information about one's self is to be considered as personal property. It is to be shared by no one but the owner. To do otherwise constitutes a breach of confidentiality and an invasion of privacy. It is an indication of disrespect and a lack of concern. It minimizes feelings of trust and increases feelings of threat. Communication and effective interaction cannot be facilitated under such conditions. Indeed, personal visibility may be of such nature that only when it can be controlled can it be tolerated.

Behavior in groups should be described rather than evaluated

In order to limit the threat factor and to make it possible for participants to be honest about their feelings, be themselves, and risk providing feedback to others, it is helpful to discourage responses in the nature of right or wrong, good or bad, to blame or not to blame. Similarly, labelling participants with such terms as insensitive, unfeeling, prejudiced, and the like more often generates defensive reactions, facade building, and double message communication than it promotes mutual sharing, support, and understanding. Because of this, it is extremely important that group members and facilitators take a self-reference when responding. Instead of saying, "You are insensitive," the member speaks of his own feelings by stating,

"I feel rejected, hurt, or angry," whatever emotion he is experiencing. Teaching members to substitute the pronoun "I" for the pronouns "you" or "they" helps them to speak of and accept their own feelings and behavior. It discourages the projection of blame on others and encourages participants to examine the effects of their own actions. The rationale for this is that no one really can know how another person sees things, how he feels, and what motivates his actions.

Judgment or evaluation of one person by another from this point of view is not possible. One can say how he feels but he should not presume to assess how others are affected. Behavior in the other direction denies other persons the right to be themselves. And not to be one's self is to sacrifice one of the salient benefits to be derived from group interaction, i.e., the opportunity to learn about one's real being and its impact upon others. One may learn of his defenses, his rationalizations, the facades that he puts up, and the games he plays but he probably will not find out what it is like to be what he would like to be. He probably will not find out how it is to be self-directed and to change according to his own determination if he must continuously defend, protect, and justify his position.

Actually, minimizing the need to defend oneself can be one of a group's most important functions. Almost nowhere else in this culture can acceptance and position be enhanced by being less than perfect, by sharing concerns, and by disclosing areas of vulnerability. There are few other places, indeed, where the ticket to membership depends upon acknowledging imperfection. As indicated by Dinkmeyer, "The group is a place where an individual may belong *because* he has defectiveness. He does not have to be more than others to get into this group." [16]

Our suggestion is to concentrate upon describing behavior and to substitute for evaluation and judgments comments in the nature of: Is it working as well as you want it to? Are you really getting what you want from your relationships with others? Was that what you wanted to communicate? The mutual influence paradigm which was described in Chapter 4 should be of value in helping group members to observe and to

[16] Don Dinkmeyer, "Group Counseling Theory and Techniques," *The School Counselor* 17 (November 1969): 148.

describe behavior to each other. Even in low threat, supportive situations, a person will probably not risk changes unless he has some idea of what needs to be modified and some reason for attempting the modification.

Stability of membership, size, and meeting time are important for process group operation

In line with the fact that every member makes a difference in a group is the corollary that the absence or presence of any member affects interaction communication patterns. Particularly this is true when a new person enters. The icebreaking, trust building process often must be repeated before the risking of high visibility and the sharing of personal concerns again is possible.

Once a group member asks for feedback about the effectiveness of his behavior and about the feelings of others toward him, or once he shares some of his own feelings with the group, it is essential that the focus of the group's attention be kept on him until he really has been heard and until he has had ample opportunity to work through or share what he had in mind (Lange, 1970). Otherwise the person is left with a visible concern that has not been dealt with and the interaction process has failed to meet a primary objective. The member may feel that people do not care about his feelings or about him. He may feel put down and demeaned. He is not so likely to try to gain feedback or to risk sharing with the group again. Rather than helping to deal with a problem, a problem has been created or intensified.

Probably, this more than any other thing accounts for the ineffectiveness and sometimes hurt that arises from sensitivity sessions. When a group is too large (eight to twelve participants is a good size), has too little time (it should have two- or three-hour sessions at least once a week), or does not meet throughout a fairly long period (there should be a minimum of ten meetings), the opportunity for active participation is not likely to be made available to some members. Rather than feeling the acceptance and support which make it safe to risk new behavior, those members are likely to feel left out and rejected. They are apt to be hurt rather than helped by the group experience.

Reality in group experience

As much as possible a group should function without crutches or gimmicks in a natural, everyday environment. Some approaches to group facilitation make a rather extensive use of activities in the nature of physical touching, game playing, confrontation exercises, and the like in order to overcome inhibitions to interaction and, so to speak, "turn participants on." But this should be held to a minimum in interpersonal process groups (Wyatt, 1970). Participants need to learn to rely upon their own abilities to interact, to verbalize feelings, and to communicate effectively. Fatigue or liquor or drugs or warming up exercises will not always be available or appropriate. If the communicative interactive abilities learned through group participation cannot be available without priming, then the value of groups for increasing human competence is open to question. Also, unless this improvement in function transfers to ordinary situations and can be used at the behaver's option to increase his influence, control, and effectiveness, his group experience may not do him much good. Furthermore, if he comes to need and to rely upon the group as a primary source for close, warm, human contacts and fails to learn how to generate these for himself, he may have lost rather than gained. Let us reemphasize—whenever a group or any activity used in conjunction with it becomes an end in itself rather than a means to an end, then it is time to look closely at reasons and objectives.

Each participant should be able to describe the competencies he wishes to gain as a result of group interaction

The procedure of specifying desired behaviors, assessing progress toward them and their effectiveness by way of feedback from one's peers, and restating and assessing further as a continuing process was described earlier as a way to self-directed personal effectiveness and as a means of converting theory into practice. Interpersonal process groups can function as human relations laboratories in which this can happen. But the process cannot be taken for granted and it cannot be expected to occur in desirable directions by chance. It is not enough that people participate in groups with the vague hope that something good will happen or because management feels that the rank and file should be more sensitive. Well-defined goals and descriptions of desired behaviors are necessary (Wyatt, 1970). A participant must formulate clearcut ideas of what he wishes to change, what needs to be done in order to do so, and how group interaction can be used to aid in the process if he wishes to be in charge of his own growth.

Desired behavior descriptions are also necessary before what is learned through group interaction can be applied in other social environments. If groups are to function as means to an end and if participants are to go beyond the thrill and sensitivity of the moment, then effective behaviors and communication skills must transfer to situations outside the group. To be maximally worthwhile, learning must be applicable in many places. This is one of the most frequently raised questions concerning the efficacy of groups. While an increasing ability with communication interaction skills is not difficult to demonstrate inside the group itself, it is much harder to show that group participation promotes more appropriate or more effective behavior elsewhere (Odiorne, 1970).

In this respect, the authors have found that the practice of requiring members to attempt, and to experiment with, clearly described desired behaviors in the interim between group meetings aids substantially with the transfer process. Personal diaries or reports that describe the setting, the behavior tried, and feedback concerning how it worked supplement this. Situations in which group members interact with their pupils, spouses, or peers plus microteaching and videotaped interactions are examples of places and ways in which experiences for these reports can be gained.

GROUP FACILITATORS

A competent facilitator is essential for a worthwhile group experience

Probably no other single factor has more effect on the capacity of a group to promote the personal growth of participants than its leader (Cooper, 1969; Lieberman, Yalom and Miles, 1973). The psychological climate, the degree of threat perceived by participants, the safety they feel, and their resultant capacity for risk taking and experimenting with new behavior all are influenced by the expertise of the facilitator. His function, in effect, is a teaching function. He uses the group as a means of helping people to learn about their behaviors and how to improve them and he does this in several different ways.

First, he serves as a model (Fullmer, 1971). Through his manner of responding, he shows participants how to facilitate self-expression for others. By his own openness and willingness to take and to give feedback, he makes it possible for group members to attempt similar behavior. He demonstrates the total commitment kind of listening that accords importance and status to all members.

Second, the facilitator acts as a referee (Yeaworth, 1970). For example, he does not permit attack, counterattack behavior to persist or to escalate beyond the point where it can be recognized and studied by the group as a learning experience. He supports and reinforces those who risk asking for feedback and he emphasizes that each is an authority concerning his own feelings. He discourages evaluative labelling and he sees to it that no participant's concern, once expressed, is brushed off. But he does all of this, plus implementing the principles for effective group operation previously mentioned, as unobtrusively as possible. If he appears to take over and to direct or control the group, the responsibility for making things go may be placed with him. Members are apt to view the experience as his show and not to participate fully. When a group is operating effectively with a good facilitator, it is difficult to tell just what it is that he does to make it work. As participants learn the rules and come to model facilitative behavior and to encourage the self-expression of other members, the referee function becomes less and less essential. A good facilitator makes that role and himself unnecesssry as soon as possible.

A third teaching and learning aspect of effective interpersonal process group facilitation lies with the leader's ability to recognize, describe, and interpret communicative interactive patterns (Johnson, 1972). If a group is to function as a behavior laboratory, it is necessary that the most is made of its opportunities to study and understand the causes and results of participant actions. If communication about communication is to take place and result in change and improvement, someone must raise questions in the nature of: What is happening? What is the level of discourse? What can be learned from this?

A fourth and related skill that a group facilitator should have is the ability to exploit emotionally upsetting problem situations. Peace-at-any-price, comfort at-all-costs behavior on his part may result in his ignoring or glossing over some of the best learning opportunities presented by group interaction. Such emotional timidity may prevent adequate attention to the feelings of participants and cause this type of facilitator to reassure when he should listen and to give advice and propose solutions before concerns and problems fully are considered. Frank described the need for maintaining a challenging level of concern.

> . . . It is necessary and desirable to maintain an optimal amount of emotional tension. . . . We know that if a person is panicky, he can't learn—and if he is completely blasé and indifferent, he is not going to learn either. . . . So we try to damp down emotion when it gets too strong, which may happen in groups, and we try to stir it up if it is too weak.[17]

In a group, as in other learning situations, there is good reason to believe that the process of dealing with problems may be more important in the long run than the solution. A process, once learned, may be applied again and again and generalize to many situations. A solution is usually specific to a particular time and place and of little use elsewhere. A personal concern with its attendant feelings has high value in a group. It offers learning opportunity and experience and a reason to interact and communicate. Whether or not it is used in this manner depends to a great extent upon the facilitator.

Finally, a facilitator should have some expertise as a counselor. Although interpersonal process groups do not have therapy as a primary objective, participants do become personally and emotionally involved. Occasionally feelings and concerns surface that, for one reason or another, are not dealt with in the group. When this happens it is necessary for the facilitator to continue the interaction and to talk these concerns out with the person or persons involved. This responsi-

[17] Jerome D. Frank, "Therapy in a Group Setting," in Morris I. Stein, ed., *Contemporary Psychotherapies* (New York: The Free Press, 1961), p. 45.

bility can be ignored only at the expense of unethical behavior and a well-deserved lack of confidence in the facilitator by the group.

Choosing facilitators

Because the role played by the facilitator is so crucial for group success and because an effective group should be able to function on a continuing basis, there are reasons to question the practice of engaging a specialist on a short-term basis from outside the school to conduct a marathon, a workshop, or a retreat. A one-shot, panacea success which lasts and which transfers to classrooms and to transactions between colleagues occurs very rarely, if at all. We agree with Lippitt and Fox (1971) that it is better to arrange for members of the school staff, counselors, psychologists, and some teachers to be trained as facilitators and then to return to involve the remainder in group communication interaction experiences. No consultant can involve a large faculty group in such a manner that each member gains feedback and insight about his own behavior and no consultant is able adequately to facilitate the interaction of several small groups at once.

We do not share the reservation that those people who must work together should not be involved in an interpersonal process group together. Rather, we think that it is precisely for this reason that attention to communication interaction processes are necessary and can return appreciable dividends. Our experience corroborates this. We have had students who functioned very effectively as group facilitators in their own schools and with their own colleagues. The key to this appears to be the ability of those involved to separate teaching and group interaction functions.

When a team is operating in a teaching capacity, participant roles, rules for transacting, appropriate behavior, and lines of authority will be different. If the primary concern is teaching, the team will deal mostly with instructional planning and discussion content will be factual and information oriented. Attention will focus upon students and effort be directed toward influencing the actions of students or persons outside the team or group. Conversely, when a team is operating as an interpersonal process group, the focus will be

279

upon persons inside the group. Emphasis will be placed upon developing participant effectiveness. Discussion content will be oriented toward the affective and personal. These two team functions, of course, are not mutually exclusive. But time should be available for both and that time should be used as designated. If it is not, teachers might fall back into the more comfortable role of discussing students, and their own inputs will neither be dealt with nor changed.

GROUP VALUE AND POTENTIAL

Do groups really work?

The answer to this question has to begin, "That depends. . . ." and because it does, it must encompass certain qualifications. First, there is not much really "hard-nosed" statistical proof that lasting personality changes can directly be attributed to a group experience (Rakstis, 1970; "Human Potential" 1970; Tuckman, 1965; Calame, 1969). There are a number of reasons for this.

(1)   Groups deal with personalities and personality variables are difficult to measure. Few, if any, psychological tests in this area can claim more than a fraction of the validity attributed to measures of aptitudes, intelligence, or interest.

(2)   The inclusion of a variety of individuals in a group tremendously compounds the number of variables that may effect personal change outcomes. The inputs of each participant exert an influence.

(3)   Every group experience is different. Generalizations from one to another are difficult to defend.

(4)   Most of the research that has been done with groups has yielded qualitative rather than quantitative results (Tuckman, 1965). Personal opinion polls and questionnaires have tended to be used rather than comparisons of carefully measured before and after differences.

(5)   Participants vary considerably with respect to amounts of self-reported, observed, and measured changes. The majority has professed to feel better and to behave more effectively but a relatively small percentage has reported unfavorable results—increased irritability, more dissatis-

faction, and the like. Almost always, individuals claim to have gained substantially more than observer ratings, pre-post observations, and personality ratings indicate (Campbell and Dunnette, 1968; Lieberman, Yalom and Miles, 1973; Luke and Seashore, 1966; "Human Potential", 1970).

Obviously, there are few assurances that honestly can be provided for prospective interpersonal process group members. No surefire guarantees are possible. A certain degree of risk must be assumed with participation, but, as we have emphasized, this can be minimized. Members and sponsoring institutions are not powerless and hence not without responsibility. Let us hazard being somewhat repetitive for purposes of emphasis. First, and like other human interaction situations, inputs tend to determine outputs. The values one derives from a group experience are proportional, in considerable degree, to the risk he is able to take and the sharing he is willing to do. Unfortunately, this supports the contention that ". . . those who benefit most are the ones who need it the least . . . and vice versa." (Rakstis, 1970, p. 25.) This phenomenon especially is observable in a group. To an appreciable extent one creates, either accidentally or purposefully, the kind of interpersonal climate within which he must function.

Second, the formulation of observable, desired behavioral descriptions will help participants to use the group experience rather than to be incapacitated or manipulated by it. The same thing applies to institutions that decide to use group interaction procedures. A series of well-planned steps in a determined direction will result in more progress than one-shot leaps with great expectations and great disillusionment.

Third, a thorough investigation of possible consultants, facilitators, and the like should be made before they are employed. Their theory of group interaction, the techniques they utilize, and their past record should be examined carefully. Exparticipants from the groups they have conducted and the sponsoring institutions should be contacted. School sponsored groups should be conducted for teaching and learning purposes or not at all. There is no place for psychological sadism, messiahlike conversions, or any exploitation of participants. The best way to prevent this is to select facilitators carefully. Such things as cost and availability should not be allowed to become primary determinants.

Innovation and the communicating team

New ideas are generated by people in contact with people. But this contact must be more than merely physical. When trust and psychological closeness can be increased through group interaction experiences, the stimulation of thinking and interchange of ideas are facilitated. This does not mean committee in touch with committee, exchanges of memos and reports, or representatives meeting with representatives. It does mean individual interacting directly with individual.

Without open channels of communication, teams exist in name only and many of the advantages which they possess for personal and professional growth fail to function. For example, the activities of analysis and feedback and teacher's learning from teachers that are recognized as so essential for in-service and change in education are not possible without communication (Bush, 1971; Lippitt and Fox, 1971). Opportunities for self-renewal, self-direction, and self-development fail to be exploited. The high-trust, low-threat, minimum defense attitudes, and feelings that enable teachers to risk and to develop new behaviors cannot be assumed. They must be created. To our way of thinking, there is no better way of doing this than to approach these things directly and to make their development the object of primary concern. Group interaction can do this. Its combination with team teaching can make each activity more meaningful and more effective.

SUMMARY

Feelings of doubt, insecurity, and loneliness beset teachers who are isolated in traditional self-contained classrooms. Communication and interaction with teaching peers can do much to overcome these feelings.

However, physical proximity without psychological closeness does not necessarily facilitate the sharing and feedback essential for self-directed teacher improvement.

A combination of team teaching to bring teachers together physically and interpersonal process group experiences which function to promote more effective communicative interaction contacts can add to the value of either or both activities for in-service purposes.

Teaching teams vary so greatly in terms of organization and function and the variables that affect them are so numerous that it is difficult to compare and to contrast between them or to claim certain results for team teaching in general.

Although teachers and students tend to prefer team teaching to more traditional methods, there is little evidence that academic achievement is affected either one way or the other by team teaching.

Considerable disagreement exists concerning the value of the interactive group experience. Some proponents may diverge so widely as to term it a communist inspired plan for thought control. Significantly, everyone respects its power to affect human behavior.

It is not the group experience of and by itself that may have good or bad consequences but the manner in which it is used that makes the difference. For various reasons, such as being forced to participate, inadequate understanding, incompetent leaders, and the feeling that to ask for help is an admission of failure, teachers tend not to interact in groups so easily as other professional groups.

Teacher reservation about groups can be minimized by keeping members informed, emphasizing each person's ability to exert control, describing rather than evaluating, keeping group composition and time stable, not relying on crutches or games, requiring participants to describe desired personal competencies, and providing for a competent facilitator.

A group facilitator's function is a teaching function. He may expedite the process by serving as a model, a referee, an interpreter of interaction patterns, by using emotionally upsetting situations as learning situations, and by counseling with group members when necessary.

Because the selection of facilitators is so crucial for group success and because the one-shot approach rarely is successful, schools should arrange for selected members of their own staffs to be trained as facilitators.

Although few assurances can be provided that a combination of team teaching and group interaction will result in more effective instruction and living, participants' reports lead to the belief that the values derived may be proportional to participant input and willingness for involvement.

SUGGESTED ADDITIONAL READINGS

Combs, Arthur W., Avila, Donald L., and Purkey, William W. *Helping Relationships*. Boston: Allyn and Bacon, Inc., 1971. Teachers who wish to examine their own helping role will find this book a most valuable source. It will acquaint them with numerous possibilities for personal change and it will furnish insights concerning some of the stumbling blocks. The reader who wishes to formulate some descriptions of desired behavior as a directive for his own actions and as a guide for obtaining pertinent feedback from others can use this book.

Fullmer, Daniel W. *Counseling Group Theory and System*. Scranton, Pa.: International Textbook Co., 1971. This author has taken a fresh look at social groups. He furnishes descriptions and insights by which a group member may understand and analyze the dynamics of his own social groups and the effects of his own inputs upon their interaction. But it should be read and considered a bit at a time. There is too much here to assimilate or practice all at once.

Knoblock, Peter, and Goldstein, Arnold P. *The Lonely Teacher*. Boston: Allyn and Bacon, Inc., 1971. This book is about teacher growth and change and the use of group interaction as a means of promoting these. It is not long or difficult to understand but it is important and authoritative in the sense that the authors have experienced what they write about. It can provide readers with a clearer concept of how teacher groups function and the type of things that such groups can be expected to deal with.

Lieberman, Morton A., Yalom, Irwin D., and Miles, Mathew B. *Encounter Groups: First Facts*. New York: Basic Books, Inc., 1973. The authors provide statistical evidence on personality changes among members of encounter groups. They performed extensive research covering outcomes, dropouts, behavior changes, leader characteristics, and group climate, among other subjects, for seventeen groups and over 200 participants. Results indicated that groups were neither as effective in changing people as protagonists claim nor as harmful as detractors believe them to be.

Moustakas, Clark. *The Authentic Teacher*. Cambridge, Mass.: Howard A. Doyle Publishing Co., 1966. The transfer of what is learned in an interpersonal process group for teachers to classroom application is one of the values gained from this book. Specifically helpful are the tips for maintaining effective interpersonal relationships with youngsters and for helping them to express and deal with their feelings.

Smith, B. Othanel, Cohen, Saul B., and Pearl, Arthur. *Teachers for the Real World*. Washington, D.C.: The American Association of Colleges for Teacher Education, 1969. This is a product of the NDEA National Institute for Advanced Study in Teaching Disadvantaged Youth. Although it focuses upon the preparation of teachers for the disadvantaged, it also is pertinent for in-service programs. The necessity for changing traditional patterns and attitudes is emphasized but the reader will need to look for specifics that apply to his situation.

CHAPTER 11

Organizing for Innovation

One realization which occurs over and over when the subject of organizing comes up is that something or someone must furnish impetus and direction. Conditions must be created, or at least manipulated, in order that certain desired activities are encouraged. Because the public schools traditionally have been authority-oriented, this function has been, and probably will continue to be, an administrative function. As Thelen (1971, p. 100) has emphasized with respect to in-service activities, ". . . the starting point or the prior condition is a decent climate and concerned faculty, and both are set by the head man."

Lest the reader begin to think that this chapter is only for administrators, remember that almost everyone is the head man of some sort of human relations system. Each person has some degree of responsibility for the organization and operation of one or more types of social interaction. This responsibility may range up the scale of authority to include self, family, peer groups, classroom, school, district, city, and so forth. It may be the ultimate authority or leadership in which power cannot be disaffirmed or it may be the incidental, organization member kind of involvement which allows some disavowal of influence and responsibility. Whatever the case, effective teacher-student and teacher-teacher human relationship transactions appear to operate on the same principles which work for the administrator-managers of progressively larger systems.

Supportive management

One of the phenomena noted by the authors during their visits in innovative schools was that some administrators appeared to generate new ideas and practices at most institutions where they were located. Also, these men showed considerable occupational mobility. They seemed to be continually moving or being moved. After two or three years, during which the school gained recognition for excellence and innovation, they switched schools and began to create or instill the innovative process at another location. Typically, the reaction to their leaving was, "We hate to see him go, but he seems to be doing well where he is now. I guess he likes a challenge."

Equally noteworthy is the fact that these schools continued to function effectively without further direction or management from the administrators credited with getting the innovative process started. These leaders appeared to have created few dependency relationships and seemed to have been able to "turn people loose" to function on their own. Snyder and Peterson (1970) describe this as a supportive as opposed to a directive role in the leadership of in-service education. With it, there is no prescription of the innovation to be tried next or any short-term importation of consultants to tell the staff of those weaknesses which need correcting. It is the type of leadership which encourages teacher self-examination and involvement and which values and rewards the thinking process of staff members.

Despite its apparent simplicity, this is not an easy role for educational managers to play. There are some traps (enticing pitfalls) to be avoided. Enthusiasm may lead to the overendorsement of an idea. A manager may become so eager to have a concept adopted and to see it function that the innovation becomes identified with him and the responsibility for carrying it out is regarded as his. Even the decision to support one idea in preference to another is bound to have repercussions. Whether he realizes it or not, the administrator-manager represents and is a part of the incumbent system. The ideas he supports have a high probability of being or becoming the status quo. Too much of this and the changes supported may add up to no real change at all.

But notice how easily we have lapsed back into valuing the product (ideas) rather than valuing and rewarding the processes by which they are generated. Most likely the administrator who is able to support teacher involvement in such activities as problem solving, cooperative planning, and brainstorming and who does not pass judgment concerning the worth of resultant ideas will have taken an important step toward dealing with a difficult problem.

Ways of looking at change

The understanding one gains about the function of a social system depends upon the frame of reference from which he observes. Even though his expectations may color his perceptions, he must know something of what to look for in order to see it. School administrators, in particular, need to establish ways of seeing more than they do see and of using these to develop both understanding and strategies for improvement. Probably there are many workable systems for gaining and for processing information in schools but the procedure should be systematic rather than accidental or intuitive. In line with previously advanced tenets, the authors have some suggestions.

Move from microcosm to macrocosm. Move from the part to the whole or from subsystem to system. One must be aware of his own manner of relating and affecting others before he can manage his own inputs in interaction situations. He must understand the dynamics of specific teacher-to-teacher relationships before he can know much about the operation of a teaching team. And he must be able to combine this knowledge with some comprehension of the other interpersonal transaction patterns within the total system for which he is held responsible. It undoubtedly is true that the whole is something more than the sum of its parts. But how much more and of what character well may be determined by the person or persons who serve as the catalyst.

A further advantage of moving from subsystem to system,

from person to group, lies with the aids this provides for understanding the larger units (Thelen, 1971). The study of human interaction often is better accomplished by observing behavior in its simpler or its most blatant aspects. Once an action or pattern with its causes and consequences is recognized in this manner, it becomes easier to spot in more complex and more ordinary situations. Thus an institution's probable defensive reaction to criticism comes to be expected through observing the responses of individuals and small groups, and the climate of a school beset with regulations can be forecast by first watching a child's reaction to overdirection and overprotection.

To a considerable extent, strategies for dealing with individuals and small groups can also be applied with success to larger groups, institutions, and organizations. For example, the principles for effective interpersonal process group operation and leader function also will work for a school administrator transacting with teaching staffs, student bodies, and PTAs. Knowledge about communication and interpersonal transaction can be applied to increasing personal and professional effectiveness in home, school, and community situations.

Tune in to the human relations aspects. A premise advanced by Goldhammer (1969) is that the human personality tends to take on the psychological characteristics of its environment. Environments are composed of people as they interact with and respond to each other. Everyone exerts some influence in such environments, and the input of no person can be overlooked if one is to understand the emotional tone, its effect on participants, and the manner in which the system perpetuates itself. This means that individuals and the manner in which they affect each other need to be objects of study and analysis if the conditions and processes which lead to change are to be established.

The person who would organize a classroom, a teaching and learning team, a school, or another social system must become informed about the interaction contacts maintained by the persons in his organization. He must know who leads and who follows and who is listened to and who is not. He must study such things as the operation of cliques, pecking orders, and dominance hierarchies and he must be able to tell whether

289

The human personality tends to take on the psychological characteristics of its environment.

these function as a part of the formal structure or whether they operate informally. Scott described organizations as social systems. He characterized each as a ". . . system of cliques, grapevines, informal status systems, and rituals; . . . a mixture of logical and nonlogical behavior." [1] If one is to deal with these systems, he needs to know how to work with, and not in opposition to, them. A knowledge that they exist is not

[1] William A. Scott, *Organization Theory* (Homewood, Ill.: Richard D. Irwin, Inc., 1967), p. 34.

enough. One needs to know how to support them and how to gain support from them. He needs to know where his inputs are apt to fit acceptably and what these should be in terms of effect and consequences.

Recognize both formal and informal interaction systems. The more authority and power a position appears to command, the more formal the interaction which it generally promotes. Conversely, the less influence an individual's job placement indicates, the more informal his communication patterns are apt to be. Two common errors in organizing and in managing organizations are either overlooking the informal systems or assuming that they coincide in structure and operation with the line and staff organization chart, through channeled representations characteristic of formal procedures. With such an orientation, the manager, supervisor, principal, or other administrator may lose individuals in the impersonalism of formal groups, committees, schedules, and representatives. He may think he is informed about his organization although his knowledge, in fact, is only sufficient to lead him into a false sense of security and a comfortable lack of awareness with respect to the human relations errors he makes.

Characteristics which may help to distinguish informal from formal interaction systems and assist in understanding their operation include:

(1) Substantial parts of the informal system operate below levels of awareness. While formal interaction communication patterns can be recognized easily in terms of administrative organization—who is headman and who are assistants, who is in charge of this and who is responsible for that—it is much more difficult to determine who influences, and what procedures and patterns form, the informal system. As many of us realize when we stop to think about it, agreements, policies, and attitudes very often are formulated in lounges, bars, and at social functions with the subsequent vote and approval mostly a formality.

(2) The informal system operates in terms of implicit understandings rather than in terms of more explicit regulations and decrees. While the formal system may be controlled directly through rules and their enforcement, the informal mostly is influenced indirectly. One may force acquiescence and obedience; he cannot force respect. An adminis-

trator may gain consent through one system but he gains commitment and support through the other.

(3)   An organization's emotional tone and psychological climate are more often indicated by the informal than by the formal system. Such intangibles as personal feelings and affect are determining factors in the function of the one system. The other is based on the assumption that organizations operate in a reasonable manner and that intellectual processes furnish a basis for their function and a means for understanding this.

(4)   Generally the more dissonance organizers and administrators sense in the informal system, the more prescription, policy, and control is applied to the formal structure. Paradoxically and conversely, the more restrictive and regulated the total organization becomes, the more restive and resistant its informal components are likely to be.

(5)   Differences between systems probably can be resolved more effectively by adapting the formal to the informal rather than the other way around. As nearly as possible, formal lines of authority and the placement of responsibility should be made, through delegation and appointment, to coincide with informal patterns of influence.

(6)   Because of the personal nature of the informal system as contrasted with the generally impersonal character of its informal counterpart, changes within that system are best accomplished through person-to-person and small group contacts. Meetings involving representatives or committees which do not bring individuals who are transacting for themselves into direct contact are more properly aspects of the formal system. The personal attitudes and feelings which people have about one another are best altered by providing opportunities for them to become directly involved with each other.

(7)   Increased emphasis with regard to the functioning of the informal system should complement, supplement, and lead to an increased understanding of the formal system. It should not be considered a substitute. One cannot overlook either system if he is to gain real perspective about the operation of an organization.

Develop a systematic approach. Only when an observer has a means of ordering and interpreting what he sees is he apt to get maximum results from supervisory management processes. Of late there has been considerable examination of the systems approach to conceptualizing and formulating organi-

Anyone can be mistaken, but if you really want to foul things up, appoint a committee!

zational structure and of systems analysis for studying and assessing the effectiveness of such systems or structures.

Basically this way of organizing and understanding is similar to the time-honored scientific method (Oettinger, 1968) or the job analysis more recently popular (Yelon, 1969). It involves not only a painstaking consideration of organization components and how they work but also a continuing effort to rearrange and restructure so they will work better. Certain components and functions are characteristic of the more formal systems approach.

1) It involves a breakdown of the organization into systems and subsystems for purposes of study. Any unit may thus be considered either as a system or a subsystem. When a unit is the primary object of analysis, it may be viewed as an entity in itself and its components may be considered as subsystems of the larger unit (Scott, 1967; Tondow, 1967). One of the values of the systems approach is that it enables an identification and analysis of each organization

293

component in a manner analogous to dealing with problems one step or one small part at a time. One may divide
and subdivide until complexities are understandable. Then
he may combine and recombine for a fresh and more
comprehensive look at total unit operation.

(2)   A systems approach employs the concepts of input and
output. First one determines the type of product (output)
he desires. Then he experiments with what he must feed
into the system (input) to get this. The outputs of the
various subsystems of a system are fed into the operation
as inputs at different points in the production, decision
making or learning process in order that certain objectives in terms of the output of the total system are
realized. Pragmatically, a system and its component
subsystems are analyzed in terms of the results achieved.
This leads to and makes the following additional characteristics or functions necessary.

(3)   The behaviors, learnings, attitudes (outputs), and similar
outcomes which are to be generated by the system must
be carefully described (Thoreson, 1969). The smaller and
more basic the subsystem, the smaller the unit of behavior
and the more specific each description needs to be. For
example, one desired behavior to be developed by team
teaching might be: "Solicits observation and feedback
from fellow teachers." This is a valuable objective for a
broad and fairly inclusive system such as a teaching team
but it is not sufficiently specific to be wholly useful. In
order to gain this specificity, it is necessary to narrow the
description so that conditions in the nature of when,
where, and how much are defined. Whether the observation is to take place as a part of a microteaching experience or during team teaching, along with what is to be
looked for and how frequently it should happen, all will
help to assess the results (output) of this particular
operation or subsystem. Hence the original objective can
be made more specific by stating such subobjectives as:

(a)   describes a desired teaching behavior,
(b)   arranges for videotaped microteaching in which this
behavior is practiced,
(c)   requests teaching team to critique tape and provide
feedback,
(d)   assesses results in terms of student reactions,
(e)   alters behavior description and performance in ways
indicated, and
(f)   practices the new teaching behavior in the classroom.

294

(4) Feedback and communication flow channels should be specified and used. A part of the results or effects of system operation thus is reintroduced for comparison with desired outcomes as specified by objectives (Hosford and Ryan, 1970). Choices, alternatives, and directions are determined on this basis. Feedback is especially important. No system, whether it be an individual teacher, a teaching team, or a total school organization, can be self-directing, self-renewing, self-actualizing, and innovative, or whatever term best describes the process in mind, in the absence of feedback. Indeed, it can be stated with confidence that the degree to which feedback is built in and utilized by a system will determine how self-directing and growth oriented the system is likely to be. But it is important when dealing with people and social systems to distinguish between feedback and those evaluative critical comments which generate defensiveness and limit risking new behavior. First of all, feedback is based upon observable, carefully described behaviors. As contrasted with opinion, it can be validated. Second, feedback is more apt to be initiated and controlled by the system, i.e., those who will use it. Because it can be internally managed rather than externally imposed, it aids in self-direction. Third, feedback is oriented toward how well a process works. It does not, of and by itself, label, evaluate, or place judgments upon people.

(5) A further distinguishing feature of a systems approach is that it lends itself to graphic portrayal through the development of flow charts. In this manner, narrative, verbal description is converted to another language. Like a road map, a flow chart prescribes a systematic best route. It helps to prevent digressions, and it helps to arrange subsystems within a system and behavior descriptions within an operation in proper sequence. Decision making points and those spots where feedback should originate plus the channels it should follow can be identified.

For the purpose of illustration, let us use the verbal example previously advanced in describing the third characteristic of the systems approach. Consider the broad objective "Solicits observation and feedback" as one of the processes or subsystems to be developed under the team teaching system, which in turn may be considered a subsystem under the more inclusive system representing instruction. In order to chart the flow of a school system, therefore, one could construct desired

295

step by step processes within the systems of instruction, administration, and maintenance (see Figure 11-1).

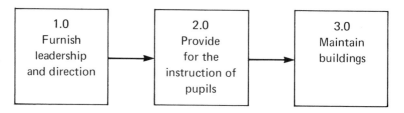

FIGURE 11-1. *A flow chart for a school system in its simplest, most comprehensive form.*

Notice that each system is designated numerically and that subsystems can be identified for each by listing second, third, and fourth digits, or more. Team teaching, for instance, might be identified as 2.3, and the third subsystem under instruction and its various components as 2.3.1, 2.3.2, and so on. It is on this level that the original desired behavior, "Solicits observation and feedback from fellow teachers," can be placed. Depending upon how the sequence representing team teaching is developed, this performance might be identified as the sixth step (2.3.6). When, and if, it is, it can be approached as a system of and by itself and the various steps, subsystems, or behavior descriptions plus the feedback channels needed for making it work can be developed. A suggested way of doing this, with feedback loops designated by the symbol Ⓕ, is advanced in Figure 11-2.

The visual picture presented by a flow chart enables the user to:

(1) know exactly where each component (system and subsystem) fits in the total organization through identifying numbers,
(2) recognize gaps and parts that are out of sequence,
(3) plan for effective communication through regular and feedback channels,
(4) establish decision making points, and
(5) understand the functioning of existing systems as well as to plan for their modification and to structure new ones.

What has been said regarding a systems approach, however, should be looked upon more as suggestion and endorsement than as prescription and guarantee. It is no panacea.

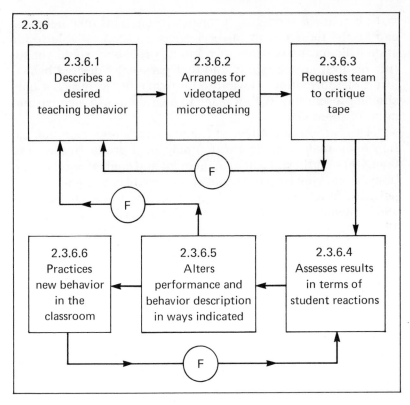

FIGURE 11-2. *A detailed flow chart showing how a teacher might work toward the objective "Solicits observation and feedback."*

While aiding in the solution of some problems it undoubtedly will create others. Hartley (1969), for example, points out twenty-five limitations of systems analysis in education. He emphasizes that "in the final analysis, the success of systems procedures is dependent upon the artistry of the user." But this is what it is all about anyway—the artistry and effectiveness of individuals. When systems analysis is conceptualized as a way of thinking which can help with the recognition and consideration of influencing factors, not as a highly technical, computer based, restricted-to-experts program, it can be valuable for anyone with responsibilities in some sort of social system, whether this includes one or two individuals, a classroom, a teaching team, a school building, or an entire district.

Emphasize and practice open communication. A most important realization for any school organization manager or supervisor is that the model he furnishes through his own behavior can be the most potent in-service experience available to his staff. This means that his own inputs probably should constitute his first area of study and that personally desired behaviors and information relevant to his own effectiveness not only should present him with a place to begin but also a consistent point of reference.

The pattern and effect of the manager's own communication upon that of his institution may be a productive way of doing this. Authorities in management and control in organizations, in viewing the communication variable as crucial for the effective functioning of such systems, tend to concur (Haney, 1967; Hughes, 1970; Bridges, Olm, and Barnhill, 1971; Scott, 1967; Tannenbaum, 1968). Generally, two implications can be made: (1) The higher the rank and the greater the responsibility of the individual, the more important his communication inputs and the more essential it is that he communicates effectively. (2) The greater the power and influence commanded by his position, the more difficult it will be for the administrator to establish and maintain open and meaningful channels of communication (Combs, Avila, and Purkey, 1971). This appears to happen because of the inverse relationship among perceived threat, trust levels, and defensive behaviors (Haney, 1967). It operates in two directions. First, when a person's potential for influencing the destiny of another is perceived by the latter to be high, the suspicion experienced in interacting and communicating will probably rise and the trust fall. He will be unable to accept at face value messages from the person he sees as having power over him. Second, an individual who feels himself to be at the mercy of another can be expected consistently to attempt to put his best foot forward. His communications are likely to omit anything which he thinks may irritate. So it is that the more influence and power one can exercise, the more his communication may be limited by what his staff thinks he wants to hear and the interpretations and advice which his staff believes he can tolerate. The responses he gets may be both limited and misleading. Certainly, much hostile behavior on the part of any executive, whether or not he means it or sees that he is antagonistic, can be expected seriously to affect the communications he maintains. It is the receiver and not the sender who really determines what is communicated.

298

The executive, then, who is estimated to spend about 75 percent of his time communicating, 75 percent of this in face-to-face situations (Haney, 1967), must be concerned about those aspects of his behavior which promote trust and limit distrust. Combs, Avila, and Purkey (1971) see this as a two-way process.[2] They describe it as the "threat counter-threat spiral in communication." Basically it operates in this manner: The administrator who withholds information senses the distrust this generates in his associates and, because he is threatened, restricts his contacts even more. Thus he promotes more distrust, more threat, and greater restriction and distortion of communication both for himself and for his subordinates in a cumulative, system reinforcing manner. The problem, of course, is to avoid the inputs which create and perpetuate such a system and to cultivate those behaviors which will reverse the spiral in a positive direction. For this purpose, some suggestions from Combs, Avila, and Purkey have been combined with ideas from other writers and from the experience of the authors.[3]

(1) The feelings of persons involved in the process of communicating should be attended to. Because schools traditionally have operated to "keep the lid on feelings," (Conlin and Haberman, 1969) it especially is important that the executive administrator model recognizes them. Much of the feeling of threat and the defensiveness which limits and distorts communication can be prevented or ameliorated by managers who can share their own feelings and who can make it possible for co-workers to verbalize theirs.

(2) The feelings of anger and hostility which result from threat need to be ventilated. When attack results and is met by counterattack, anger is intensified. When its verbalization is encouraged, its force is spent and it does not need to be acted out. But the manager is responsible for many things and his sensitivity and vulnerability to criticism and attack can be expected to be proportional to this responsibility. For this reason, he especially must be aware of his own inclination to defend and to counterat-

[2] See also the paradigm of mutual influence described in Chapter 4.
[3] Arthur W. Combs, Donald L. Avila, and William W. Purkey, *Helping Relationships: Basic Concepts for the Helping Professions* (Boston: Allyn and Bacon, Inc., 1971), pp. 265–66.

299

tack. A few slips and open communication with him will become too risky.

(3) Personal feelings of security and importance must be generated in co-workers. When a person feels positively about himself, knows that what he does makes a worthwhile difference and feels accepted and appreciated, there is a greater tolerance for threat and less tendency to be defensive on his part. Interpersonal competition and the oneupmanship which puts people down and makes them feel inadequate seriously will interfere with open communication.

(4) The differences of individuals should be recognized in terms of their tolerance for threat if their ability to listen and respond is not to be impaired. While feedback can be accepted and used profitably to direct behavior change by some, others will feel criticized and be incapacitated by it. A manager of social interaction systems needs to bear these differences in mind if he is to be an effective communicator.

(5) An overt recognition of the impact which associates have and one's areas of dependence upon them is a necessary aspect in developing an effective interaction perspective. This serves to deter the tendency to overassume responsibility and to take unilateral action and it keeps the distinction between the organizer and those with whom he works from becoming a communication gap.

(6) Straight line, open, explicit communication should be modeled and encouraged. Whenever a person is forced to speculate concerning another's intent and feelings, his levels of threat, insecurity, and defensiveness rise and his own ability to transfer meaning is restricted. Remember, the greater the power of the communicator, the more disruptive any inability to communicate openly on his part can be.

(7) Actions calculated to reverse the threat counter-threat spiral must be applied consistently over an extended period of time before results may become apparent. The reason for this is that behavior tends to outlast eliciting conditions. Failures of communication may continue long after the reasons for them have disappeared, and it is rare indeed that results occur as quickly as we would like. The danger is that instant cure expectations may lead to abandoning a promising approach before it has had a chance to work.

The organizer's personal needs should be considered. A person's own attitude is an important determinant in his performance. When the demands of a position are too stringent and psychological pressure is high, he feels controlled by, instead of feeling in control of, the situation. He is apt to resist rather than be enthusiastic about what needs to be done.

One of the least recognized aspects of the high influence positions is that those who occupy them are likely to be made more, rather than less, vulnerable because of the power and competence they represent. Despite the fact that the urge for security often leads people to strive for more control and strength in social situations, the role they are forced to play in order to get and to keep this can generate anything but assurance and comfort. Two ways in which this can happen substantiate this assertion.

The first of these concerns the dependence which competence and power tend to promote in others, for in our culture the strong are expected to help the weak. A state of powerlessness and inadequacy carries with it the right to demand assistance and direction. It is this demand that raises the question, "Who really directs whom?" A social system may come in fact to manage its managers and even to victimize those who guide its operation. After all, the persons with the power cannot avoid the responsibility for making the system work. Those without it experience comparatively little of this kind of pressure. It is not uncommon for the person in charge to become spread so thinly by the demands of his associates and his job (Peter, 1967) that he is unable to focus his efforts enough to do anything very well. Instead of satisfaction and status, his position brings him frustration and feelings of inadequacy.

A second reason for the increase in vulnerability with influence and prestige lies with the high personal visibility these promote. To a considerable degree this is a competetive, scapegoating culture. Someone must be identified as responsible and culpable when things do not turn out as expected. Too often, a head or two must fall, even though the original situation may not be improved by the sacrifice. In addition, giant killing and psychological oneupmanship may be ego gratifying for those who suffer by comparison. Attack sometimes is mounted just to "take down a peg" those with status.

One needs to have done nothing more to be a victim. The poet Yevtushenko described such a situation:

Enormity commands everyone
To hunt for it.
Whoever is big is stupid
Who's smaller is wiser.[4]

But the picture is not all bleak. Knowledge of the possibilities allows a look for alternatives. Some suggestions are: Consciously put yourself first sometimes. Retain the right to manage your time by reserving some for yourself and your family which you hold relatively inviolable. Refuse, on suitable occasions, to respond as expected. Don't always put things right even if you can. Insist that someone else assumes the responsibility occasionally. Remember that the organizer can be free only to the extent that his associates are able to act independently. Purposely do some things to destroy the exalted image you may have developed in the eyes of your associates. Practice enough of what Peter (1967) has described as "creative incompetence" so that you retain the right to be mistaken. Own up to, and point out, your weaknesses often enough to tone down the expectancies and the consequent disillusionments people generate for you. If you have no weaknesses, it may be wise to create a few, for it is hard to relate to, and communicate meaningfully with, perfection. One can decrease the pressure with which he must deal this way and paradoxically sometimes become more competent by purposely becoming less competent.

THE DILEMMAS OF ORGANIZATION MANAGEMENT

There is a disquieting ambivalence which besets human affairs, which renders unshakable convictions difficult, and which often makes really decisive behavior a task of no mean proportions. It exists because there is a vast middle ground between right and wrong and between never and always.

[4] Yevgeny Yevtushenko, "Cemetery of Whales." From STOLEN APPLES by Yevgeny Yevtushenko. Copyright © 1971 by Doubleday & Company, Inc. Reprinted by Permission of Doubleday & Company, Inc.

Things seldom arrange themselves with the preponderance of evidence on one side and convincing arguments often can be advanced for any one of many alternatives. Often the more comprehensive one's knowledge and the more objective his outlook, the more elusive the clear-cut perspective. An awareness of ambiguity does not lend itself to easy decisions or to comfort in administrative positions.

But it may be that certainty, insofar as it locks one in to a course of action and limits flexibility, must give way to the tentative position. A certain amount of freedom to take advantage of something better must be maintained despite the insecurity which a lack of closure and suspended decision tend to promote. As Erikson has observed:

> Psychoanalysts, of course, are consulted primarily by those who cannot stand the tension between alternatives, contrasts, and polarities which governs the American style of today: the increasing necessity to remain tentative to be free for bigger and better opportunities.[5]

Unfortunately, conditions combine to increase this stress for the organizer or administrator. Along with the needs to withhold commitment and to tolerate uncertainty, there inevitably is pressure to decide, to say how it should be, to take a stand, and to "tell us what is expected." This push can be expected to increase with status and position in a power hierarchy. It can be expected to be applied with most insistence by those who themselves are least secure, most threatened, most in need of structure, and most doubtful about their own abilities.

But no matter what the degree of certainty, decisions must be made and positions must be taken. One cannot remain tentative or uncommitted for very long. There always is the dilemma—the pressure to decide and the threat of being judged wrong and incompetent when one does so.

Other dilemmas which must be faced by the supervisor or organizer or manager are described below. They are advanced as examples, with no claims for breadth of coverage or for correctness of any solutions mentioned or implied. The pur-

---

[5] Erik H. Erikson, *Identity, Youth, and Crisis* (New York: W. W. Norton and Co., 1968), p. 65.

pose is to point out the perennial, persistent, and often paradoxical nature of the dilemmas faced by organizers and to provide any comfort which may come from a knowledge of the fact that those dilemmas mentioned as well as others of a similar nature have been solved over and over again without every really having been solved at all.[6] This may be good as far as the organizer or manager is concerned. Conclusive and lasting settlements and answers would eliminate the need for his services. If he were to be as completely successful as he strives to be and his decisions anything but transitory, he would no longer be needed.

It may be necessary to give away authority in order to keep it.

Self-directing teachers remove some of the pressure and responsibility for ordering and managing from administrators. Students who are capable of individual, self-directed study decrease the tension which pushing and directing rouses for teachers. The question of how to make this happen is akin in difficulty to that faced by the authority figure who orders his subordinates to be democratic. The more he pushes and directs, the more he defeats what he tries to accomplish. Indeed, the very use of incentives and actions provides evidence that authority is not accepted (Scott, 1967).

Just as some structure and direction are necessary to provide the security and support needed for risk taking, so too much rigidity and too many regulations will operate to prevent it. Certainly it is tempting as well as traditional to issue additional directives and to increase regulations when things do not go well. It is customary to tighten the screws when others fail to behave responsibly and it is standard procedure to correct mistakes and to set people straight when they fail. But then the dilemma arises. How can individuals learn to direct their own actions and begin to make decisions for themselves under these conditions?

Fortunately, this does not have to be an either/or situation, i.e., total application or total abstention. Miller offers this clarification:

[6] For an excellent description of additional educational dilemmas see Robert Goldhammer, *Clinical Supervision* (New York: Holt, Rinehart and Winston, Inc., 1969), pp. 44–49.

304

. . . You do not need complete authority over a social organization in order to reform it. The important thing is not to control the system, but to understand it. Someone who has a valid conception of the system as a whole can often introduce relatively minor changes that have extensive consequences throughout the entire organization. Lacking such a conception, worthwhile innovations may be total failures.[7]

This process is one of delegating rather than of exercising authority and control. It entails understanding the organization well enough to know when, where, what kind, and how much direction is needed. If one is to err either way, it probably is better to provide too little rather than too much. But, here again, the quality of the relationship maintained rather than the quantity imposed is apt to make the real difference. The essence of this type of leadership was caught by Hall.

The responsibility of the leader—be he president, chairman, coach, director, chief-of-staff—is not primarily to provide directives but to maintain an evocative situation. Though he may be relatively inconspicuous, his role is crucial in keeping the goal in sight, creating a warm and permissive atmosphere for participation, recognizing consensus, helping persons find their parts in a cooperative effort.

We measure the effectiveness of the leader, not in terms of leadership he exercises, but in terms of the leadership he evokes—not in terms of his power over others, but in terms of the power he releases in others—not in terms of the goals he sets up and the directions he gives, but in terms of the goals and plans of action persons work out for themselves with his help—not in terms alone of products and projects completed, but in terms of growth in competence, sense of responsibility and the personal satisfactions among many participants.

Under this kind of leadership it may not always be clear at any given moment just who is leading—nor is this very important. What is important is that many may learn how to set their teeth into a problem, to apply their minds to it, to work it out together.

[7] George A. Miller, "Psychology as a Means of Promoting Human Welfare," *American Psychologist* 24 (1969): 1063–1075.

Leadership of this kind gets more done—more thinking, more action, more final product—and of even greater importance—more enhancement of human values.[8]

So the most effective leader actually leads as little as he can. Leadership remains a means toward an end with him. It is not allowed to become an end in itself. The more unnecessary he can become the better his job has been done. As the Chinese philosopher, Lao Tse, phrased it thousands of years ago:

A leader is best
When people barely know he exists,
Not so good, when people obey and acclaim him,
Worst, when they despise him.

. . . But of a good leader, who talks little,
When his work is done, his aim fulfilled,
They will say, 'We did this ourselves.' [9]

Although structure and direction are necessary, prescription may discourage the creative innovative process.

The application of a method already devised really cannot be considered as creative or new any more than the adoption of a previously developed idea honestly can be regarded as innovative. Whenever administrative structures specify which innovation to put into practice and decide who will do this and how it will be done, the word "innovate," in its strictest sense, is deceptive. "Conform" may be the more appropriate term.

But how about authors whose writing appears to tell others what and how? Is it not hypocritical to speak of self-direction and innovation at the same time that suggestions for doing things this way or that way are provided? We have pondered these questions and the saving grace we see is that, with books of this nature, reader choice always is possible. There is the option to agree with all or none or any part or to create any combination. One need not read to adopt any more

[8] L. K. Hall, "Leadership," quoted by Paul Talbot in United Business Investment Report 61 (December 1, 1969): 471.
[9] Quoted in Ruth Strang, *Group Work in Education* (New York: Harper and Row, Publishers, Inc., 1958), p. 82.

than he reads to experience a variety of stimuli which he may be able to use to generate creative ideas on his own. Our defensible purpose and that of supportive managers and organizers is to provide the bases for creative selection and recombination.

If good working accord is to be maintained some conflict must be allowed.

Petty jealousies, competitions, and resentments inevitably are generated among people in social organizations (Knoblock and Goldstein, 1971). More frequently than we care to admit, the assessment of another's ideas or projects and the support given to them result from feelings about the person involved rather than from an objective evaluation of the workability of his idea. Gaining the endorsement of one individual or group too often means ensuring the automatic opposition of another. Inexplicable and unexpected results are generated by organizations in which possibilities of this nature are ignored and consequently not dealt with.

It is possible that concern for a salubrious working climate may lead to a peace-at-any-price, emotional timidity on the part of organizers. They may avoid confronting issues and individuals and they may discourage this in others. The net result, of course, is a build up of tension, one small thing piled on another, with no means either for preventing its accumulation or for dispelling it after it has generated. There is a great difference between recognizing that human interaction does generate friction and providing some means for dealing with it and ignoring or attempting to suppress it. Its expression can be channeled and controlled but it can't be banished. Comfort at all costs usually turns out to be no comfort at all.

Particularly, interpersonal tension may become an issue in situations where change is sought. The process of changing provides for challenge, stimulation, interaction, disagreement, and pressure upon individuals (Combs, Avila, and Purkey, 1971). Empires are bound to be invaded, psychological security upset, negative emotions generated, and the traditional and usual is bound to be questioned. It is hard to see how innovation can be attempted without triggering at least some of these disruptions. It is hard to see how it can continue with any chance of success unless some means of resolving these feelings is provided as a part of the innovative process or package. Our recommendation already has been made (see Chapter 9, pp. 237–38). It involves the use of small groups as communication laboratories which function both to prevent and to dispell the defensive, limiting behaviors resulting from ineffective interpersonal relationships.

Certainty concerning the process of change and innovation involves the toleration of uncertainty.

It is common practice to want some assurance of success before moving, to want some guarantee that an idea will work before it is put into practice, and to require that certain results will be obtained as a condition for trying something different. We do not mean to imply that this attitude is wrong and to advocate indiscriminate change just for the sake of change, but here, as with many dilemmas, it is hard to tell when the show-me, prove-it attitude becomes unnecessarily restrictive. Being sure that something will work suggests that results are already known which in turn suggests that nothing new or really innovative will be allowed a trial.

There is a vast and often undistinguished difference between changing and merely trying harder. While the first requires a fresh look and a different approach, the second may involve an intensification of effort on the very thing that didn't work in the first place. Such perennial problems, from school dropouts to study assignments, are cases in point. In too many instances, time, money, and concern are expended to get youngsters back into the same situations they were unable to tolerate. When learning does not take place as expected, the too frequent remedy is to increase the length and difficulty of assignments.

As the amount of criticism, attack, and pressure experienced by a system—be this classroom, teaching team, school or school district—rises, the tendencies to become locked in to established procedures and to try harder rather than to change increase. In such systems the expenditure of effort perpetuates and intensifies rather than solves problems.

It probably is true that those institutions and individuals who most need to change find it most difficult to do so (Combs,

Avila, and Purkey, 1971). Defensive rigidity stems from feelings of threat and uncertainty. In such cases the risk felt is already so strong that any increase is intolerable. Ideas or behavior which might upset a precarious balance are opposed with a vehemence disproportional to their probable impact. Banning long hair or short skirts, for example, becomes a matter of much concern while issues and needed changes of a far graver nature are ignored in this preoccupation with trivia.

A couple of descriptive rules of thumb can be advanced. The amount of threat, feelings of inadequacy, uncertainty, and insecurity being experienced by an organization and its directors and supervisors is indicated by their resistance to change and by their refusal to consider different behaviors. The more creative, innovative, and inventive a proposal or idea, the more resistance it is apt to provoke in high threat level individuals and institutions (Taylor, 1968). So it may be that if any assurance is to be gained that innovation and change will function in an organization, its organizers must be willing to encourage those processes without demanding anything approaching a complete assurance concerning what the products will be.

Pressure to change may prevent its happening. The need to change, to innovate, and to invent depends upon a dissatisfaction with what is. The idea that things can be improved carries the implication that present functioning and those who are responsible for it are not doing their job well, that they in a sense are deficient or incompetent. Particularly this may be true when the impetus for change comes from a supervisory, systems management position and it may increase with the amount of power and authority represented.

When this happens a number of things inimical to the innovative process may take place in those who are urged to make the changes or do the changing.

(1) Because of the lack of confidence implied in them, they may come to doubt both themselves and the degree of leader support they can expect.
(2) Some degree of immobilizing threat and defensiveness may be generated (Conlin ahd Haberman, 1969, p. 213).
(3) Larger degrees of responsibility for the modification and effective operation of the system will come to bear upon those in supervisory roles.

Pressure to change may prevent its happening!

(4)   The more the responsibility for change and for directing the organization becomes the manager's, the less the others involved will identify with the project and the less interest and commitment they will feel for making it work (Likert, 1967).

(5)   Because feelings of powerlessness and a lack of identification with the organization may be promoted in others by pressuring them to change, some degree of resistance and perverseness may be manifest by system members.

In this respect, Lippitt and Fox (1971, p. 133) advance the assumption, "Typically the stimulus to participate in inservice training is an unwelcome imposition of authority. . . ." But that is what makes a dilemma. No organizer can afford to let his organization stagnate. He must do something even if it is wrong. Here we reiterate, both for comfort and for emphasis, *the process of innovating and changing is likely, in the long run, to prove more important than its products.* One never knows for sure how well an idea will work until after it is put into practice and even then he never knows whether another alternative would have worked better.

Probably the best suggestion is that change will occur

most easily and results will be more lasting when ideas and impetus are generated inside a teaching staff than when these are imposed from exterior sources (Lippitt and Fox, 1971). After all, the major value of an idea may lie in the enthusiasm and involvement it generates. The excellence of any innovation is likely to be no greater than the commitment to put it into practice (Glasser, 1969; Rogers, 1969).

The major value of an idea may lie in the enthusiasm and involvement that it generates.

Teaching teams have great potential for involving teachers and starting the innovative process from the inside. When teachers are communicating and when they have responsibilities for planning and implementing, suggestions for improvement are bound to result. Effective organizers are quick to recognize and support these. If they fail to do so, a climate for innovation is not likely to be generated in their school.

Evaluation, though a necessary aspect of management, may hinder its purposes.

Successful social system management depends upon a knowledge of the functional competence of components. Although evaluation is necessary in order to achieve this, the judging,

311

rating, and labelling often involved in this process usually do not engender feelings of trust nor lead to the open communication necessary for effective operation. As Combs, Avila, and Purkey point out, ". . . the net effect of evaluation externally applied often boomerangs to destroy the very motivations it sought to produce." [10]

People are generally defensive and especially alert when being rated and assessed. The best foot is forward and the rater is likely to get anything but a look at usual behavior. This especially is true of teachers whose tenure, promotions, salary, and recommendations depend upon supervisor impressions. It is even more likely with those teachers who need improvement and the helpful suggestions which supervision ostensibly is conducted to provide. For no matter how hard one tries to prevent it and no matter how vociferously it may be denied, supervision, when performed by principals, superintendents, and other authorities, tends to be perceived as evaluative (Sybouts, 1969). It is avoided by teachers and sometimes even considered as a personal attack (Guss, 1969).

Even though supervision should function as an integral part of classroom based in-service education, teacher distrust must be overcome before this profitably can be done (Rutrough, 1969). McNeil (1971) reports that, although 75 percent of superintendents and principals express confidence in their supervisory programs, 50 percent of their teachers do not. He also indicates that the median number of observations during a school term is two for elementary teachers and only one for secondary teachers. No more than 50 percent of these observations are followed up by conferences. Hence there is a considerable gap between supervision in practice and supervision in terms of in-service education theory.

In order to reduce the threat and distrust which teachers feel toward the supervisory process and to ensure its being used regularly and consistently in service, here are some suggestions to bear in mind:

(1)   The process probably can be handled more effectively by fellow teachers. Colleagues can be valuable resource persons and their use can minimize much of the threat

---

[10] Arthur W. Combs, Donald L. Avila, and William W. Purkey, *Helping Relationships* (Boston: Allyn and Bacon, Inc., 1971), p. 116.

involved in asking for help (Sybouts, 1969). There doesn't have to be a superior or an authority—just people helping each other. An additional advantage is that the supervisor can learn too: He is helped, through helping, to become a better teacher.

(2) Observation and supervision will be more effective when it is solicited rather than imposed. People who can exercise some control over a situation are not so threatened by it. In this instance, teachers are more likely to see supervision as an opportunity than as something to be endured and resisted (Flanders, 1970).

(3) In-service-supervisory activities will be less threatening and more productive when observation and feedback are based upon the teacher's own objectives. Despite the age-old dispute about whether we know (Hamacheck, 1969, p. 341) or do not know (White, 1969, p. 595) what constitutes good teaching and how to measure it, teachers can be helped and encouraged by feeling that they are making progress. We think this particularly is true when they are able to direct the process. We agree with Foster's endorsement of Clark's research that, "whenever a teacher was using any kind of reasonable method and was enthusiastic about that method, pupils learned." [11]

(4) As much as possible, supervision and observation processes should be nonevaluative (Corey, 1969; Foster, 1969). These should provide feedback regarding the degree to which the observed teacher is behaving as he has specified and might also include how well this appears to be working, but evaluation in terms of right or wrong, good or bad, competent or incompetent should be avoided.

(5) Supervision should operate to enhance the self-image of the person supervised (Combs, Avila, and Purkey, 1971; Neville, 1969). When it is demeaning, it will be resisted. When it builds self-esteem and makes people feel more adequate, it will be sought.

(6) The administrator or organizer who does not become involved in evaluative supervision (and it probably will be perceived this way if he does it) may be able to maintain more meaningful, personally satisfying relationships with

[11] Richard L. Foster, "Poise Under Pressure," in Robert R. Leeper, ed., *Supervision: Emerging Profession* (Washington, D.C.: Association for Supervision and Curriculum Development, National Education Association, 1969), p. 17. Harold Clark, Teachers College, Columbia University, conducted a study of "quality education."

313

his staff. When supervision is handled by teachers, a part of the threat is removed from the relationships they maintain. Traditionally, principals and superintendents have come to know, or to know about, only those individuals who were deficient or in trouble. Their job has been a lonely one involving little sharing and much pressure. The idea that it may not have to be this way is intriguing.

Some parting thoughts

The points have been made, and we hope with clarity and emphasis, that:

(1)   Learning and the growth of youngsters as individuals depend upon teachers who themselves are growing, self-directed, and creative.
(2)   A warm nonthreatening acceptive psychosocial climate is necessary for this to happen.
(3)   This type of working/learning atmosphere best is generated by team or group learning activities which bring teachers into productive contact with peers.
(4)   The attitudes and behavior of the organizing head man in furnishing a flexible, nonthreatening model are most crucial in determining whether such a climate will be established.

In our visits to innovative schools, we experienced school climates of this nature and we saw such teachers and administrators in action. We believe these outcomes to be a possibility in most schools. A quotation frequently used by Senator Robert Kennedy and originating with George Bernard Shaw portrays our feeling. "Other people," Shaw said, "see things and say, 'Why?' But I dream of things that never were—and say, 'Why not?' "

SUMMARY

Some school administrators appear to generate innovative climates and processes at whatever school they are located.

A systematic procedure for examining how a school functions and for conceptualizing needed changes is necessary in order to do this.

Macrocosms and complex situations can be understood by studying the manner in which microcosms and simpler situations operate.

Human relations aspects need to be included if the study of an organization is to be either comprehensive or systematic and if a real understanding of its functioning is to result.

A common error in assessing organizations and planning for change is a tendency to overlook the informal system and in the assumption that it conforms in structure and operation to the line and staff, organization chart, formal system.

A recent emphasis in education involves the systems analysis approach as a means of dividing and subdividing until complexities become understandable. The operation of the subsystem thus identified can be made more intelligible through assessing the inputs needed to achieve specified behavioral products or outputs and through graphically portraying the process with flow charts.

Provisions for feedback in a system are especially important if the system is to become self-directed and growth oriented.

The value of open communication can best be emphasized when the supervisor or organizer realizes that his own behavior is his most potent means of influencing others to behave in this manner.

The organizer or administrator must consider his personal needs if he is to maintain the type of competence required for effective leadership. Spreading himself too thinly and trying for too much influence are likely to be self-defeating.

Decision making is difficult because of the paradoxical nature of human beings and the social interactions which they maintain. The most insoluble of problems are replays of these continuing dilemmas. They may be solved again and again without really being solved at all.

If good working accord is to be maintained some conflict must be permitted. Peace-at-any-price management does not permit interpersonal issues to be faced and resolved.

In order to entertain any certainty about the process of change, some uncertainty must be tolerated. Being sure that something will work suggests that results already are known which in turn suggests that nothing new or really innovative will be allowed a trial.

Pressure to change may prevent its happening. This is likely to make the process of innovation the responsibility of the administration, and creates a lack of identification with, and a resistance toward, the development of new programs for teacher in-service education.

Evaluation, conducted to determine what and who needs to change, may also inhibit the change process. The rating and assessment which ordinarily accompany evaluation tend to produce defensiveness, game playing, and "best-foot-forward" behavior. Hence observers are not likely to see how things function normally.

Supervision, though essential for classroom-based, in-service programs, is often viewed with suspicion and considered as a personal attack on themselves by teachers.

More effective, less threatening supervision is possible when inspection is:

(1) Conducted by fellow teachers,
(2) Solicited rather than imposed,
(3) Based upon the teacher's own objectives,
(4) Nonevaluative in nature, and
(5) Conducted to enhance the self-image of the supervised person.

SUGGESTED ADDITIONAL READINGS

Avila, Donald L., Combs, Arthur W., and Purkey, William W., eds. *The Helping Relationship Sourcebook.* Boston: Allyn and Bacon, Inc., 1971. A collection of readings intended to supplement the book, *Helping Relationships.* Although phenomenological and humanistic in tone and orientation, it also presents other points of view. Particularly, it is valuable for conceptualizing the behaviors necessary in order to prepare an effective human interaction climate.

Goldhammer, Robert. *Clinical Supervision.* New York: Holt, Rinehart and Winston, Inc., 1969. Methods for supervising teachers including the observation, postobservation, analysis, and conference stages of the process are presented with philosophy, theory, humor, and human understanding interspersed. Though primarily for supervisors, this book also can be an aid to teachers in understanding their own behavior and the supervisory process.

Leeper, Robert R., ed. *Supervision: Emerging Profession.* Washington, D.C.: Association for Supervision and Curriculum Development, National Education Association, 1969. Teacher points-of-view and feelings concerning supervision are presented in this book of readings. It represents more of a grass roots approach and opinions than the readings edited by Rubin and thus should furnish a different and needed perspective on in-service supervisory relationships and processes for teachers, supervisors, and administrators.

Rubin, Louis J., ed. *Improving In-Service Education.* Boston: Allyn and Bacon, Inc., 1971. This book contains selections from recognized authorities in the field of teacher in-service education. It includes introductions and analyses by the editor which integrate its message to a far greater extent than in most books of readings. Among the important unifying concepts advanced are the need for self-directing and self-evolving teachers and the necessity for the involvement of teachers' peers in the supervisory process.

Ryans, David G. "System Analysis in Planning." In *Long Range Planning in Higher Education.* Owen A. Knorr, ed. Boulder, Colo.: Western Interstate Commission for Higher Education, 1965. An easily read description of the manner in which the systems approach can be adapted to meet the needs of educational organizations. Those who are undecided about its use as well as those who wish to learn more about it will find this article well worth the reading.

Scott, William A. *Organization Theory.* Homewood, Ill.: Richard D. Irwin, Inc., 1967. Unlike the other recommended readings for this chapter, this book is business management rather than education oriented. Even so, its communication, human interaction emphasis can provide much of pertinence and value for teachers and administrators. The reader may be surprised, as the authors were, to discover that organization based on effective human relations has many similarities no matter what the setting.

Glossary

ACCOUNTABILITY   The concept that educators should be held responsible for achieving specified goals that are observable and measurable, within a given time limit.

ACHIEVEMENT MOTIVATION   The desire and drive a pupil has to succeed in school and fulfill parental hopes and expectations.

AMBIVALENCE   Simultaneously having feelings that are opposites, e.g., love vs. hate, interest vs. boredom, self vs. other, anger vs. affiliation.

AMPLIFICATION SYSTEM   Any tool or technique or combination of these which can be used to increase physical and intellectual power or psychological or social impact and influence.

ANTHROPOLOGY   The study of man. Inquiry into the behavior that individuals learn and transmit, consciously or unconsciously, in various cultures and subcultures.

BEHAVIOR MODIFICATION   A technique for encouraging learning and behavioral change through the management of reinforcement schedules.

BRANCHING PROGRAMS   Programmed materials, endorsed by N. A. Crowder, that provide for alternate routes and supplementary sections, depending on students'·specific needs and answers on preceding materials. Errors are thus corrected by using varied routes. See also LINEAR PROGRAM.

COMPUTER ASSISTED INSTRUCTION (CAI)   The presentation of programmed instructional material by computers with data storage and

319

retrieval capacities utilized for progress reports and to indicate needed remedial action.

COMPUTER MEDIATED INSTRUCTION (CMI)   A type of instruction using programmed learning techniques and the data storage and retrieval capacities of computers for assessing learner progress but without direct contact between student and computer.

CONTINGENT RELATIONSHIP   A partnership in which that done by one element helps direct the course of what another does; mutuality of action. For instance, the pupil can, on occasion, be a teacher because the teacher is a learner. Pupils have some choice in the curriculum and its pacing.

CONTINUOUS PROGRESS   The practice of permitting each pupil to progress in the mastery of subject matter at his own pace without regard for age or grade classification.

CONVERGENT THINKER   One who tends to reach conclusions that are in agreement with popular notions, who agrees with authority, and accepts commonly held beliefs. One who reaches conclusions from observable data.

CULTURAL DEPRIVATION   Denial of access to the understandings and advantages of dominant culture because of membership in a different culture.

CULTURE   The man-made aspects of human environment—customs, beliefs, institutions, and modes of living. The aggregation of mores, arts, science, education, and social organization that man creates.

DEVELOPMENTAL TASK   A level of achievement that, in a given society and at a given age, is considered appropriate and necessary for socially acceptable functioning. Its attainment contributes to happiness and success with later tasks whereas failure contributes to unhappiness and the inability to master later tasks.

DIALOGUE   Verbal transaction in which participants both listen and are listened to. May be contrasted to one-way verbal action such as lecturing, telling, advising, and assigning.

DISCOVERY   The process of learning in which the pupil, through his own work, classifies and relates knowledge so he can make his own predictions.

EMPATHY   The emotional bond that characterizes understanding relationships between individuals; sensing the feeling of another.

EXPECTANCY HYPOTHESIS   See SELF-FULFILLING PROPHECY.

EXTRINSIC PROGRAM   See LINEAR PROGRAM.

FEEDBACK   Reintroducing a part of the production of a system as a guide for its operation. For example, the reactions of others to one's behavior help him to gauge its effectiveness.

HARDWARE   The tools for automated instruction or for audiovisual aids; the projectors, computer terminals, recording machines, televisions, radios, and the like.

HAWTHORNE EFFECT Improvement of performance or motivation and morale because of some announced experimental change in conditions. Either more or less of something results in salutary effects. The name derives from numerous experiments conducted at the Hawthorne plant of the Western Electric Company.

HETEROSTASIS The urge to grow, to be active, and to become; the urge or tendency to explore and to satisfy one's curiosity. See also HOMEOSTASIS.

HEURISTIC Helping one to discover for himself; learning by argument.

HOMEOSTASIS The tendency to preserve a stable or constant internal self or state; keeping in balance.

IDIOSYNCRATIC Individual, unique, being peculiarly oneself.

INDIVIDUALLY PRESCRIBED INSTRUCTION (IPI) A computer mediated instructional program in which paraprofessionals are used for checking student progress through a series of learning activity packets. Teachers prescribe additional or remedial packets on the basis of computer printouts.

INNOVATIVE PACKAGE Combining several novel educational ideas so that each in itself become more workable. Independent study becomes more feasible as pupil autonomy, programmed learning, teacher guidance, individual choice, and self-evaluation are included in a total learning milieu.

INTERACTION ANALYSIS A means of rating teacher communication with students, on a ten-point scale in terms of direct and indirect approaches, developed by Ned Flanders.

INTERPERSONAL PROCESS GROUPS About eight to twelve persons who meet for the specific purpose of learning how they impress others and who seek understanding and control of the affective and social phases of their lives. Also erroneously called sensitivity groups, T-groups, or basic encounter groups.

INTERPERSONAL PROCESS RECALL (IPR) A means of reconstructing a counseling or teaching experience through the use of videotaping and playback for critique and feedback purposes.

INTERVENING VARIABLE A condition which operates between a stimulus and response to influence the probability and intensity of that response. Habit strength and fatigue, for example, are intervening variables.

INVOLVEMENT The feeling that one really has a voice in his own destiny; believing that one's presence makes a difference.

LEARNING ACTIVITY PACKET (LAP) A self-contained unit of study which frequently is employed in independent study and continuous progress. Its use enables students to learn on their own with a minimum of teacher supervision and direction.

LEVEL OF ASPIRATION   The height to which one aspires. The degree of difficulty of a response that an individual will accept as a personal challenge.

LINEAR PROGRAM   Programmed materials, endorsed by B. F. Skinner, in which students progress through an established sequence of frames. Skinner believes that material should be at such a level that errors are avoided. In contrast, Crowder believes that programs should be in large units and that errors should be corrected by alternate branches.

METACOMMUNICATION   Communication about the process of communication. Discussing what is going on, while it is going on, in interpersonal transactions.

MICROTEACHING   Teaching small groups under observation with feedback for short periods of time with the development of certain behaviors in mind.

MOBILITY   That phenomenon in socioeconomic status by which one may move up or down the hierarchical order of classes.

MODULAR SCHEDULING   Scheduling, generally with computer assistance, to avoid class conflicts, and utilizing small units or modules of time of fifteen to thirty minutes in length.

NEUROTIC   A person subject to any of a number of minor, handicapping emotional disturbances. One who has heavy components of anxious or depressed feelings; he is handicapped but not usually disabled.

NONGRADED SCHOOL   An administrative device in which conventional class lines are obliterated and which allows continuous progress education to function.

PERCEPTUAL FIELD   The way a person sees things—not necessarily as others would describe reality—in terms of his biological makeup, experience, and cultural conditioning. Things prominent on one person's perceptual field might go unnoticed in another's orientation.

PERFORMANCE CONTRACTING   An agreement between the school and some outside organization to conduct a school so as to achieve specified learning outcomes with pupils or no payment will result.

PSYCHOTIC   One who is victim of any of a number of serious emotional or mental disorders that render him incapable of effective adjustment; he is usually detached from, or has gross misinterpretations of, reality.

SCHOOL CLIMATE   The psychological tone of an educational institution. It results from the myriad interpersonal transactions which take place within a school and the effects of these upon the self-regarding attitudes of participants.

SELF-FULFILLING PROPHECY   The tendency for an individual to be or become as others expect him to act or be; or, the tendency for one to live up to his own aspirations of what he is or can be.

SENSITIVITY GROUP   A group which has the same or similar purposes as T-groups—training participants to become more sensitive to their own feelings and those of others. Because most human relationship groups have this objective in some degree, this term has come into use to describe these kinds of group activities in general. Included are such interactions as confrontation groups and encounter groups.

SOCIOLOGY   The study of behavior in groups; study of the formal and informal institutions of society.

SOCIOMETRY   The graphical or columnar representation of interpersonal attractions (or avoidances) of persons in group situations. Grouping persons according to their likes and preferences for one another.

SOFTWARE   The curriculum materials, learning packages, films, slides, and syllabi which are used with and in educational hardware.

TEACHER'S CODE   An informal but widespread belief among educators that the best teacher is one who can handle discipline and instructional problems by himself. He requires little supervision and he does not question the status quo or cause problems for the administration.

TEAM TEACHING   Two or more teachers share the responsibility for the instruction of a distinct group of students. This responsibility extends over a substantial period of time with mutual cooperative relationships as contrasted with a mere division of teaching duties.

THERAPY GROUP   A group which operates to cure or ease the ills of the psychologically unhealthy in contrast with T-groups or sensitivity groups which function to increase the competence of healthy individuals.

TRANSACTION ANALYSIS   An approach, developed by Drs. Eric Berne and Thomas Harris, for describing and understanding behavior by characterizing it as typical of either the child, the parent, or the adult.

YERKES-DODSON LAW   The relationship between threat and performance. While a very low level of anxiety is insufficient to motivate corrective behavior or learning, a moderate amount energizes and therefore improves performance. A high degree of pressure, on the other hand, is likely to impair and to disrupt learning and adaptive behavior.

Bibliography

Abrahamson, Mark. *Interpersonal Accommodation.* Princeton, N. J.: D. Van Nostrand Co., 1966.

Adams, Raymond S., and Biddle, Bruce J. *Realities of Teaching Explorations with Videotape.* New York: Holt, Rinehart and Winston, Inc., 1970.

Aiken, Henry D. "Toward a New Humanist Manifesto." *The Humanist* 33 (January-February 1973): 14–15.

Allen, Dwight, and Ryan, Kevin. *Microteaching.* Reading, Mass.: Addison-Wesley Publishing Co., 1969.

Allport, Gordon W. *The Person in Psychology.* Boston: Beacon Press, 1968.

Anderson, Robert H. "Organizing and Staffing the School." In National Society for the Study of Education, 72d Yearbook, Part II, *The Elementary School in the United States.* Chicago: The University of Chicago Press, 1973.

————. "Public Relations." In Shaplin, Judson T., and Olds, Henry F., Jr. (eds.). *Team Teaching.* New York: Harper and Row, Publishers, Inc., 1964.

Bair, Medill, and Woodward, Richard G. *Team Teaching in Action.* Boston: Houghton Mifflin Co., 1964.

Barro, Stephen M. "An Approach to Developing Accountability Measures for the Public Schools." *Phi Delta Kappan* 52 (December 1970): 196–205.

Barron, Frank. *Creativity and Psychological Health,* Princeton, N. J.: D. Van Nostrand Co., 1963.

324

Becker, Ernest. *The Birth and Death of Meaning.* New York: The Macmillan Co., 1962.

Becker, Wesley C. "Applications of Behavior Principles in Typical Classrooms." In National Society for the Study of Education, 72d Yearbook, Part I, *Behavior Modification in Education.* Chicago: The University of Chicago Press, 1973.

Beggs, David W., III, and Buffie, Edward G. (eds.). *Nongraded Schools in Action.* Bloomington: Indiana University Press, 1967.

Beier, Ernst G. *The Silent Language of Psycho-therapy.* Chicago: Aldine Publishing Co., 1966.

Berdyaev, Nicholas. *Dostoevsky.* New York: World Publishing Co., Meridian Books, 1957.

Bernard, Harold W. *Child Development and Learning.* Boston: Allyn and Bacon, Inc., 1973.

————. *Human Development in Western Culture,* 3d ed. Boston: Allyn and Bacon, Inc., 1970.

————. *Mental Health in the Classroom.* New York: McGraw-Hill Book Co., 1970.

————, and Huckins, Wesley C. *Dynamics of Personal Adjustment.* Boston: Holbrook Press, 1971.

Berne, Eric. *Games People Play.* New York: Grove Press, Inc., 1964.

Biller, H. B., and Bahm, R. M. "Father-absence, Perceived Maternal Behavior, and Masculinity of Self-Concept among Junior High School Boys." *Developmental Psychology* 4 (1971): 178–81.

Binzen, Peter H. "Education in the World of Work." *Change* 5 (1973): 31–34.

Birdwhistell, Ray L. *Kinesics and Context.* Philadelphia: University of Pennsylvania Press, 1970.

Birnbaum, Max. "Sense About Sensitivity Training." *Saturday Review* 52 (November 15, 1969): 82–83.

Bloom, Benjamin S. *Stability and Change in Human Characteristics.* New York: John Wiley and Sons, 1964.

Bonner, Hubert. *On Being Mindful of Man.* Boston: Houghton Mifflin Co., 1965.

Borden, George A., Gregg, Richard B., and Grove, Theodore G. *Speech Behavior and Human Interaction.* Englewood Cliffs, N. J.: Prentice-Hall, Inc., 1969.

Borton, Terry. "What's Left When School's Forgotten?" *Saturday Review* April 18, 1970, pp. 69–71.

Boyer, William H. "Education for Survival." *Phi Delta Kappan* 52 (January 1971): 258–62.

Brenton, Myron. "Troubled Teachers Whose Behavior Disturbs Our Kids." *Today's Health* 49 (November 1971): 17–19.

325

Breslaw, Elaine G. "Behaviorism in the Classroom." *Change* 5 (April 1973): 52–56.

Brickell, Henry M. *Organizing New York State for Educational Change.* Albany: New York State Education Department, 1961.

Bridges, Francis J., Olm, Kenneth W., and Barnhill, J. Allison. *Management Decisions and Organizational Policy.* Boston: Allyn and Bacon, Inc., 1971.

Bromage, Dorothy. *The Oakmont Nongraded Primary Program.* Claremont, Calif.: Claremont Unified School District, 1967.

Brookover, Wilbur B., and Erickson, Edsel L. *Society Schools and Learning.* Boston: Allyn and Bacon, Inc., 1969.

Brophy, Jere E., and Good, Thomas L. "Teacher Expectations: Beyond the Pygmalion Controversy." *Phi Delta Kappan* 54 (December 1972): 276–78.

Brown, B. Frank. "The Nongraded High School." *Phi Delta Kappan* 44 (1963): 206–09.

Brown, Roger, and Bellugi, Ursula. "Three Processes in the Child's Acquisition of Syntax." *Harvard Educational Review* 34 (1964): 133–51.

Bruce, Paul. "Three Forces in Psychology and Their Ethical and Educational Implications." *Educational Forum* 30 (1966): 277–85.

Bruner, Jerome S. *The Process of Education.* Cambridge, Mass.: Harvard University Press, 1960.

―――. "The Growth of the Mind." *American Psychologist* 20 (December 1965): 1007–17.

―――. "Culture, Politics, and Pedagogy." *Saturday Review*, May 18, 1968, pp. 69–72.

Brunswick, Joan M. "My Ten Commandments to Creative Teaching." *Journal of Creative Behavior* 5 (1971): 199–200.

Buber, Martin. *I and Thou.* Translated by Ronald Gregor Smith. New York: Charles Scribner's Sons, 1958.

Buffie, Edward G. "Potentials for Team Teaching in the Junior School." In Beggs, David W., III (ed.), *Team Teaching: Bold New Venture*, Indianapolis: Unified College Press, Inc., 1964.

Bugenthal, James F. T. *Challenges of Humanistic Psychology.* New York: McGraw-Hill Book Co., 1967.

Bundy, Robert F. "Computer Assisted Instruction—Where Are We?" *Phi Delta Kappan* 49 (April 1968): 424–29.

Bush, Robert N. "Curriculum-Proof Teachers." In Rubin, Louis J. (ed.). *Improving In-Service Education.* Boston: Allyn and Bacon, Inc., 1971.

Caffrey, John. "Higher Education and the Computer." *NEA Journal* February 1967.

Calame, Byron E. "The Truth Hurts." *Wall Street Journal*, July 14, 1969.

Campbell, John P., and Dunnette, Marvin D. "Effectiveness of T-Group Experiences in Managerial Training and Development." *Psychological Bulletin* 70 (August 1968): 73–104.

Carson, Robert C. *Interaction Concepts of Personality.* Chicago: Aldine Publishing Co., 1969.

Casey, Virginia M. "A Summary of Team Teaching—Its Patterns and Potentials." In Beggs, David W., III, and Buffie, Edward G., eds. *Team Teaching: Bold New Venture.* Indianapolis: Unified College Press, Inc., 1964.

Cass, James. "Are There Really Any Alternatives?" *Phi Delta Kappan* 54 (March 1973): 452–53.

————. "Profit and Loss in Education." *Saturday Review*, August 15, 1970, pp. 39–40.

Cawelti, Gordon. "Innovative Practices in High Schools." *Nations Schools* 79 (April 1967): 56–88.

Chesler, Mark, and Fox, Robert. "Teacher Relationships and Educational Change." *NEA Journal* 56 (May 1967): 25–26.

Christie, T. "Environmental Factors in Creativity." *Journal of Creative Behavior* 4 (Winter 1970): 13–31.

Clark, L. H., Klein, R. L., and Burks, J. B. *The American Secondary School Curriculum.* New York: The Macmillan Co., 1965.

Cohen, Arthur M. "Technology: Thee or Me?" *Educational Technology* 10 (November 1970): 57–60.

Cole, Natalie. *The Arts in the Classroom.* New York: The John Day Co., 1940.

Coleman, James S. *Adolescents and the Schools.* New York: Basic Books, Inc., 1965.

————. "The Children Have Outgrown the Schools." *Psychology Today* 5 (February 1972): 72–82.

"The Coleman Report." *NEA Journal* 56 (September 1967): 26, 27.

Colman, Clyde H., and Budahl, Leon. "Necessary Ingredients for Good Team Teaching." *National Association of Secondary School Principals Bulletin* 57 (January 1973): 41–46.

Combs, Arthur W., ed. *Perceiving, Behaving, Becoming.* Washington, D. C.: Association for Supervision and Curriculum Development, National Education Association, 1962.

————. *The Professional Education of Teachers.* Boston: Allyn and Bacon, Inc., 1965.

————, Avila, Donald L., and Purkey, William W. *Helping Relationships: Basic Concepts for the Helping Professions.* Boston: Allyn and Bacon, Inc., 1971.

Coombs, Orde. "The Necessity of Excellence: Nairobi College." *Change* 5 (1973): 38–44.

Conant, James B. *The American High School Today.* New York: McGraw-Hill Book Co., 1959.

Conlin, Marcia R., and Haberman, Martin. "Supervising Teachers of the Disadvantaged." In Leeper, Robert R. (ed.). *Supervision: Emerging Profession.* Washington, D. C.: Association for Supervision and Curriculum Development, National Education Association, 1969.

Cooper, Gary L. "The Influence of the Trainer on Participant Change in T-Groups." *Human Relations* 22 (1969): 515–30.

Corey, Darryl. "Continuous Progress in the Joseph G. Wilson Elementary School." Lecture given at The Dalles, Oregon, May 12, 1970.

Cottle, Thomas J. "Bristol Township Schools Strategy for Change." *Saturday Review,* September 20, 1969, pp. 70–71.

Craig, Robert C. *The Psychology of Learning in the Classroom.* New York: The Macmillan Co., 1966.

Crutchfield, Richard S. "Independent Thought in a Conformist World." In Farber, Seymour M., and Wilson, Richard H. L. (eds.). *Conflict and Creativity.* New York: McGraw-Hill Book Co., 1963.

Culbert, Samuel A. *The Interpersonal Process of Self Disclosure: It Takes Two to See One.* Washington, D. C.: National Training Laboratory Institute for Applied Behavioral Science, 1968.

Cummings, Susan N. *Communication for Education.* Scranton, Pa.: International Textbook Co., 1971.

Darling, David W. "Team Teaching." *NEA Journal* 54 (May 1965): 24–25.

Dayton, Delbert H. "Early Malnutrition and Human Development." *Children* 6 (1969): 210–17.

Dennison, George. *The Lives of Children.* New York: Random House, Inc., 1969.

DeVault, M. Vere, and Kriewall, Thomas E. "Differentiation in Mathematics Instruction." In National Society for the Study of Education 69th Yearbook, Part I, *Mathematics Education.* Chicago: The University of Chicago Press, 1970.

Dinkmeyer, Don. "Group Counseling Theory and Techniques." *The School Counselor* 17 (November 1969): 148–52.

DiVirgilio, James. "Guidelines for Effective Interdisciplinary Teams." *The Clearing House* 47 (December 1972): 209–11.

Dobzhansky, Theodosius. *Mankind Evolving.* New Haven: Yale University Press, 1962.

Dubos, René. "Man and His Environment: Scenarios for the Future." *New York University Education Quarterly* 11 (Summer 1971): 2–7.

Easch, Maurice J. "Is Systems Analysis for Supervisors?" In Leeper, Robert R. (ed.). *Supervision: Emerging Profession.* Washington, D. C.: Association for Supervision and Curriculum Development, National Education Association, 1969.

Ebel, Robert L. "Some Limitations on Basic Research in Education." *Phi Delta Kappan* 49 (October 1967): 81–84.

Edmonds, Ronald, et al. "A Black Response to Christopher Jenck's Inequality and Certain Other Issues." *Harvard Educational Review* 43 (1973): 76–91.

Elam, Stanley. "The Age of Accountability Dawns in Texarkana." *Phi Delta Kappan* 51 (June 1970): 509–14.

Ellison, Alfred. "The Myth Behind Graded Content." *Elementary School Journal* 72 (1972): 212–21.

Engler, David. "Instructional Technology and the Curriculum." *Phi Delta Kappan* 51 (March 1970): 379–81.

Erikson, Erik H. *Identity, Youth, and Crisis.* New York: W. W. Norton and Co., 1968.

Fabun, Don. *Communications: The Transfer of Meaning.* Beverly Hills: Glencoe Press, 1968.

Fairbank, Ruth E. "The Subnormal Child Seventeen Years After." *Mental Hygiene* 17 (1933): 177–208.

Farson, Richard E. "Emotional Barriers to Education." *Psychology Today* 1 (October 1967): 32–35.

"Feelings of a Group Member Concerning the Risk of Personal Involvement." Unpublished class paper, 1969.

Ferguson, Charles W. *The Male Attitude.* Boston: Little Brown and Co., 1966.

Finley, Robert M. "How Team Teaching Fits into the Elementary School." In Beggs, III, David W., ed. *Team Teaching: Bold New Venture.* Indianapolis: Unified College Press, Inc., 1964.

Finn, James D. "The Technological Revolution in Education." In Burke, John C. ed. *The New Technology and Human Values.* Belmont, Calif.: Wadsworth Publishing Co., 1966.

Flanders, Ned A. *Analyzing Teacher Behavior.* Reading, Mass.: Addison-Wesley Publishing Co., 1970.

———. *Teacher Influence, Pupil Attitudes, and Achievement.* Washington, D. C.: Office of Education, United States Department of Health, Education, and Welfare, 1965.

Foster, Richard L. "Poise Under Pressure." In Leeper, Robert R., ed. *Supervision: Emerging Profession.* Washington, D. C.: Association for Supervision and Curriculum Development, National Education Association, 1969.

Frank, Jerome D. "Therapy in a Group Setting." In Stein, Morris I., ed. *Contemporary Psychotherapies.* New York: The Free Press, 1961.

Frankel, Charles. "The Awful Idea of Being an Individual." In The University of Denver, Centennial Symposium. *The Responsible Individual and a Free Society in an Expanding Universe.* Denver: Big Mountain Press, 1965.

Freud, Sigmund. "Analysis Terminable and Interminable." In *Collected Papers*, vol. 5. London: Hogarth Press, 1950.

——. *Beyond the Pleasure Principle.* New York: Liveright Publishers, 1920.

Friedenberg, Edgar Z. "Comment on 'Revolutionaries Who Have to be Home by 7:30.'" *Phi Delta Kappan* 50 (1969): 566–67.

——. "The Generation Gap." *The Annals of the American Academy of Political and Social Science* 382 (1969): 32–42.

Fullmer, Daniel W. *Counseling, Group Theory and System.* Scranton, Pa.: International Textbook Co., 1971.

——, and Bernard, Harold W. *Counseling: Content and Process.* Chicago: Science Research Associates, 1964.

Gage, Nathan L. "IQ Hereditability, Race Differences, and Educational Research." *Phi Delta Kappan* 58 (1972): 308–12.

Gagné, Robert M. *The Conditions of Learning.* 2d ed. New York: Holt, Rinehart and Winston, Inc., 1970.

——. "Learning Research and Its Implications for Independent Learning." In Gleason, G. T., ed. *The Theory and Nature of Independent Learning.* Scranton, Pa.: International Textbook Co., 1967.

Gallagher, James J. *Teaching the Gifted Child.* Boston: Allyn and Bacon, Inc., 1964.

Gardner, John W. *Self-Renewal: The Individual and the Innovative Society.* New York: Harper and Row Publishers, Inc., 1964.

Getzels, Jacob W., and Jackson, Philip W. *Creativity and Intelligence.* New York: John Wiley and Sons, Inc., 1962.

Gibb, Jack R. "Fear and Facade: Defensive Management." In Farson, R. E., ed. *Science and Human Affairs.* Palo Alto, Calif.: Science and Behavior Books, Inc., 1965.

Gibran, Kahlil. *The Prophet.* New York: Alfred A. Knopf, 1923.

Glasser, William. *Schools Without Failure.* New York: Harper and Row Publishers, Inc., 1969.

Glenn, Edward E. "Plan Ahead for Team Teaching." *American School Board Journal* 154 (June 1967): 33–36.

Goldhammer, Keith. "Local Organization and Administration of Education, Supplementary Statement." In Morphet, E. L., and Ryan, C. O., eds. *Implications for Education of Prospective Changes in Society.* Denver: Designing Education for the Future, 1967.

Goldhammer, Robert. *Clinical Supervision.* New York: Holt, Rinehart and Winston, Inc., 1969.

Goldstein, K. *Language and Language Disturbance.* New York: Grune and Stratton, 1948.

Goldstein, William. "Problems in Team Teaching." *The Clearing House* 42 (October 1967): 83–86.

Golembiewski, Robert T. "Enriching Marriages through the Laboratory Approach: Tentative Steps Toward the 'Open Couple.' " In Golembiewski, Robert T., and Blumberg, Arthur, eds. *Sensitivity and the Laboratory Approach.* Itasca, Ill.: F. E. Peacock Publishers, Inc., 1970.

————. "What is O. D.?" In Golembiewski, Robert T., and Blumberg, Arthur, eds. *Sensitivity and the Laboratory Approach.* Itasca, Ill.: F. E. Peacock Publishers, Inc., 1970.

Goodlad, John I. "Curriculum: A Janus Look." *The Record, Teachers College* 70 (1968): 95–107.

————. *Educational Change: A Study for Study and Action.* Dayton, Ohio: Institute for the Development of Educational Activities, 1968.

————. "The Educational Program to 1980 and Beyond." In Morphet, E. L., and Ryan, C. O., eds. *Implications for Education of Prospective Changes in Society.* Denver: Designing Education for the Future, 1967.

————. "Individual Differences and Vertical Organization of the School." In National Society for the Study of Education, 61st Yearbook, Part I, *Individualizing Instruction.* Chicago: The University of Chicago Press, 1962.

————. "The Schools vs. Education." *Saturday Review,* April 19, 1969, pp. 59–61.

Goodman, Paul. "Freedom and Learning: The Need for Choice." *Saturday Review,* May 18, 1968, pp. 73–75.

Gordon, Ira J. "The Beginnings of Self: The Problem of the Nurturing Environment." *Phi Delta Kappan* 50 (1969): 375–78.

Gordon, W. J. "On Being Explicit About Creative Process." *Journal of Creative Behavior* 6 (1972): 295–300.

Gorman, Alfred H. *Teachers and Learners in the Interactive Process of Education.* Boston: Allyn and Bacon, Inc., 1969.

Gorman, Burton W. "Change in the Secondary School: Why and How?" *Phi Delta Kappan* 54 (May 1972): 565–68.

Grannis, Joseph C. "Team Teaching and the Curriculum." In Shaplin, Judson T., and Olds, Henry F., eds. *Team Teaching.* New York: Harper and Row, Publishers, Inc., 1964.

Green, Thomas F. "Can History of the Future Be Written?" Presentation given at IMPACT (Invitational Meeting on the Preparation of Administrators, Counselors, and Teachers), Phoenix, Arizona, May 1969.

Gross, Beatrice, and Gross, Ronald. "A Little Bit of Chaos." *Saturday Review,* May 16, 1970, pp. 71–73.

Guba, Egon G., and Horvat, John J. "Evaluation During Development." *Bulletin of the School of Education, Indiana University* 46 (1970): 21–45.

Guilford, J. P. "Three Faces of Intellect." *American Psychologist* 14 (1959): 469–79.

―――. *The Nature of Human Intelligence.* New York: McGraw-Hill Book Co., 1967.

Guss, Carolyn. "How Is Supervision Perceived?" In Leeper, Robert R., ed. *Supervision: Emerging Profession.* Washington, D. C.: Association for Supervision and Curriculum Development, National Education Association, 1969.

Haddan, Eugene E. *Evolving Instruction.* New York: The Macmillan Co., 1970.

Hall, Edward T. *The Silent Language.* Greenwich, Conn.: Fawcett Publications, Inc., 1959.

―――. "Listening Behavior: Some Cultural Differences." *Phi Delta Kappan* 50 (March 1969): 379–80.

Hall, L. K. "Leadership." Quoted by Paul Talbot in *United Business Investment Report* 61 (December 1, 1969): 471.

Hallman, Ralph J. "Techniques of Creative Teaching." *Journal of Creative Behavior* 1 (1967): 325–30.

Hamachek, Don. "Characteristics of Good Teachers and Implications for Teacher Education." *Phi Delta Kappan* 50 (February 1969): 341–44.

Hammer, Bernard. "Grade Expectations, Differential Teacher Comments, and Student Performance." *Journal of Educational Psychology* 63 (1972): 454–58.

Haney, William V. *Communication and Organizational Behavior.* Homewood, Ill.: Richard D. Irwin, Inc., 1967.

Harrington, Michael. *The Accidental Century.* New York: The Macmillan Co., 1965.

Harris, Thomas A. *I'm O.K. You're O.K.* New York: Harper and Row, Publishers, Inc., 1969.

Harrison, Charles H. "South Brunswick, N. J.: Schools Put a Town on the Map." *Saturday Review*, February 21, 1970, pp. 66–68.

Hart, Leslie A. "Learning at Random." *Saturday Review*, April 19, 1969, pp. 62–63.

Hartley, Harry J. "Limitations of Systems Analysis." *Phi Delta Kappan* 50 (May 1969): 515–19.

Hausmann, Louis. "The ABC's of CAI." *American Education* November 1967, p. 15.

Havighurst, Robert J. *Developmental Tasks and Education.* 3rd ed. New York: David McKay, 1972.

———, and Neugarten, Bernice L. *Society and Education.* 3rd ed. Boston: Allyn and Bacon, Inc., 1967.

Heathers, Glen. "School Organization: Nongrading, Dual Progress, and Team Teaching." In National Society for the Study of Education, 65th Yearbook, Part II, *The Changing American School.* Chicago: The University of Chicago Press, 1966.

———. "Team Teaching and the Educational Reform Movement." In Shaplin, Judson T., and Olds, Henry F., eds. *Team Teaching.* New York: Harper and Row, Publishers, Inc., 1964.

Heller, Melvin P. "Qualities for Team Members." In Begg, III, David W., ed. *Team Teaching: Bold New Venture.* Indianapolis: Unified College Press, Inc., 1964.

Hetherington, E. Mavis. "Girls Without Fathers." *Psychology Today* 6 (1973): 46–52.

Hillson, Maurice. "The Nongraded School: A Dynamic Concept." In Beggs, David W., III, and Buffie, Edward G., eds. *Nongraded Schools in Action.* Bloomington, Ind.: Indiana University Press, 1967.

Hoehn, Lilburn P., ed. *Teaching Behavior Improvement Program.* Detroit: Michigan-Ohio Regional Education Laboratory, 1969.

Holland, James G. "Teaching Psychology by a Teaching Machine Program." Paper given at the American Psychological Association Convention, Cincinnati, Ohio, September 8, 1959.

Hollomon, J. Herbert. "Creative Engineering and the Needs of Society." In DeSimone, Daniel V., ed. *Education for Innovation.* Long Island City, N. Y.: Pergamon Press, Inc., 1968.

Holt, John. *How Children Fail.* New York: Pitman Publishing Corp., 1964.

———. "Introduction" to Kohl, Herbert R. *Teaching the "Unteachable."* New York: The New York Review, 1967.

Honzik, M. "Personality Consistency and Change." *Vita Humana* 7 (1964): 139–42.

Hosford, Ray E., and Ryan, T. Antoinette. "Systems Design in the Development of Counseling and Guidance Programs." *Personnel and Guidance Journal* 49 (1970): 221–30.

Howard, Eugene R. "Developing Student Responsibility for Learning." *Bulletin of the National Association of Secondary School Principals*, 50 (1966): 235–46.

Hughes, E. W. *Human Relations in Management.* New York: Pergamon Press, Inc., 1970.

Hughes, Marie M. "Learning and Becoming—New Meanings to Teachers." In Waetjen, Walter B., and Leeper, Robert R., eds. *Learning and Mental Health in the School.* Washington, D. C.: Association for Supervision and Curriculum Development, National Education Association, 1966.

Hull, Clark L. *A Behavior System: An Introduction to Behavior Theory Concerning the Individual Organism.* New Haven: Yale University Press, 1952.

"Human Potential: The Revolution in Feeling." *Time* (November 9, 1970): 54–58.

Humphrey, Hubert H. "Keynote Address." American Personnel and Guidance Association National Convention, Washington, D. C., April 4, 1966.

Hurley, Rodger. *Poverty and Mental Retardation.* New York: Random House, Inc., Vintage Books, 1969.

Huxley, Aldous. "Can We Be Well Educated?" *Esquire,* December 1956, pp. 112ff.

———. "Human Potentialities." In Farson, R. E., ed. *Science and Human Affairs.* Palo Alto, Calif.: Science and Behavior Books, Inc., 1965.

"Instructional Technology." *Today's Education* 59 (November 1970): 33–40.

Janowitz, Morris. "Institution Building in Urban Education." In Streed, David, ed. *Innovation in Mass Education.* New York: John Wiley and Sons, Inc., 1969.

Jencks, Christopher. "Social Stratification and Higher Education." *Harvard Educational Review* 38 (1968): 277–316.

Jenkins, Joseph R., and Deno, Stanley L. "A Model for Instructional Objectives." *Educational Technology* 10 (December 1970): 11–16.

Jensen, Arthur R. "How Much Can We Boost IQ and Scholastic Achievement?" *Harvard Educational Review* 39 (1969): 1–123.

Jersild, Arthur T. "The Voice of the Self." *NEA Journal* 54 (October 1965): 23–25.

———, and Lazar, Eva A., with Brodkin, Adele M. *The Meaning of Psychotherapy in the Teacher's Life and Work.* New York: Teachers College, Columbia University, 1962.

Johnson, David W. *Reaching Out.* Englewood Cliffs, N. J.: Prentice-Hall, Inc., 1972.

Jones, Richard M. *Fantasy and Feeling in Education.* New York: New York University Press, 1968.

Jones, Richard V. "Tuning up the Staff for Organizational Change." *Journal of Secondary Education* 44 (December 1969): 339–45.

Jourard, Sidney M. *The Transparent Self.* Princeton, N. J.: D. Van Nostrand Co., 1964.

Kagan, Jerome. "Biological Aspects of Inhibition Systems." *American Journal of Disabled Children* 114 (1967): 507–12.

———. "The Concept of Intelligence." *The Humanist* 32 (January–February 1972): 7–8.

Kagan, Norman, Schauble, Paul, Resnikoff, Arthur, Danish, Steven J., and Krathwohl, David R. "Interpersonal Process Recall." *The Journal of Nervous and Mental Disease* 148 (1969): 365–74.

———. "Issues in Encounter." *The Counseling Psychologist* 2 (1970): 62–65.

Kaplan, Abraham. "The Life of Dialogue." Lecture given at Nobel Conference, Gustavus Adolphus College, St. Peter, Minn., January 8–9, 1969.

Kelley, Harold H. "Interpersonal Accommodation." *American Psychologist* 23 (June 1968): 399–410.

Kelly, G. A. *The Psychology of Personal Constructs*, vol. 1. New York: W. W. Norton and Co., 1955.

Kibler, Robert J., Barker, Larry L., and Miles, David T. *Behavioral Objectives and Instruction.* Boston: Allyn and Bacon, Inc., 1970.

Kilpatrick, William H. *A Reconstructed Theory of the Educative Process.* New York: Teachers College, Columbia University, 1935.

King, Paul T., and Neal, Robert. *Ego Psychology In Counseling.* Boston: Houghton Mifflin Co., 1968.

Knoblock, Peter, and Goldstein, Arnold P. *The Lonely Teacher.* Boston: Allyn and Bacon, Inc., 1971.

Koerner, James. "Educational Technology." *Saturday Review of Education* (May 1973): 43–46.

Korner, Anneliese F. "Individual Differences at Birth: Implications for Early Experience and Later Development." *American Journal of Orthopsychiatry* 41 (1971): 608–19.

Kounin, Jacob S., and Gump, Paul V. "The Comparative Influence of Punitive and Nonpunitive Teachers Upon Children's Concepts of School Misconduct." *Journal of Educational Psychology* 52 (1961): 44–49.

Kowitz, Gerald T. "The Management of Motivation." *Phi Delta Kappan* 49 (October 1967): 77–80.

Kozol, Johnathan. *Death at an Early Age.* Boston: Houghton Mifflin Co., 1967.

Kubie, Lawrence S. "Hidden Brain Power." *Saturday Review* (October 13, 1956): 26.

Lakin, Martin. "Some Ethical Issues in Sensitivity Training." *American Psychologist* 24 (1969): 923–28.

Lamont, Corliss. "Toward a New Humanist Manifesto." *The Humanist* 33 (January–February 1973): 15.

Lange, Sylvia. "Esalen—and Afterward." *Nursing Outlook* 18 (June 1970): 33–35.

Langer, John H. "The News Media and Social Science Teaching." *Phi Delta Kappan* 51 (1970): 318–20.

Lee, Dorris M. "Views of the Child." In National Society for the Study of Education, 72d Yearbook, Part II, *The Elementary School in the United States.* Chicago: The University of Chicago Press, 1973.

Lee, Gordon C. "The Changing Role of the Teacher." In National Society for the Study of Education, 65th Yearbook, Part II, *The Changing American School.* Chicago: The University of Chicago Press, 1966.

Leeper, Robert R., ed. *Humanizing Education.* Washington, D. C.: Association for Supervision and Curriculum Development, National Education Association, 1967.

Leonard, George B. *Education and Ecstasy.* New York: The Delacorte Press, 1968.

Lessinger, Leon. "Engineering Accountability for Results in Public Education." *Phi Delta Kappan* 52 (December 1970): 217–25.

Levitt, Eugene E. *The Psychology of Anxiety.* Indianapolis: The Bobbs-Merrill Co., 1967.

Lieberman, Morton A., Yalom, Irvin D., and Miles, Matthew B. "Encounter: The Leader Makes the Difference." *Psychology Today* 6 (March 1973): 69–72.

Lieberman, Myron. "An Overview of Accountability." *Phi Delta Kappan* 52 (December 1970): 217–25.

Likert, Rensis. "Measuring Organizational Performance." In Fleishman, Edwin A., ed. *Studies in Personnel and Industrial Psychology.* Homewood, Ill.: The Dorsey Press, 1967.

Lippitt, Ronald, and Fox, Robert. "Development and Maintenance of Effective Classroom Learning." In Rubin, Louis J., ed. *Improving In-Service Education.* Boston: Allyn and Bacon, Inc., 1971.

Long, Barbara Ellis. "A Climate for Learning." *Today's Education* 61 (September 1972): 50–52.

Longfellow, Layne A. "Body Talk, the Game of Feeling and Expressing." *Psychology Today* 4 (October 1970): 45–54.

Lopez, Felix M. "Accountability in Education." *Phi Delta Kappan* 52 (December 1970): 231–43.

Lortie, Dan C. "The Teacher and Team Teaching." In Shaplin, Judson T., and Olds, Henry F., eds. *Team Teaching.* New York: Harper and Row, Publishers, Inc., 1964.

Loughary, John W. "The Computer Is In." *Personnel and Guidance Journal* 49 (November 1970): 185–91.

Loukes, Harold. "Passport to Maturity." *Phi Delta Kappan* 46 (October 1964): 54–57.

Lowe, Linda. "Team Teaching Is——." *Teacher* 90 (December 1972): 41.

Luft, J. *Group Processes: An Introduction to Group Dynamics.* Palo Alto, Calif.: National Press, 1963.

Luke, Bob, and Seashore, Charles. "Generalizations on Research and Speculations from Experience Related to Laboratory Training Design." Washington, D.C.: National Training Laboratory Institute for Applied Behavioral Science, 1966.

McClelland, David C. "IQ Tests and Assessing Competence." *The Humanist* 32 (January–February 1972): 9–12.

McCully, C. Harold, and Miller, Lyle L. *Challenge for Change in Counselor Education.* Minneapolis: Burgess Publishing Co., 1969.

MacDonald, W. Scott. *Battle in the Classroom.* Scranton, Pa.: International Textbook Co., 1971.

MacKinnon, Donald W. "Conditions for Effective Change." In Passow, A. Harry, ed. *Nurturing Individual Potential.* Washington, D. C.: Association for Supervision and Curriculum Development, National Education Association, 1964.

————. "Conditions for Effective Personality Change." In Passow, A. Harry, ed. *Nurturing Individual Potential.* Washington, D. C.: Association for Supervision and Curriculum Development, National Education Association, 1964.

McLoughlin, William P. "The Phantom Nongraded School." *Phi Delta Kappan* 49 (1968): 248–50.

McNeil, John D. *Toward Accountable Teachers.* New York: Holt, Rinehart and Winston, Inc., 1971.

Mager, Robert F. *Preparing Instructional Objectives.* Palo Alto, Calif.: Fearon Publishers, 1962.

──────. *Developing Attitude Toward Learning.* Palo Alto, Calif.: Fearon Publishers, 1968.

Martin, John Henry. "School Role of the Computer Debated." *Education U. S. A.* (November 11, 1967), p. 57.

Maslow, Abraham H. "Creativity in Self-Actualizing People." In Anderson, H. H., ed. *Creativity and Its Cultivation.* New York: Harper and Brothers, 1959.

──────. *Motivation and Personality.* 2nd ed. New York: Harper and Row, Publishers, Inc., 1970.

──────. "Music Education and Peak Experience." *Music Educators Journal* 54 (February 1968): 72–75.

May, Rollo. "Freedom, Responsibility, and the Helping Relationship." Presentation given at Arden House, Teachers College, Columbia University, January 6–10, 1963.

──────. *Psychology and the Human Dilemma.* Princeton, N. J.: D. Van Nostrand Co., 1967.

Meacham, Merle L., and Wiessen, Allen E. *Changing Classroom Behavior.* Scranton, Pa.: International Textbook Co., 1970.

Menninger, Karl, with Mayman, M., and Pruyser, P. *The Vital Balance.* New York: The Viking Press, 1963.

Metcalf, Lawrence E., and Hunt, Maurice P. "Relevance and the Curriculum." *Phi Delta Kappan* 51 (1970): 358–61.

Meyer, Richard I. "Do Teachers Promote Change?" *Journal of Secondary Education* 44 (March 1969): 107–11.

Michael, Donald N. "Cybernation and Changing Goals in Education." In Bushnell, Don D., and Allen, Dwight, eds. *The Computer and American Education.* New York: John Wiley and Sons, Inc., 1967.

Mickelson, Norma I., and Galloway, Charles G. "Art and the Hidden Vocabulary of Indian Children." *Studies in Art Education* 13 (1972): 27–29.

Miller, George A. "Psychology as a Means of Promoting Human Welfare." *American Psychologist* 24 (1969): 1063–75.

Miller, John K. "Not Performance Contracting But the OEO Experiment Was a Failure." *Phi Delta Kappan* 54 (1973): 394–96.

Miller, Paul A. "Major Implications for Education of Prospective Changes in Society, One Perspective." In Morphet, E. L., and Ryan, C. O., eds. *Implications for Education of Prospective Changes in Society.* Denver: Designing Education for the Future, 1967.

Miller, Richard I., ed. *Perspectives on Educational Change.* New York: Appleton-Century-Crofts, 1967.

Moore, Raymond S., and Moore, Dennis R. "The Dangers of Early Schooling." *Harper's Magazine*, July 1972, pp. 58–62.

Moustakas, Clark. *The Authentic Teacher.* Cambridge, Mass.: Howard A. Doyle Printing Co., 1966.

Nations, Jimmy E. "Caring for Individual Differences in Reading Through Nongrading." Seattle: Seattle Public Schools, May 3, 1967.

Neale, Daniel C. "Aversive Control of Behavior." *Phi Delta Kappan* 50 (1969): 335–38.

Neville, Richard F. "The Supervisor We Need." In Leeper, Robert R., ed. *Supervision: Emerging Profession.* Washington D. C.: Association for Supervision and Curriculum Development, National Education Association, 1969.

Odiorne, George S. "The Trouble with Sensitivity Training." In Golembiewski, Robert T., and Blumberg, Arthur, eds. *Sensitivity and the Laboratory Approach.* Itasca, Ill.: F. E. Peacock Publishers, Inc., 1970.

Oettinger, Anthony G. "The Myths of Educational Technology." *Saturday Review*, May 18, 1968, pp. 76–77.

Olivero, James L. "Evaluation Considerations for Team Teaching." In Beggs, III, David W., ed. *Team Teaching: Bold New Venture.* Indianapolis: Unified College Press, Inc., 1964.

Olson, Carl O., Jr. "Why Teaching Teams Fail." *Peabody Journal of Education* 45 (July 1967): 15–20.

Parker, John L., and Withycombe, Richard J. "Mediation in an Alternative Teacher Training Program." *Phi Delta Kappan* 54 (1973): 483–85.

Parnes, Sidney J. "Creativity: Developing Human Potential." *Journal of Creative Behavior* 5 (1971): 19–36.

Patrick, Catherine. *What Is Creative Thinking?* New York: Philosophical Library, 1955.

Penfield, Wilder. "The Uncommitted Cortex: The Child's Changing Brain." *Atlantic* 214 (July 1964): 77–81.

"Performance Contracting." *Phi Delta Kappan* 52 (December 1970): 225.

Perls, Frederick. *Ego, Hunger, and Aggression.* London: George Allen and Unwin, 1947.

Perrone, Vito. *Open Education: Promise and Problems.* Bloomington, Ind.: Phi Delta Kappa Educational Foundation, 1972.

Peter, Lawrence J. "The Peter Principle: We're All Incompetent." *Phi Delta Kappan* 48 (March 1967): 339–41.

Petrequin, Gaynor. *Individualizing Learning Through Modular-Flexible Programming.* New York: McGraw-Hill Book Co., 1968.

Pfeil, Mary Pat. "Everybody's Somebody." *American Education* 5 (December 1969): 21–24.

Pierson, George A. *Counselor Education in Regular Session Institutes.* Washington, D. C.: United States Government Printing Office, 1965.

Pilcher, Paul S. "Teacher Centers: Can They Work Here?" *Phi Delta Kappan* 54 (January 1973): 340–43.

Pine, Patricia. "Where Education Begins." Interview with J. McVicker Hunt in *American Education* 4 (1968): 15–19.

Plunkett, William T. "Independent Study at Syosset High School." *Phi Delta Kappan* 50 (1969): 350–52.

Rakstis, Ted J. "Sensitivity Training: Fad, Fraud, or New Frontier?" *Today's Health* (January 1970): 20–25, 86–87.

Randazzo, Joseph D., and Arnold, Joanne M. "Does Open Education Really Work in an Urban Setting?" *Phi Delta Kappan* 54 (1972): 107–10.

Rarick, John R. "Sensitivity International—Network for World Control." *Congressional Record-House* (January 19, 1970), pp. 228–31.

Reese, Hayne W., and Parnes, Sidney J. "Programming Creative Behavior." *Child Development* 41 (1970): 413–23.

"Research Discloses Clues to Failure." *Education, U. S. A.* (September 25, 1967).

Riessman, Frank. "The Strategy of Style." *Teachers College Record* 65 (1964): 484–89.

———. "Styles of Learning." *NEA Journal* 55 (1966): 15–17.

Rippey, R. M. "A Study of Differences in Achivement Due Personality Differences in Four Classroom Environments." *School Review* 73 (1965): 374–83.

Roberts, Wallace. "No Place to Grow." *Saturday Review* (March 21, 1970): 62–64.

Robinson, Donald W. "Alternative Schools: Do They Promise System Reform?" *Phi Delta Kappan* 54 (March 1973): 433, 443.

Roethlisberger, F. J., and Dickson, W. J. *Management and the Worker.* Cambridge, Mass.: Harvard University Press, 1939.

Rogers, Carl R. "A Humanistic Conception of Man." In Farson, R. E., ed. *Science and Human Affairs.* Palo Alto, Calif.: Science and Behavior Books, Inc., 1965.

———. *Freedom To Learn.* Columbus, Ohio: Charles E. Merrill Publishing Co., 1969.

———. "Interpersonal Relationships: U.S.A. 2000." *Journal of Applied Behavioral Sciences* 4 (1968): 265–80.

———. *On Becoming A Person.* Boston: Houghton Mifflin Co., 1961.

————. "The Process of the Basic Encounter Group." In Bugenthal, James F. T., ed. *Challenges of Humanistic Psychology.* New York: McGraw-Hill Book Co., 1967.

————. "Toward a Theory of Creativity." In Anderson, H. H., ed. *Creativity and Its Cultivation.* New York: Harper and Row, Publishers, Inc., 1959.

Rogers, Vincent R. "Open Education in Hartford: Exciting, Significant, Underrated." *Phi Delta Kappan* 54 (1972): 110.

Rollins, Sidney P. "Ungraded High Schools: Why Those Who Like Them Love Them." *Nation's Schools* 73 (April 1964): 110, 130.

Rosenfeld, Howard, and Zander, Alvin. "The Influence of Teachers on Aspirations of Students." *Journal of Educational Psychology* 52 (1961): 1–11.

Rosenthal, Robert, and Jacobson, Lenore. *Pygmalion in the Classroom.* New York: Holt, Rinehart and Winston, Inc., 1968.

Ruark, Henry C. "Programmed Instruction: Don't Sell the Process Short." *Educational Screen and Audiovisual Guide* (May 1967): 19, 41.

Ruesch, Jurgen. *Therapeutic Communication.* New York: W. W. Norton and Co., 1961.

————, and Bateson, Gregory. *Communication.* New York: W. W. Norton and Co., 1951.

Rugg, Harold. *Foundations for American Education.* Yonkers-on-Hudson, N. Y.: World Book Co., 1947.

Ruitenbeek, Hendrick M. *The Individual and the Crowd.* New York; Mentor Books, 1964.

Rutrough, James E. "The Supervisor's Role in Personnel Administration." In Leeper, Robert R., ed. *Supervision: Emerging Profession.* Washington, D. C.: Association for Supervision and Curriculum Development, National Education Association, 1969.

Ryans, David G. "System Analysis in Planning." In Knorr, Owen A., ed. *Long Range Planning in Higher Education.* Boulder, Colo.: Western Interstate Commission for Higher Education, 1965.

Sartain, Harry W. "Organizational Patterns of Schools and Classrooms for Reading Instruction." In Robinson, Helen M., ed. *National Society for the Study of Education, 67th Yearbook, Part II, Innovation and Change in Reading Instruction.* Chicago: The University of Chicago Press, 1968.

Scanlan, Burt K. "Sensitivity Training—Clarifications, Issues, Insights." *Personnel Journal* 50 (July 1971): 246–52.

Schockley, William. "Dysgenics, Geneticity, Raceology: A Challenge to the Intellectual Responsibility of Educators." *Phi Delta Kappan* 58 (1972): 297–307.

Schofield, William. *Psychotherapy: The Purchase of Friendship*. Englewood Cliffs, N. J.: Prentice-Hall, Inc., 1964.

Schrag, Francis. "Freedom and Authority in the Educative Process." *School Review* 80 (1972): 551–71.

Schutz, William C. *Joy*. New York: Grove Press, Inc., 1967.

Scobey, Mary-Margaret, and Graham, Grace, eds. *To Nurture Humaneness*. Washington, D. C.: Association for Supervision and Curriculum Development, National Education Association, 1970.

Scott, William A. *Organization Theory*. Homewood, Ill.: Richard D. Irwin, Inc., 1967.

Seashore, Charles. "What Is Sensitivity Training?" In Golembiewski, Robert T., and Blumberg, Arthur, eds. *Sensitivity and the Laboratory Approach*. Itasca, Ill.: F. E. Peacock Publishers, Inc., 1970.

Shaplin, Judson T. "Description and Definition of Team Teaching." In Shaplin, Judson T., and Olds, Henry F., Jr., eds. *Team Teaching*. New York: Harper and Row, Publishers, Inc., 1964.

Shostrom, Everett L. "Group Therapy: Let the Buyer Beware." *Psychology Today* 2 (May 1969): 36–40.

———. *Man, the Manipulator*. Nashville, Tenn.: Abingdon Press, 1967.

Sigel, Efrem. "General Learning." *Saturday Review of Education* 1 (May 1973): 46–47.

Silverman, Irwin William, and Stone, Judith M. "Modifying Cognitive Functioning Through Participation in a Problem-Solving Group." *Journal of Educational Psychology* 63 (1972): 603–08.

Skinner, B. F. *Beyond Freedom and Dignity*. New York: Alfred A. Knopf, 1971.

———. "Freedom and the Control of Men." In Burke, J. G., ed. *The New Technology and Human Values*. Belmont, Calif.: Wadsworth Publishing Co., 1966.

———. "Teaching Machines." *Science* 128 (1958): 969–77.

———. "Why We Need Teaching Machines." *Harvard Educational Review* 31 (1961): 377–89.

Slaughter, Robert E. "The Educator and the Industrialist." *NEA Journal* (February 1967): 27–29.

Smith, B. Othanel. "Conditions of Learning." In Morphet, E. L., and Ryan, C. O., eds. *Implications for Education of Prospective Changes in Society*. Denver: Designing Education for the Future, 1967.

———, Cohen, Saul B., and Pearl, Arthur. *Teachers for the Real World*. Washington, D. C.: The American Association of Colleges for Teacher Education, 1969.

Snyder, Fred A., and Peterson, R. Duane. *Dynamics of Elementary School Administration*. Boston: Houghton Mifflin Co., 1970.

Snygg, Donald. "A Cognitive Field Theory of Learning." In Waetjen, Walter B., and Leeper, Robert R., eds. *Learning and Mental Health in the School*. Washington, D. C.: Association for Supervision and Curriculum Development, National Education Association, 1966.

Stalcup, Robert J. *Sociology and Education*. Columbus, Ohio: Charles E. Merrill Publishing Co., 1968.

Stearns, Marian S. "Early Education: Still in Its Infancy." *American Education* 6 (August–September 1970): 3–5.

Sterns, Harvey N. "Team Teaching in Teacher Education Programs." *The Journal of Teacher Education* 23 (Fall 1972): 318–22.

Storr, Anthony. *Human Aggression*. New York: Atheneum Publishers, 1968.

Strang, Ruth. *Group Work in Education*. New York: Harper and Row, Publishers, Inc., 1958.

Strom, Robert D. *Psychology for the Classroom*. Englewood Cliffs, N. J.: Prentice-Hall, Inc., 1969.

Sybouts, Ward. "Supervision and Team Teaching." In Leeper, Robert R., ed. *Supervision: Emerging Profession*. Washington, D. C.: Association for Supervision and Curriculum Development, National Education Association, 1969.

Tannenbaum, Arnold S. *Control in Organizations*. New York: McGraw-Hill Book Co., 1968.

Tanner, R. Thomas. "The Science Curriculum: Unfinished Business for an Unfinished Country." *Phi Delta Kappan* 51 (1970): 353–57.

Taylor, Calvin W. *Creativity: Progress and Potential*. New York: McGraw-Hill Book Co., 1964.

————. "Cultivating New Talents: A Way to Reach the Educationally Deprived." *Journal of Creative Behavior* 2 (1968): 83–90.

————. "Factors Influencing Creativity." In DeSimone, Daniel V., ed. *Education for Innovation*. Long Island City, N. Y.: Pergamon Press, Inc., 1968.

Thayer, Lee. *Communication and Communication Systems*. Homewood, Ill.: Richard D. Irwin, Inc., 1968.

Thelen, Herbert A. "A Cultural Approach to In-Service Teacher Training." In Rubin, Louis J., ed. *Improving In-Service Education*. Boston: Allyn and Bacon, Inc., 1971.

Thoreson, Carl E. "The Systems Approach and Counselor Education: Basic Features and Implications." *Counselor Education and Supervision* 9 (Fall 1969): 3–17.

343

Thorndike, E. L. *Educational Psychology: Briefer Course.* New York: Teachers College, Columbia University, 1924.

————. *Fundamentals of Learning.* New York: Teachers College, Columbia University, 1932.

Thorndike, Robert L. "Pygmalion in the Classroom." [Book review] *The Record, Teachers College* 70 (1969): 805–07.

Tomcheck, David. "A Teacher Comments on Team Teaching." In Beggs, David W., III, ed. *Team Teaching: Bold New Venture.* Indianapolis: Unified College Press, Inc., 1964.

Tondow, Murray. "Systems Analysis and Innovation." *Journal of Secondary Education* 42 (May 1967): 261–67.

Torrance, E. Paul. *Constructive Behavior: Stress, Personality and Mental Health.* Belmont, Calif.: Wadsworth Publishing Co., 1965.

————. *Guiding Creative Talent.* Englewood Cliffs, N. J.: Prentice-Hall, Inc., 1962.

————, and Torrance, Pansy. "Combining Creative Problem-Solving with Creative Expressive Activities in the Education of Disadvantaged Young People." *Journal of Creative Behavior* 6 (1972): 1–10.

————, and Ziller, R. C. *Risk and Life Experience: Development of a Scale for Measuring Risk Taking Tendencies.* Lackland, Tex.: Air Force Personnel and Training Research Center, 1957.

Trusty, Francis M. "An Administrator Looks at Team Teaching." In Beggs, David W., III, ed. *Team Teaching: Bold New Venture.* Indianapolis: Unified College Press, Inc., 1964.

Tuckman, Bruce W. "Developmental Sequence in Small Groups." *Psychological Bulletin* 63 (1965): 284–97.

Tyler, C. Edward. *Team Teaching.* Eugene, Ore.: University of Oregon, Curriculum Bulletin No. 286, 1968.

Tyler, Leona E. "Minimum Change Therapy." In Ard, Ben N., Jr., ed. *Counseling and Psychotherapy.* Palo Alto, Calif.: Science and Behavior Books, Inc., 1966.

Tyler, Ralph W. "Purposes, Scope, and Organization of Education." In Morphet, E. L., and Ryan, C. O., eds. *Implications for Education of Prospective Changes in Society.* Denver: Designing Education for the Future, 1967.

Vars, Gordon F. "Can Team Teaching Save the Core Curriculum?" *Phi Delta Kappan* 47 (January 1966): 258–62.

Vriend, John. "Report on the Harvard Invitational Conference on Computer Assisted Systems in Guidance and Counseling." *Educational Technology* 10 (March 1970): 15–19.

Waetjen, Walter B., and Leeper, Robert R., eds. *Learning and Mental*

Health in the School. Washington, D. C.: Association for Supervision and Curriculum Development, National Education Association, 1966.

Wallas, Graham. *The Art of Thought.* New York: Harcourt, Brace and Co., 1926.

Watzlawick, Paul, Beavin, Janet, and Jackson, Don D. *The Pragmatics of Human Communication.* New York: W. W. Norton and Co., 1967.

Weiner, Bernard. "Attribution Theory, Achievement Motivation, and the Educational Process." *Review of Educational Research* 42 (1972): 203–15.

White, Burton L. "When Should Schooling Begin?" *Phi Delta Kappan* 53 (1972): 610–12.

White, Mary Alice. "Memo to a Future Superintendent." *Phi Delta Kappan* 50 (June 1969): 595–97.

Whiteley, John M. "Ethical Questions." *The Counseling Psychologist* (special issue on encounter groups) 2 (1970): 62–65.

Wilhelms, Fred T. "The Curriculum and Individual Differences." In National Society for the Study of Education, 61st Yearbook, Part I, *Individualizing Instruction.* Chicago: The University of Chicago Press, 1962.

Wolf, Stewart, and Goodell, Helen. *Harold G. Wolff's Stress and Disease.* Springfield, Ill.: Charles C Thomas, Publisher, 1968.

Wright, Richard. *Black Boy: A Record of Childhood and Youth.* New York: Harper and Brothers, 1937.

Wyatt, Wendy C. "Responsible Use of Sensitivity Training." *Nursing Outlook* 18 (June 1970): 39–40.

Yamamoto, K. "Relationships Between Creative Thinking Abilities of Teachers and Achievement and Adjustment of Pupils." *Journal of Experimental Education* 32 (1963): 2–25.

Yeaworth, Rosalee. "Learning Through Group Experience." *Nursing Outlook* 18 (June 1970): 29–32.

Yelon, Stephen L. "Toward the Application of Systems Analysis to Counselor Education." *Educational Technology* 9 (March 1969): 55–60.

Yevtushenko, Yevgeny. "Cemetery of Whales." *Stolen Apples.* Doubleday & Co., 1971.

Name Index

Abrahamson, M., 55, 74
Adams, R. S., 74, 118, 150, 159, 163
Aiken, H. D., 5
Alexander, W. M., 225
Allen, D. W., 152, 163
Allport, G. W., 39
Anderson, R. H., 200, 250, 252, 253, 254, 260
Arnold, J. M., 184
Avila, D. L., 284, 298, 299, 307, 309, 312, 313, 316

Bahm, R. M., 9
Bair, M., 252, 254, 259
Barker, L. L., 153
Barnhill, J. A., 298
Barro, S. M., 159, 160
Bateson, G., 76
Bauer, D. H., 238
Beavin, J., 76
Becker, E., 35, 78, 82
Beggs, D. W., 220, 225
Beier, E. G., 62, 68, 81, 82, 83, 86
Bellugi, U., 201
Bennet, A., 230
Berberich, J. P., 194
Berdyaev, N., 270
Bernard, H. W., 10, 53, 99, 103, 202
Berne, E., 89, 103, 160, 323
Berscheid, E., 20
Biddle, B. J., 74, 118, 150, 159
Biller, H. B., 9
Binzen, P. H., 10

Birdwhistell, R. L., 86
Birnbaum, M., 266
Bloom, B. S., 31
Bogue, E. G., 47
Bonner, H., 4, 23
Borden, G. A., 100
Boyer, W. H., 106
Brenton, M., 123
Breslaw, E. G., 218
Brickell, H. M., 117
Bridges, F. J., 298
Bromage, D., 201
Brookover, W. B., 8
Brophy, J. E., 124
Broudy, H. S., 238
Brown, B. F., 201, 210
Bruce, P., 5
Bruner, J. S., 109, 202
Brunswick, J. M., 192
Buber, M., 97
Budahl, L., 241, 242, 248, 250, 254, 255, 261
Bundy, R. F., 148
Bush, R. N., 282

Caffrey, J., 145
Calame, B. E., 280
Campbell, J. P., 281
Casey, V. M., 249, 255
Cass, J., 245
Cawelti, G., 245, 248
Chesler, M., 259
Christie, T., 235
Clark, L. H., 313

Cohen, A. M., 136
Cohen, S. B., 158, 285
Cole, N., 179
Coleman, J. S., 21, 25, 26, 41, 61, 176, 187, 194, 241
Colman, C. H., 242, 248, 250, 254, 255, 261
Combs, A. W., 5, 50, 118, 120, 284, 298, 299, 307, 308, 312, 313, 316
Conant, J. B., 187
Conlin, M. R., 299, 309
Cooper, G. L., 276
Corey, D., 210, 313
Cottle, T. J., 33, 45
Cronback, L., 260
Crowder, N. A., 170, 172, 319, 322
Crutchfield, R. S., 118
Culbert, S. A., 265, 269
Cummings, S. N., 128

Darling, D. W., 248
Dayton, D. H., 26
Dennison, G., 176
Deno, S. L., 153, 163
DeSimone, D. V., 106
DeVault, M. V., 233, 234
Dewey, J., 172
Dickson, W. J., 121
Dinkmeyer, D., 273
DiVirgilio, J., 246, 251, 252
Dobzhansky, T., 106
Dubos, René, 106, 128
Dunnette, M. D., 281

Ebel, R. L., 260
Edmonds, R., 173, 213
Elam, S., 11, 13
Ellison, A., 21, 25, 202
Erickson, D. A., 21
Erickson, E. L., 8
Erikson, E. H., 41, 67, 118, 303

Fabun, D., 75, 89, 101, 103
Fairbank, R. E., 15
Fantini, M. D., 221
Ferguson, C. W., 109
Finley, R. M., 252
Finn, J. D., 138

Flanders, N. A., 15, 16, 17, 41, 48, 118, 129, 152, 313
Foster, R. L., 313
Fox, R., 259, 279, 282, 310, 311
Frank, J. D., 278
Frank, L. K., 41
Freud, S., 6, 175
Friedenberg, E. Z., 41, 78, 176
Fullmer, D. W., 99, 277, 284

Gage, N. L., 10
Gagné, R. M., 233
Gallagher, J. J., 186
Galloway, C. G., 34
Gardner, J. W., 217
Getzels, J. W., 29, 191
Gibran, K., 56
Glasser, W., 65, 311
Glenn, E. E., 251, 255, 260
Goldhammer, K., 18, 60, 289
Goldhammer, R., 304, 316
Goldstein, A. P., 284, 307
Goldstein, K., 78, 242, 251, 256
Goldstein, W., 260, 264
Golembiewski, R. T., 265
Good, T. L., 124
Goodale, R. A., 238
Goodell, H., 63
Goodlad, J. I., 18, 25, 114, 202, 214
Goodman, P., 25, 201
Gordon, I. J., 78
Gordon, W. J., 39
Gorman, A. H., 48, 60, 74, 163
Gorman, B. W., 243, 249
Graham, G., 49, 50
Grannis, J. C., 252
Green, T. F., 50, 107, 121
Gregg, R. B., 100
Gross, B., 25, 183
Gross, R., 25, 183
Grove, T. G., 100
Guba, E. G., 214
Guilford, J. P., 178, 186, 187
Gump, P. V., 17
Guss, C., 312
Guthrie, E. R., 172

Haberman, M., 299, 309
Haddan, E. E., 150, 163

Hall, E. T., 82, 86, 89, 103, 109
Hall, L. K., 305, 306
Hamachek, D., 118, 129, 313
Hammer, B., 27
Haney, W. V., 298, 299
Harrington, M., 106
Harris, T. A., 269, 323
Harrison, C. H., 33, 40, 45, 63, 78, 203
Hart, L. A., 19, 23, 202
Hartley, H. J., 297
Hatch, W. R., 230
Hausmann, L., 143
Havighurst, R. J., 10, 79
Heathers, G., 200, 214, 250, 254
Heller, M. P., 255, 256
Hetherington, E. M., 9
Hillson, M., 203
Hines, V. A., 225
Hoehn, L. P., 152, 153
Holland, J. G., 167, 173
Hollomon, J. H., 106
Holt, J., 176
Honzik, M., 175
Horan, J. D., 190
Horvat, J. J., 214
Hosford, R. E., 295
Howard, E. R., 228
Huckins, W. C., 103
Hughes, E. W., 298
Hull, C. L., 172
Humphrey, H. H., 134
Hunt, M. P., 78, 200, 229
Hurley, R., 39
Huxley, A., 215

Jackson, D. D., 29, 30, 76
Jackson, P. W., 191
Jameson, M., 207
Janowitz, M., 125
Jencks, C., 10
Jenkins, J. R., 153, 163
Jensen, A. R., 10, 30, 31, 213
Jensen, L. C., 164
Jersild, A. T., 40, 229, 256
Johnson, D. W., 277
Jones, R. M., 60
Jones, R. V., 115
Jourard, S. M., 265

Kagan, J., 10, 175
Kagan, N., 150, 262
Kaplan, A., 98
Kelley, H. H., 55
Kelly, G. A., 30
Kilpatrick, W. H., 185
King, P. T., 78
Knoblock, P., 242, 256, 264, 284, 307
Koerner, J., 142, 175
Kounin, J. S., 17
Kowitz, G. T., 255
Kriewall, T. E., 233, 234
Kubie, L. S., 126

Lakin, M., 265, 266
Lamont, C., 5
Lange, S., 274
Langer, J. H., 227
Lazar, E. A., 40, 229
Lee, D. M., 229
Lee, G. C., 19
Leeper, R. R., 17, 50, 118, 317
Leonard, G. B., 176
Lessinger, L., 156, 160
Levitt, E. E., 83, 122
Lieberman, M. A., 266, 276, 281, 284
Lieberman, M., 157
Likert, R., 310
Lippitt, R., 279, 282, 310, 311
Long, B. E., 88
Longfellow, L. A., 86
Lopez, F. M., 156
Lortie, D. C., 251
Loughary, J. W., 143, 146
Loukes, H., 72
Lowe, L., 254
Luft, J., 269
Luke, B., 281

McClelland, D. C., 10
McCully, C. H., 202
MacDonald, W. S., 129
MacKinnon, D. W., 119, 187, 191
McLoughlin, W. P., 197, 213
McMahon, M. B., 175
McNeil, J. D., 312
Mager, R. F., 153, 164
Martin, G. C., 172

Martin, J. H., 141
Maslow, A. H., 4, 5, 23, 26, 98, 119, 184
May, R., 55, 67, 68, 90, 138
Meacham, M. L., 74, 139, 164
Mead, M., 41
Mecklenberger, J. A., 194
Menninger, K., 23
Metcalf, L. E., 200, 229
Meyer, R. I., 114
Michael, D. N., 134
Mickelson, N. I., 34
Miles, D. T., 153
Miles, M. B., 266, 276, 281, 284
Miller, G. A., 305
Miller, J. K., 14
Miller, L. L., 202
Miller, P. A., 18, 38
Miller, R. I., 115
Mitzel, H. E., 221
Moore, D. R., 236
Moore, R. S., 236
Moustakas, C., 47, 284
Musgrove, F., 41

Nations, J. E., 27
Neal, R., 78
Neale, D. C., 218
Neugarten, B. L., 10
Neville, R. F., 313

Odiorne, G. S., 265, 276
Oettinger, A. G., 142, 293
Ojemann, R. H., 194
Olds, H. F., 244, 247
Olivero, J. L., 250, 261
Olm, K. W., 298
Olson, Carl O., Jr., 251, 252, 261

Parker, J. L., 45
Parnes, S. J., 231, 238
Pearl, A., 47, 158, 285
Penfield, W., 43
Perls, F., 70
Perrone, V., 183
Peterson, R. D., 118, 287
Petrequin, G., 203
Pierson, G. A., 55
Pilcher, P. S., 53, 54
Plunkett, W. T., 225, 228, 238

Purkey, W. W., 284, 298, 299, 307, 309, 312, 313, 316

Rakstis, T. J., 262, 266, 280, 281
Randazzo, J. D., 183, 184
Rarick, J. R., 262
Reese, H. W., 231
Riessman, F., 27, 177
Rippey, R. M., 236
Roberts, W., 202
Robinson, D. W., 17, 221
Roethlisberger, F. J., 121
Rogers, C. R., 5, 17, 18, 23, 36, 55, 100, 261, 264, 269, 311
Rogers, V. R., 184
Rollins, S. P., 215
Rosenthal, R., 30, 124
Ruark, H. C., 141, 145
Rubin, L. J., 317
Ruesch, J., 76, 84
Rugg, H., 134
Rutrough, J. E., 312
Ryan, K. A., 152, 163
Ryan, T. A., 295
Ryans, D. G., 317

Sartain, H. W., 249
Scanlan, B. K., 263, 266
Schockley, W., 10, 263, 266
Schofield, W., 67, 79, 80
Schrag, F., 222
Schultz, W. C., 265
Scobey, M. M., 49, 50
Scott, W. A., 290, 293, 298, 304, 317
Seashore, C., 266, 281
Shannon, D. C., 211
Shaplin, J. T., 244, 247, 249, 250, 253, 254, 258
Shaw, G. B., 314
Sherif, C., 41
Sherif, M., 41
Shostrom, E. L., 62, 70, 81, 83, 103, 266
Silverman, I. W., 255
Skinner, B. F., 6, 37, 63, 166, 172, 322
Slaughter, R. E., 142
Smith, B. O., 158, 285

Snyder, F. A., 118, 287
Snygg, D., 159
Stalcup, R. J., 10
Stearns, M. S., 28, 34
Sterns, H. N., 244, 245, 249, 250
Stone, J. M., 255
Strang, R., 306
Strom, R. D., 201
Sybouts, W., 312, 313

Tannenbaum, A. S., 298
Tanner, R. T., 200
Taylor, C. W., 30, 107, 159, 187, 188, 189, 260, 309
Thayer, L., 57, 75, 84, 86, 89
Thelen, H. A., 286, 289
Thoreson, C. E., 294
Thorndike, E. L., 6, 172
Tomcheck, D., 258
Tondow, M., 293
Torrance, E. P., 62, 119, 122, 123, 129, 185, 186, 191, 195, 231, 235
Trusty, F. M., 258
Tsitrian, J., 47
Tuckman, B. W., 269, 280
Tyler, C. E., 244
Tyler, L. E., 38, 126
Tyler, R. W., 18

Vars, G. F., 248, 249, 251, 252, 253
Vriend, J., 142

Waetjen, W. B., 50, 118
Walster, E., 20
Watzlawick, P., 35, 76, 84, 89, 103
Weiner, B., 4, 5, 9
Weissen, A. E., 74, 139, 164
White, B. L., 31
White, M. A., 313
Whiteley, J. M., 267
Withycombe, R. J., 45
Wolf, S., 63
Woodward, R. G., 252, 254, 259
Wright, R., 26
Wyatt, W. C., 275, 276

Yalom, I. D., 266, 276, 281, 284
Yamamoto, K., 235
Yeaworth, R., 277
Yelon, S. L., 293
Yevtushenko, Y., 302
Young, J. I., 164

Ziller, R. C., 119
Zirkel, P. A., 47

Subject Index

Academic mind, myth of, 178, 180
Acceleration, 211n
"Accidental Century," 106
Accountability, 11, 156ff.
Achievement:
  and adjustment, 235
  in nongraded schools, 197, 213
  overemphasis on, 197
  in programmed learning, 173
  tests of, 213
Administrators:
  and communication, 299
  as models, 314
  role of, in innovation, 114, 258
  and team teaching, 244, 253
Affect, in teaching, 61
Affiliation, importance of, 36
Alienation, 182
Ambiguity, in communication, 85
Amplification systems, 109
Anthropologists, contributions of, 10
Anthropology, and learning, 9
Anxiety, 80
Approval, role of, in learning, 43
Aptitude tests, and ego concept, 187
Art, climate for, 192
Attitudes, learning of, 64
Attribution theory, 4
Authoritarianism, 37
Authority, management of, 304
Autonomy:
  and behavior modification, 135
  need for, 227
  role of, 214
Average, tyranny of, 188

Basic needs, and learning, 184
Behavior:
  causes of, 219
  and change, 49
  control of, 70
  and educational goals, 154
  pupil, and nongraded school, 214
Behavior modification, 135
Behavioral objectives, 153
Behaviorism, 136
Branching program, 170–72
Business, and education, 11

Change:
  and behavior, 49
  control of, 71
  difficulties in planning for, 107
  implications of, for schools, 121
  initiation of, 113, 117, 259
  pressure to, 309
  reactions to, 125, 288
  and threat, 121
  types of, 115
Change agents, characteristics of, 118
Choice, 222
  need for, 228

Competition, 232
Commitment, and innovation, 310
Communication, 75–101
    and administrators, 299
    facilitating open, 297
    in groups, 276
    limits on, 298, 300
    in team teaching, 242
Communicative interaction, 89
Compensatory education, 34
Computers, in education, 142
Computer assisted instruction (CAI), 143
Computer dialogue, 145
Computer mediated instruction (CMI), 147
Conflict, normality of, 307
Conformists, 180
Connectionism, 6
Consultants, in group process, 281
Continuous learning, need for, 225
Continuous progress, 196–220
Control:
    exercise of, 305
    in groups, 270
    of self, 68
Convergent-divergent thinking, 166
Counselors, as group facilitators, 278
Creative persons, 119
Creative thought, stages of, 190
Creativity, 185–93
    conditions of, 189
    encouragement of, 235, 306
    learning of, 231
    and programmed learning, 166
Critical periods, 43
Criticism, effect of, 308
Culturally different children:
    in nongraded school, 200
    and study, 226, 234
    tests for, 187
Culture:
    competitive, 301
    machine oriented, 141
    varieties of, 235

Curiosity, 218
Curricular content, 38
    vs. feelings, 41
Curriculum:
    basics in, 184, 201
    and life of pupil, 227

Decisions, inevitability of, 303
Defensiveness:
    origins of, 309, 312
    in process groups, 270, 273
Determinism, 5
Developmental tasks, 79n
Dialogue, computer, 145
Differential ability tests, 187
Dilemmas, normality of, 302
Discipline, 86
Disadvantaged children (see Culturally different children)
Divergent pupils, 29
Double message communication, 87, 258
    feelings in, 40

Education, aims of, 61, 202, 232
Educational aims, testing of, 261
Educational costs, and team teaching, 250
Educational outcomes, and teachers, 158
Egocentrism, in teaching, 57
Ego-concept, in learning, 179
Elementary school, ungraded, 204
Emotions, dealing with, 62, 66
    release of, 67
    in teaching, 60
Evaluation, roles of, 311
Existentialism, 137

Facilitators (see Group facilitators)
Facts, learning of, 38
Feedback, 6, 149, 173
    channels for, 295
    in groups, 277

teachers' need for, 243
and team teaching, 241
Feelings, and verbalization, 36
Flow chart, 295, 296
Freedom, 222
in the classroom, 183
concept of, 68
need for, in classroom, 231
psychological, 79

Gifted children, 191
Goals, in groups, 276
statement of, 153
Grading, fallacy of, 197
Group facilitators, 266, 276–80
choice of, 279
Grouping, fallacy of, 201
Groups:
goals in, 275
hazards of, 277, 278
participant's rights in, 272
stability of membership in, 274
value of, 270
Guilt, teachers' feelings of, 58

Hawthorne Effect, 120
Hazards, in learning milieu, 50
Heterostasis, 23, 218
High school, ungraded, 208
Holistic concept, 25, 51
Homeostasis, 23
Hostility, in communication, 83
Human problems, 5
Human relations, in innovation, 286
Humanistic orientation, 4
Humanistic psychology, 137
Humanity, and prescription, 235

Independence, need for, 227
Independent study, 222–37
Individual differences, 196
in learning styles, 177
Individual learning program, 223
Individualized instruction, 200
Individually prescribed instruction (IPI), 147, 236

Innovation:
and commitment, 310
and group process, 282
organizing for, 286–316
perpetuation of, 112
risks in, 119
and school climate, 314
and self-examination, 250
and stress, 123
success of, and teachers, 249
team approach to, 245
threats to, 309
types of, 116
value of, 217, 219
Innovative package, 203, 260
In-service training, attitudes toward, 310
Institutions, and change, 124
Instruction, improvement of, 255
Interest:
need for, 249
role of, 233
Interpersonal process groups, 261–76
Interpersonal relations:
improvement of, 77
and team teaching, 252, 256
Interpersonal tension, tolerance for, 307
Involvement, 36
learning of, 65
need for, 216
IQ, changes in, 30

Job analysis, 293
Judgment, in groups, 273

Knowledge explosion, 3
and independent study, 226

Language, learning of, 201
Leader, characteristics of, 302, 305
Learning:
continuous, 14
dynamics in, 37
facilitation of, 22–47

factors in, 172, 205
and feelings, 63
as human process, 17
incentives to, 12
interdisciplinary nature of, 7
practice in, 31
propositions on, 23ff.
and self-concept, 28
teachers' influence on, 16, 314
and team teaching, 250, 260
tools of, 202
Learning activity packet (LAP), 223
Learning groups, 263
Learning milieu, 48–72
Learning styles, 27, 175–83
and independent study, 224
in nongraded school, 198
and programmed learning, 14
Levels of discourse, 94
Life styles, 175, 181
and teachers, 5
Linear program, 166–70
Listening, barriers to, 100
role of, 99

Man, vs. machines, 133
Management:
processes of, 292
supportive, 287
Manipulation, in communication, 81
"Mechanical" mind, 178, 180
Metacommunication, 269
use of, 84, 88, 93
Models, teachers as, 251, 252
Motivation:
internal vs. external, 229
and programmed learning, 173
and team teaching, 251, 261
Mutual Influence Paradigm, 91

Needs:
basic, and learning, 184
hierarchy of, 26
varied, of pupils, 176
Nongraded schools, 196–220

Nonverbal communication, 86, 101

Objectives, stating of, 294
Open education, 183–85
Organization chart, 291
Overcontrol, 70
Overlearning, 7

Paraprofessionals, in team teaching, 247
Parental influence, 53
Parents, and grades, 208
Peak experiences, 98
Peer influences, 32, 41
Performance contracting, 11
Personal growth, 126
Personality:
ascendent, 181
effect of nongradedness on, 217
factors in, 289
submissive, 181
Philosophy:
and curriculum, 229
of nongraded elementary school, 204
of nongraded high school, 211
Physiology, and learning, 26
Planning, teachers' role in, 288
Policy, teachers' participation in, 256
Potential, unused, of humans, 126
Power:
and communication, 301
in peer groups, 42
Pressure, and change, 123
Product vs. process, 37
Programmed learning:
and creativity, 190
results of, 13
Psychoanalytic theory, 6
Psychological theories, 134–37
rapprochement of, 139
Psychological well-being, factors in, 118
Psychology:
application of, 140

systems of, 6
and technological aids, 149
Punishment, in learning, 172, 218

Readiness, 43
Reading, and adjustment, 235
Reality, in group processes, 275
Reinforcement, 4
Reinforcement psychology, 166
Relevance, meaning of, 229
Research, need for, 214
Responsibility, 222
in communication, 92
Rewards, hazards of, 174
Risk, need for, 160
Routine, as learning factor, 44

Safety, in groups, 271
Schedules, role of, in learning, 45
School climate, 48
School patrons, expectations of, 54
School regulations, 42
School success, and independent study, 230
Schools, "failure" of, 3
Sciences, and psychology, 138
Security, role of:
in learning, 44
in teamwork, 279
Self, and communication, 78
Self-actualizers, 119
Self-concept:
factors in, 219
and learning, 28, 29
origins of, 31
of slow learner, 223
and supervision, 313
Self-direction:
and feedback, 243
of teachers, 61
Self-disclosure, 265
Self-fulfilling prophecy, 30
and institutions, 124
Self-management, 69
Self-paced learning, 223, 233
Sensitivity groups, 262, 271
Social organizations, 111

Social relations, in learning, 182
Social structure, and amplification of power, 110
Social systems, 290
Sociology, and learning, 8
Special classes, 196
Specialization, of teachers, 248
Stereotypes, in teaching, 56
Stimulus-response gap, 67
Stimulus-response psychology, 136
Student unrest, 3
Styles of learning (see Learning styles)
Success, role of, 205
Supervision, attitudes toward, 312
Systems, formal and informal, 291
Systems analysis, 253, 259
limitations of, 297
Systems approach, 293–95

Talent, encouragement of, 186
Talking, and learning, 33
Teacher effectiveness, 123
Teacher improvement, and videotapes, 150
Teacher-pupil relations, 251
Teachers:
accountability of, 156
as agents of change, 105–27
attitudes of, 217, 246, 264
centrality of, 52
and communication, 76
and creativity, 192
effect of nongradedness on, 215
growth of, 25
and independent study, 236
influence of, 15, 200
innovative, 19
as models, 39
as persons, 17
pressures on, 159
recalcitrant, dealing with, 216
role of, 7, 19, 233
satisfactions of, 55, 255
self-directing, 304
vs. technicians, 22

and technology, 133–61
  using talents of, 133
"Teachers Code," 267
Teacher-teacher interaction, 254
Teaching:
  concepts of, 18, 52
  core of, 56
  evaluation of, 313
  improvement of, and team
    teaching, 254
  limitations to, 57ff.
  rewards of, 54
Teaching methods, need for var-
    ied, 176
Team teaching, 241–83
  and group process, 279
Technological aids, 141, 224
  cost of, 145
Technology:
  hazards of, 51
  and teachers, 133, 159, 161
Testing:
  advantages of, 187
  limitations of, 260
Tests:
  in nongraded schools, 208
  as incentives, 187

Texarkana schools, 11
Theory, application of, 241, 247,
    259
Therapy groups, 263
Thinking, types of, 178
Thinking styles, 230
Tolerance, for uncertainty, 308
Trust:
  and communication, 298
  generation of, 312

Values:
  and education, 214
  role of, in learning, 43
Variety, need for, 230
Verbalization, 35
Videotape recorders, 150

World, changing nature of, 34

Yerkes-Dodson Law, 122